November 2002

Dear Ingenix Customer:

Enclosed is *Ingenix Coding Lab: Implementing ICD•10*:

This book helps you prepare for release of ICD-10-CM. It compares the pre-release draft of the ICD-10 code set as written by the World Health Organization (WHO) and and clinically modified by the National Center for Health Statistics (NCHS). These are the codes that are expected to replace the current ICD-9-CM system for medical documentation and reimbursement pending legislative approval.

The codes in ICD-10-CM are not currently valid for any purpose or use. Testing of ICD-10-CM will occur using this pre-release version. It is anticipated that updates and corrections to this draft will be made by NCHS prior to implementation of ICD-10-CM.

There is not yet an anticipated implementation date for the ICD-10-CM. Implementation will be based on the process for adoption of standards under the Health Insurance Portability and Accountability Act of 1996 (HIPAA). There will be a two- year implementation window once the final notice to implement has been published in the *Federal Register*. But it is imperative to begin preparing for this major change now. Staff must be trained, software must be selected, and health information management strategies must ship.

Thank you for choosing to be an Ingenix customer. If you have any questions please call our customer service department, toll free at (800) INGENIX (464-3649).

Cordially,

Elizabeth Bovdre

Vice President, Publisher

2003 ICD-9-CM Code Books for Physicians Volumes 1 & 2

ICD-9-CM Professional for Physicians, Vols. 1 & 2

Softbound
ISBN: 1-56329-872-4   Item No. 3650 **$64.95**
Available: September 2002

Compact
ISBN: 1-56329-873-2   Item No. 3661 **$64.95**
Available: September 2002

ICD-9-CM Expert for Physicians, Vols. 1 & 2

Spiral
ISBN: 1-56329-874-0   Item No. 3652 **$84.95**
Available: September 2002

Updateable Binder
ISBN: 1-56329-875-9   Item No. 3534 **$144.95**

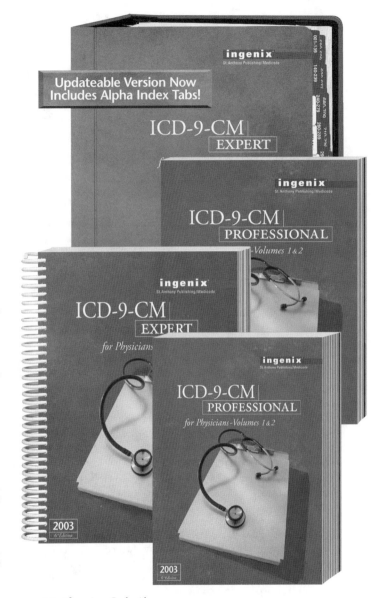

Our page design, featuring intuitive symbols, exclusive color-coding, and additional resources provides a new approach to pertinent coding and reimbursement information. New codes and changes to the ICD-9-CM make our 2003 code books a must buy! Order today and keep currenton all changes!

Professional and Expert Editions of ICD-9-CM for Physicians Feature:

• New and Revised Code Symbols

• Fourth-and Fifth-digit Requirement Alerts

• Complete Official Coding Guidelines

• Age and Sex Edits

• Clinically Oriented Definitions and Illustrations

• Medicare as Secondary Payer Indicators

• Manifestation Code Alerts

• "Other" and "Unspecified" Diagnosis Alerts

• Symbols Identifying V Codes Designated for only Primary or only Secondary Diagnosis Use

Expert Editions Also Include These Enhancements:

• Special Reports Via E-mail.

• Code Tables--Complex coding issues are simplified in coding tables, as developed for I-9 Express

• Valid Three-digit Category List

The Expert Updateable Binder Subscriptions Feature:

• Money Saving Update Service

• Three Updates per Year [October (full text), January and July]

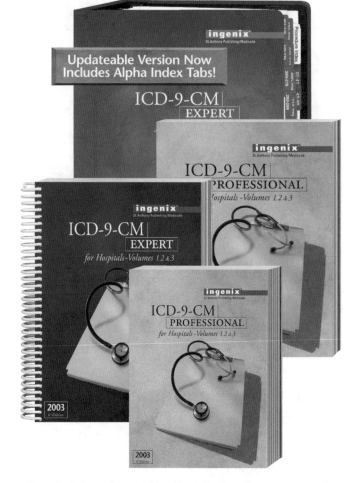

St. Anthony Publishing/Medicode

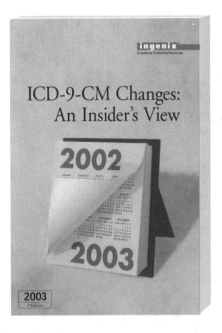

NEW!
CPT® Changes 2003: An Insider's View

7" x 10" Perfect Bound

The American Medical Association and Ingenix Publishing present *CPT® Changes 2003: An Insider's View*, a must-have resource for Physicians' Current Procedural Terminology (CPT®) Professional users! This book serves as a reference tool to understanding each of the CPT® code changes found in CPT® 2003.

In both books you'll find:

- **Every new, revised and deleted code change**—Listed along with a detailed rationale for the change. Index changes, convention changes and instructional note changes are also explained.

- **Organized by ICD-9-CM and CPT® code section and code number**—Includes a separate section that discusses index changes.

- **Illustrated**—Helps orient you to change in code.

- **Clinical Examples/Diagnostic or Procedural Descriptions**—Helps you understand the practical application of the code.

CPT is a registered trademark of the American Medical Association

NEW!
ICD-9-CM Changes 2003: An Insider's View

7" x 10" Perfect Bound

Item No. 4951 **$54.95**

Available: November 2002

A must have resource for ICD-9-CM users! *ICD-9-CM Changes 2003: An Insider's View* serves as a reference tool to understanding each of the ICD-9-CM code changes found in ICD-9-CM 2003.

CPT® Changes for 2003:
- 204 New Codes
- 23 Deleted Codes
- 203 Revised Codes
- Place of Service section added to appendices

ICD-9-CM Changes for 2003:
- 163 New Diagnosis Codes
- 23 Revised Diagnosis Codes
- 25 New Procedure Codes
- 3 Revised Procedure Codes
- New chapter on New Technology and Medical Services in Volume 3
- Changes to conventions and to the index

Call Toll-Free 1.877.INGENIX (1.877.464.3649) or Shop Online at www.IngenixOnLine.com

Also Available from your Medical Bookstore or Distributor

2003 Publications

St. Anthony Publishing/Medicode

The Best CPT® Reference in the Industry!

2003 CPT® Expert

Spiral bound
ISBN: 1-56329-855-4   Item No. 4529 **$84.95**

Compact
ISBN: 1-56329-856-2   Item No. 4508 **$74.95**
Available: December 2002

If you are not using the current information , your Medicare claims will be rejected! In 2002, there were more changes in *Physicians' Current Procedural Terminology* (CPT®) codes than ever. Be ready this year for what is expected to be another significant year in CPT® code revisions. With full descriptions, *CPT® Expert* will help you interpret these changes and speed reimbursement. Order today to see for yourself!

Features and Benefits Include:

- **Comprehensive**—Includes EVERY CPT® code with FULL descriptions

- **Exclusive**—Complete index helps you find codes quickly

- **Exclusive**—Color keys and icons revealing Correct Coding Initiative Comprehensive codes, Medicare, CLIA and other common coding rules

- **Exclusive**—Code-specific definitions, rules, and tips compiled from the *Medicare Carriers Manual and Coverage Issues Manual,* and other sources speed reimbursement

- **Illustrated**—Detailed illustrations orient you to the procedures

Publisher's Note: CPT Expert is not a replacement for the American Medical Association's CPT 2003 Standard and Professional code books.

CPT is a registered trademark of the American Medical Association

Call Toll-Free 1.877.INGENIX (464.3649) or Shop Online at www.IngenixOnLine.com
Also Available from your Medical Bookstore or Distributor

ingenix®
St. Anthony Publishing/Medicode

The Expert Coding Solution

Encoder Pro

Item No. D4178   Subscriptions Start at **$499.95**

CALL TODAY FOR A FREE DEMO ON CD-ROM!

Available: October 2002

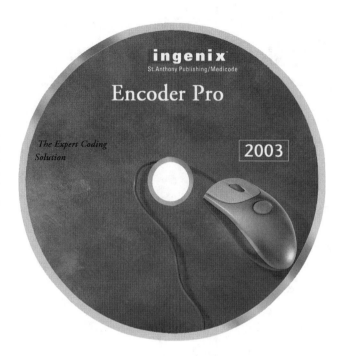

The best only gets better. Ingenix CodeLogic™ search technology now gives you intuitive results for even faster coding. More search terms! Faster results! Larger reference library to support every level of code selection.

Encoder Pro gives users a complete code and reference library at their fingertips. Complete with Sticky Notes, Bookmarks, and Notepad features, Encoder Pro provides a customizable user experience, with annotations and icons for powerful medical coding!

- **Ingenix CodeLogic™ Search Engine.** Searches simultaneously across all three code sets. Employs built-in spell-check, abbreviations, and narrow functions for finding the right codes fast.

- **"Code Book" Navigation.** Gives users the familiarity they'll need to use Encoder Pro exclusively for all medical coding needs.

- **Surgical Cross Codes.** Help the user verify the right match among code sets.

- **Notepad, Bookmarks, and Sticky Notes.** Make the most out of code searches and allow for a customizable experience.

- **CCI Unbundling Edits.** Up-to-date Medicare NCCI edits for comprehensive unbundling rules.

- **Lay Descriptions, Annotations, and Icons.** Help improve Physicians Current Procedural Terminolgy (CPT™), ICD-9-CM, and HCPCS Level II code selection.

- **Continuing Education Units (CEUs).** Earn 8 CEUs through AAPC.

REQUIREMENTS	
Local Deployment Recommended Hardware	**ASP Deployment Recommended Hardware**
• 256 MB of RAM	• 128 MB of RAM
• 800X600 SVGA	• 800X600 SVGA
• PIII 800 MHZ	• PII 233 MHZ
• 125 MB Disk Space	• 60 MB Disk Space
	• Requires High-speed Internet Access

CPT is a registered trademark of the American Medical Association

Call Toll-Free 1.877.INGENIX (464.3649) or Shop Online at www.IngenixOnline.com

Also Available from your Medical Bookstore or Distributor

New! DRG Desk Reference— The Book You've Been Requesting!

DRG Desk Reference

Compact, Softbound
ISBN: 1-56329-929-1   Item No. 4282 **$199.95**
Available: September 2002

A truly comprehensive resource that creates an inpatient coding resource that functions to work efficiently and effectively with either *DRG Expert* or *DRG Guidebook*.

A must-have resource for anyone who assigns DRGs or audits claims for inpatient cases!

DRG Desk Reference **will bring you:**

- **Optimal Reimbursement Indicators**—Quickly identify the top ICD-9-CM diagnosis or procedure codes and key indicators for each DRG to ensure optimal payment while ensuring compliance.

- **Tips for the Encoder Use**r—Many decisions faced by coders using grouper software, or encoder, have significant impact on final DRG assignment. Tips are provided on how to avoid making the wrong decisions.

- **New Technology and Medical Services**—Descriptions of the new technology and medical services and which services will receive add-on payment under the Medicare inpatient prospective payment system.

- **Key Abstracting Field Items**—An in-depth look at the significance of key abstracting fields for DRG assignment and the impact on reimbursement.

- **DRG Assignment Tutorial**—This tutorial will explain the DRG assignment process in clear and understandable language.

- **Coding and Documentation Guidelines for DRG Validation**—Uncover potential coding problems and ensure the accuracy and validity of DRG assignment.

- **Key Complication and Comorbidity Condition (CC) Indicators:**
  Drug Usage and Treatment
  Durable Medical Equipment
  Noninvasive Diagnostic Test Outcomes
  Abnormal EKG Findings
  Abnormal Laboratory Values
  Major Cardiovascular Complications
  Complex Diagnoses
  Organisms

- **DRG Decision Trees**

- **Complete CC List**

- **CC Principal Diagnosis Exclusion List**

- **Relative Weights of Valid DRG**

St. Anthony Publishing/Medicode

DRG System Changes Impact 12 of the Top 25 DRGs!

2003 DRG Expert
(formerly called the DRG Guidebook)

Compact, Spiral

ISBN: 1-56329-891-0

Available: September 2002

Item No. 3575 **$99.95**

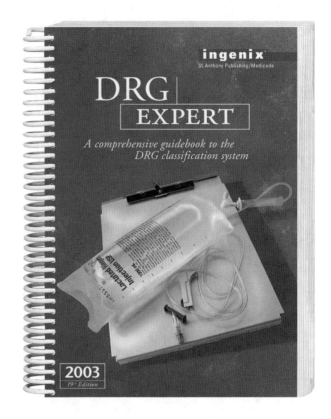

Trust the nation's DRG experts to bring you the DRG guidebook designed specifically for those who need a comprehensive resource for accurate assignment of DRGs, concurrently and retrospectively. The most trusted and comprehensive guidebook to the DRG classification system for 19 years should be your guide to navigate the changes in the DRG system!

NEW—Exclusive Color Coding Helps Hospitals to:

- See at a glance surgical/medical partitioning
- Know if CCs must be assigned and when age limits apply
- Know when certain qualifications for principal or secondary diagnosis must be met
- Identify DRGs targeted for audits

Other Features Include:

- **Organized by Major Diagnositic Category (MDC)**

- **Transfer DRG Alert**—Indicates a DRG selected as a qualified discharge that may be paid by per diem rate

- **Main Term Code Search**—Customized code descriptions that list main conditions or operative terms first

- **Average National Payment**—Listed with every DRG for quick benchmark comparisons

- **Surgical Hierarchy Table**—Quickly shows DRG hierarchy for multiple procedure cases

- **Invalid DRG Conversion Table**—Easily track the reassignment of codes to the new DRG

- **Full Listing of All Dx Within a MDC**

- **Numeric and Alphabetic ICD-9-CM Indexes**

- **Current CMS Rate Structure** (RW, AMLOS, GMLOS)

- **QuickFlip Color Tabs**—Find the right code in half the time of traditional thumb tabs

8 Out of 10 Surveyed Coders Prefer *Coders' Desk Reference*

Coders' Desk Reference

ISBN: 156329-854-6   Item No. 5762 **$119.95**
Available: December 2002

No matter how much experience you have using ICD-9-CM, Physicians' Current Procedural Terminology (CPT®), and HCPCS Level II codes, there are always tough questions that hold up the billing process. And because billing errors can result in fines, you can't afford to guess. Now you can get easy-to-understand answers to your coding questions without leaving your desk, with the 2003 *Coders' Desk Reference*.

- **NEW—Updated with 2003 CPT® Codes.** Includes accurate descriptions for more than 7,000 CPT® procedures, plus an anesthesia crosswalk and an E/M chapter.

- **More Than 6,000 Lay Descriptions of Procedures and Tests.** Improve your coding accuracy by consulting these easy-to-understand explanations of procedures.

- **Update on the CPT®-5 Project.** Keep current on changes to the CPT® codes and guidelines.

- **ICD-10-CM and ICD-10-PCS Preparation.** Learn how each will affect you and discover ways to make the transitions as smooth as possible.

- **CPT® "New," "Changed," and "Grammatically Changed" Icons from the Previous Year.** Official CPT® headings and subheadings denoting anatomical and procedural sections help users determine the codes associated with lay descriptions.

- **Earn 5 CEUs from AAPC.**

CPT is a registered trademark of the American Medical Association

Call Toll-Free 1.877.INGENIX (464.3649) or Shop Online at www.IngenixOnline.com
Also Available from your Medical Bookstore or Distributor

060102

2003 Publications

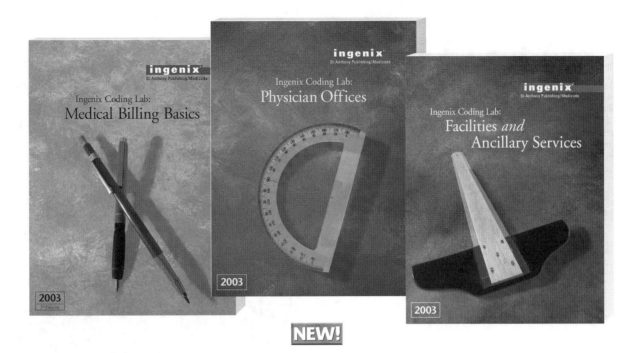

NEW!

A New Coder's Training System

These comprehensive education modules help beginning and advanced coders in the office, the facility, or the classroom. Designed to allow you to understand and master the skills needed to be an effective coder, each module includes a CD containing a student workbook and a teacher's guide, along with a three-month subscription to the popular *Code It Fast* look-up program.

All Books Include:

- **Student Workbook on CD**—Student workbook helps you convert information in the book to hands-on experience

- **Teacher's Guide on CD**—Teacher's guide helps instructors and managers tutor and challenge their students

- **Three-month Code It Fast CD**—*Code it Fast* look-up CD includes the latest ICD-9-CM, HCPCS, and CPT® codes

- **Complex Coding Scenarios**—Complex coding scenarios help assure fast and accurate physician reimbursement through example

NEW! Ingenix Coding Lab: Medical Billing Basics

Complete Foundation for Coding and Billing—Broad overview of coding, payers, and the reimbursement process for the entry-level coder or billing professional

ISBN: 1-56329-921-6   Item No. 5772 **$74.95**

Available: December 2002

NEW! Ingenix Coding Lab: Physician Offices

Complete Foundation for Physician Coding and Billing—Broad overview of physician reimbursement process for the coder or billing professional

ISBN: 1-56329-908-9   Item No. 3268 **$74.95**

Available: December 2002

NEW! Ingenix Coding Lab: Facilities and Ancillary Services

Complete Foundation for Facility Coding and Billing—Broad overview of facility reimbursement process for the coder or billing professional

ISBN: 1-56329-920-8   Item No. 3227 **$99.95**

Available: December 2002

CPT is a registered trademark of the American Medical Association

Call Toll-Free 1.877.INGENIX (464.3649) or Shop Online at www.IngenixOnLine.com

Also Available from your Medical Bookstore or Distributor

060102

ingenix
St. Anthony Publishing/Medicode

Get Your Claims in the Right Hands the First Time

Insurance Directory

ISBN: 1-56329-834-1   Item No. 2933 **$64.95**
Available: September 2002

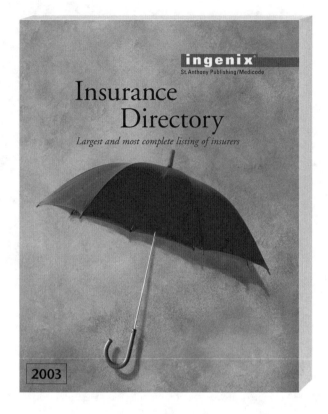

The majority of insurance companies experienced changes this past year in their addresses, phone, or fax numbers. For timely and accurate payment of claims, having the latest edition of the *Insurance Directory* is essential. We personally call each carrier to insure the validity of each company listed.

• **NEW** — Improved format makes it easy and fast for you to locate the insurance carrier.

• **State and Local Listings.** Insurers don't always list their claims offices in the phone book. Our Insurance Directory can help you find them.

• **E-mail and Web Addresses.** Now contacting the payer is as easy as logging onto your computer.

• **State Insurance Commissioner Listings.** Complete addresses and phone and fax numbers of the Insurance Commissioner for each state.

• **Prior Authorization.** Find out whether an insurer requires prior authorization for contracted plans.

• **Alphabetized Index of Nationwide Companies with Centralized Claims Offices.** Identify which insurance companies have centralized their claims operations.

Get Expert Coding and Reimbursement Advice—Every Month

Our newsletters are a great companion to your code book. Your facility will get timely, concise, and reliable information—targeted to your specialty—month after month.

Ambulatory Coding and Payment Report

Inside each 16-page issue of *Ambulatory Coding and Payment Report*, you'll find:

- **Answers You Need to Manage APC Operations Effectively**. We'll help you prevent costly billing mistakes and collect and manage essential data properly.

- **Improve Coding Accuracy to Get Every Medicare Dollar You're Entitled To**. We'll help you train your staff on correct coding so you can avoid medical necessity denials, support additional payment where appropriate, and audit your outpatient claims for costly mistakes.

- **Stay Abreast of New Developments as APC Implementation Moves Forward**. A regular Q&A column will clarify specific operational and coding issues and give you an opportunity to ask your own questions.

Item No. 2428 **$249.95**

Clinical Coding and Reimbursement

Inside each monthly issue of *Clinical Coding and Reimbursement*, you'll find:

- **In-Depth Clinical Analysis of Diseases and Procedures**. So you can choose the right code the first time. Use to train your staff!

- **Up-To-Date News on ICD-9-CM, CPT®, and HCPCS Coding Systems and Reimbursement Methodologies**. Keeps you current so you receive the appropriate reimbursement.

- **Actual Case Studies and "Question and Answer" Column**. Offers real-life solutions to your difficult coding scenarios.

Item No. 4031 **$179.95**

Part A Insider

Part A Insider is a bi-weekly publication—co-published with the Healthcare Financial Management Association (HFMA)—designed to help give you the news and analysis you need to plan, implement, and survive the regulatory, compliance, billing, and legal changes affecting your facility.

Inside *Part A Insider*, you'll find:

- **Regulatory Updates**. PPS for outpatient (APCs), inpatient, SNFs, HHA, and inpatient rehab; Medicare coverage issues that affect billing and reimbursement; HIPAA regulations and implementation, and more.

- **Compliance Updates**. OIG's advisory opinions, annual work-plan initiatives, high risk areas, audit reports, and more.

- **Billing Updates**. HCFA-1450/UB-92 and Medicare billing policy changes; common problem billing areas; correct coding and other Medicare edits.

Item No. 4281 **$349.95**

HIPAA and E-Health for Facility Management

Co-published with the Healthcare Financial Management Association (HFMA), this 12-page monthly newsletter provides:

- **Coverage on HIPAA Regulations**. Concise and to the point. Know what the latest provisions, developments, and delays are and how they affect your facility.

  - **Strategies and Guidance**. Learn what's working and what's not for your colleagues through consultant interviews, guest authors, and case studies.

  - **E-health Tools and Technology Updates**. Evaluate the need for EDI, electronic patient records, and point-of-care advancements.

  - **HIPAA and E-health Links**. Utilize hard-to-find information from sources like digests, listservs, Web sites, white papers, and more.

Item #2431 **$299.95**

CPT is a registered trademark of the American Medical Association.

2003 Publications

St. Anthony Publishing/Medicode

Specialty Coding Changes and Best Practice Tips— Every Month

Our newsletters are a great companion to your code book. Your practice will get timely, concise, and reliable information—targeted to your specialty—month after month.

Inside each of our specialty newsletters you'll find:

- **Expert Advice.** You'll get the help you need to code more accurately—reducing delays and denials.

- **Questions and Answers.** You'll get answers to difficult coding questions—without hiring consultants or spending hours on research.

- **Timely Coverage of Regulatory Decisions.** Our experts keep you on top of complicated government regulations and tell you how they will impact your practice.

$179.95 /year, per title

Newsletter	Item No.
Coding and Reimbursement for:	
Behavioral Health Services	6543
Cardiovascular Specialties	6542
ENT & Allergy	4276
General Surgery	4277
Oncology & Hematology	4278
Ophthalmology	4053
Ob/Gyn	4091
Orthopaedics	4097
Pediatrics	4270
Primary Care Specialties	4034
Radiology	4114
Urology	4279

Practical Guidance on HIPAA and E-Health for the Physician Practice

News, analysis, innovative strategies, case studies, and practical "how-to" articles to help you implement the administrative simplification provisions under HIPAA and related e-health technologies. Your subscription includes:

- **HIPAA News.** The latest information on HIPAA regulations and deadlines.

- **E-health Updates.** Solid information on how your practice can prepare for technology enhancements and security requirements—and even profit!

- **Practical Articles.** Strategies for upgrading computer systems, designing a workflow that protects privacy, evaluating hardware and software, and other HIPAA-related operational challenges.

- **Legislative Analysis.** Interviews with legal analysts in the field.

Item No. 4231 **$269.95**
(12 issues annually)

Part B Insider

With *Part B Insider*, you will receive clear and current coverage of the changing Part B regulatory, compliance, and legal environment. *Part B Insider* is your guide to:

- **News.** Stay informed of new and proposed regulations, coding and billing guidelines, judicial decisions, compliance developments, and more.

- **Impact.** Learn how these developments will affect your organization—and your bottom line.

- **Action.** Discover practical ways to implement the new policies and procedures.

Item No. 4272 **$349.95** (24 issues annually)

Call Toll-Free 1.800.INGENIX (464.3649) or Shop Online at www.IngenixOnLine.com

Also Available from your Medical Bookstore or Distributor

020917

2003 Publications

20% Discount ($143.95) for AAO-HNS Members

Specialty-Specific Comprehensive Illustrated Guides to Coding and Reimbursement

Coding Companions

These comprehensive illustrated coding guides for 10 specialties link coding and clinical information to help you code the common procedures for your specialty with greater ease and accuracy.

- **EXCLUSIVE — Physicians' Current Procedural Terminology (CPT®) Codes Included, Updated for 2003.** Find many of the codes you need, since Surgery, Medicine, E/M, Radiology, and Path/Lab sections of the CPT® manual relating to your specialty are covered in one resource.

- **NEW—Medicare National Correct Coding Initiative (NCCI) Edits Delivered Quarterly via E-mail.** Identify which coding combinations cannot be billed together to reduce the risk of audit.

- **Coding and Reimbursement Tips.** Help you reduce surgical coding errors and curb claim denials.

- **Easy-to-Understand Descriptions of Each CPT® Code.** Compare the explanation to the medical record and make an informed choice on which CPT® code is appropriate.

- **Annotations and Definitions Associated with Surgical Procedures.** Help you easily interpret the documentation.

- **ICD-9-CM Codes, HCPCS Level II Codes, and Anesthesia Codes Cross-referenced to the Related CPT® Code.** Easily find out which CPT® procedure goes with which ICD-9-CM code and HCPCS Level II code.

$179.95 each

6 CEUs from AAPC

ISBN No.	Acronym	Item Description	Item No.	Available
1-56329-844-2	ATCR	Coding Companion for Cardiology/Cardiothoracic Surgery/Vascular Surgery	5270	December 2002
1-56329-849-X	AENT	Coding Companion for ENT/Allergy/Pulmonology	5271	January 2003
1-56329-843-0	AGEN	Coding Companion for General Surgery/Gastroenterology	5272	December 2002
1-56329-846-5	ATNN	Coding Companion for Neurosurgery/Neurology	5273	January 2003
1-56329-844-9	ATOB	Coding Companion for OB/GYN	5274	December 2002
1-56329-845-7	ATEY	Coding Companion for Ophthalmology	5275	December 2002
1-56329-847-3	ATLE	Coding Companion for Orthopaedics — Lower: Hips & Below	5276	December 2002
1-56329-848-1	ATUE	Coding Companion for Orthopaedics — Upper: Spine & Above	5277	December 2002
1-56329-850-3	ATPR	Coding Companion for Plastics/OMS/Dermatology	5278	December 2002
1-56329-851-1	ATUN	Coding Companion for Urology/Nephrology	5279	January 2003

CPT is a registered trademark of the American Medical Association

Call Toll-Free 1.877.INGENIX (464.3649) or Shop Online at www.IngenixOnline.com

Also Available from your Medical Bookstore or Distributor

4 Easy Ways to Order

CALL toll-free
1.800.INGENIX
(464.3649)
and mention the
Source Code: FOBA3

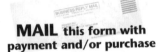

SHOP on line at
www.IngenixOnline.com

MAIL this form with
payment and/or purchase
order to:
PO Box 27116
Salt Lake City, UT 84127-0116

FAX this order form with
credit card information and /or
purchase order to 801.982.4033

Customer Service Hours
7:00am to 5:00pm MT
9:00am to 7:00pm ET

100% Money Back Guarantee

If our merchandise* ever fails to meet
your expectations, please contact our
Customer Service Department toll-free
at 1.800.INGENIX (464.3649) for an
immediate response. We will resolve
any concern without hesitation.

*Software: Credit will be granted for
unopened packages only.

No. of Items	Fee
Shipping and Handling	
1	$9.95
2-4	$11.95
5-7	$14.95
8-10	$19.95
11+	Call

PUBLICATION ORDER AND FAX FORM

FOBA3

Customer No._____ Contact No._____

Purchase Order No._____ Source Code_____
(Attach copy of Purchase Order)

Contact Name _____ Title_____

Company_____

Address _____
(no P.O. Boxes, please)

City_____ State_____ Zip_____

Phone (_____)_____ Fax (_____)_____
(in case we have questions about your order)

IMPORTANT: E-MAIL REQUIRED FOR ORDER CONFIRMATION AND SELECT PRODUCT DELIVERY.

E-mail _____

❑ YES, I WANT TO RECEIVE SPECIAL REPORTS AND INFORMATION VIA E-MAIL.
❑ YES, I WANT TO RECEIVE NEW PRODUCT ANNOUNCEMENTS VIA E-MAIL.

Item #	Qty	Item Description	Price	Total
4025	1	(SAMPLE) DRG Guidebook	$89.95	$89.95

Sub Total _____
TX, UT, OH, and VA residents please add applicable sales tax _____
Shipping & handling (see chart) _____
(11 plus items, foreign and Canadian orders, please call for shipping costs)
Total enclosed _____

Payment Options

❑ Check enclosed. (Make payable to Ingenix, Inc.)

❑ Charge my: ❑ MasterCard ❑ VISA ❑ AMEX ❑ Discover

Card # | | | | | | | | | | | | | | | | | | | Exp. Date: | | | |
MM   YR

❑ Bill Me P.O.#_____

Signature _____

Ingenix Coding Lab: Implementing ICD·10

ingenix™

St. Anthony Publishing/Medicode

PUBLISHERS NOTICE

Ingenix Coding Lab: Implementing ICD•10 is designed to be an accurate and authoritative source regarding coding and every reasonable effort has been made to ensure accuracy and completeness of the content. However, Ingenix, Inc. makes no guarantee, warranty, or representation that this publication is accurate, complete, or without errors. It is understood that Ingenix, Inc. is not rendering any legal or other professional services or advice in this publication and that Ingenix, Inc. bears no liability for any results or consequences that may arise from the use of this book. Please address all correspondence to:

Product Manager, Ingenix, Inc.
2525 Lake Park Blvd
Salt Lake City, UT 84120

AMERICAN MEDICAL ASSOCIATION NOTICE

CPT codes, descriptions, and other CPT material only are copyright © 2001 American Medical Association. All Rights Reserved. No fee schedules, basic units, relative values, or related listings are included in CPT. AMA does not directly or indirectly practice medicine or dispense medical services. AMA assumes no liability for data contained or not contained herein.

CPT is a registered trademark of the American Medical Association.

ACKNOWLEDGMENTS

Elizabeth Boudrie, *Publisher*
Lynn Speirs, *Senior Director, Publishing Services Group*
Sheri Poe Bernard, CPC, *Director, Essential Regulatory Products*
Brad Ericson, MPC, *Product Manager*
Wendy Dickie, *Project Editor*

Jean Parkinson, *Project Editor*
Lori Becks, RHIA, *Clinical/Technical Editor*
Kerrie Hornsby, *Desktop Publishing Manager*
Greg Kemp, *Desktop Publishing Specialist*

ABOUT THE AUTHORS

LORI BECKS, RHIA

Lori Becks has functioned as a coding specialist at the University of Utah and served as Assistant Director of Health Information Management. Her areas of expertise include the ICD-9-CM and CPT coding systems. She also has a background in teaching English to foreign speakers and technical writing.

SHERI POE BERNARD, CPC

Sheri Bernard has contributed to the development of coding products for Ingenix for more than 10 years, and her areas of expertise include ICD-9-CM and ICD-10 coding systems. A member of the National Advisory Board of the American Academy of Professional Coders, Ms. Bernard chairs its committee on ICD-10, and is a nationally-recognized speaker on ICD-10 coding systems. Prior to joining Ingenix, Ms. Bernard was a journalist specializing in business and medical writing and editing.

COPYRIGHT

First edition copyright ©2002 Ingenix, Inc., First printing, November 2002
Printed in the United States of America.
ISBN 1-56329-945-3

Contents

Introduction

It is a reality in today's modern medical science that the codes within ICD•9•CM fall woefully short of today's medical reporting needs. ICD•9•CM was created more than 25 years ago as a modern and expansive system that was then only partially filled. Thousands of codes have been added to ICD•9•CM to classify new procedures and diseases over the years, and today the remaining space in ICD•9•CM procedural and diagnostic coding systems cannot accommodate our new technologies or our new understanding of diseases. An overhaul of our coding systems is needed.

New coding systems have been developed. Through the World Health Organization (WHO), ICD•10 was created and adopted in 1994. This is the system upon which the new U.S. diagnostic coding system, ICD•10•CM, is based. Concurrent to the clinical modification of ICD•10 by the National Center for Health Statistics (NCHS), the Centers for Medicare and Medicaid Services (CMS) commissioned 3M Health Information Management to develop a new procedural coding system to replace Volume 3 of ICD•9•CM, used for inpatient procedural coding.

Now that the coding systems have been designed and written, they need only be implemented; but progress is slow. The government is moving very cautiously toward implementation, partly because (1) the medical reimbursement industry is already reeling under the impact of the Health Insurance Portability and Accountability Act of 1996; (2) the scope of change is massive and will have a profound effect upon all care providers, payers, and government agencies; and (3) the change is big enough and costly enough to carry considerable political impact.

Two important events occurred late in 2002 that affected ICD•10•CM and ICD•10•PCS and their implementation: First, a subcommittee on coding for the National Center for Vital and Health Statistics (NCVHS) forwarded a recommendation to the full committee that ICD•10•CM and ICD•10•PCS be adopted by the Secretary of Health and Human Services (HHS). The recommendation of the subcommittee is important and will most likely pass the full committee and be sent to the Secretary of HHS. That takes ICD•10•CM and ICD•10•PCS one step closer to national rule making, which opens up a formal public comment period. The second event was the posting of a near-final draft of ICD•10•CM on the CMS website. While an earlier draft included only the tabular section of ICD•10•CM, this draft included the index as well. (The final draft of ICD•10•PCS has been available for more than a year.)

Any way you look at it, the system changes cannot occur before October 2005 or 2006. That's because, at the time of publication of *Ingenix Coding Lab: Implementing ICD•10*, we are still months away from any official designation of these code sets, and the law is written in such a way that everyone affected by a new coding system will have at least two years' notification before the codes are required. That's not a long way off, considering the innumerable issues you must understand today to ensure a smooth transition.

 DEFINITION

WHO. World Health Organization. The international agency that maintains an international nomenclature of diseases, causes of death, and public health practices. WHO, with advice from participating countries, developed ICD•9 to track morbidity and mortality statistics worldwide. It recently updated diagnostic coding with ICD•10. Find WHO at: http://www.who.org/

CMS. Centers for Medicare and Medicaid Services, formerly the Health Care Financing Administration (HCFA). A federal agency that provides health insurance for more than 74 million Americans through Medicare, Medicaid, and Child Health. CMS contracted for the development of a new procedural coding system by 3M HIS. Find CMS at: http://www.cms.hhs.gov/

NCHS. National Center for Health Statistics. The U.S. government agency that, jointly with CMS, refines the diagnostic portion of ICD•9•CM and is responsible for the clinical modification of ICD•10. NCHS holds several hearings a year to consider changes or additions in diagnostic coding. Find NCHS at: http://www.cdc.gov/nchswww/

The purpose of this book is to explain those issues. First, *Ingenix Coding Lab: Implementing ICD•10* provides a comprehensive introduction to ICD•10•CM. This reference analyzes the similarities and differences between ICD•9•CM and ICD•10•CM and provides a preview of ICD•10•PCS. Most importantly, *Ingenix Coding Lab: Implementing ICD•10* teaches you how to prepare your business office for the significant changes the new coding systems will bring. Everyone in your facility will be affected: human resources staff, accountants, information systems staff, physicians — just to name a few. The proposed codes provide tremendous opportunities for disease and procedure tracking, but also create enormous challenges. Computer hardware and software, medical documentation, and the reimbursement cycle are just three of the foundations of medical reimbursement that will be shaken when implementation occurs.

You can take many actions today to help reduce the impact of implementation in the years to come. This book will guide you in identifying the strategies you can employ to make implementation easier for your business office. A heightened awareness of the issues surrounding ICD•10•CM can do the following:

- Prevent your organization from investing in potentially obsolete equipment.
- Guide you in cultivating the right skill sets required for ICD•10•CM implementation.
- Allow your financial managers to prepare for the added capital and personnel investments required by the change.
- Minimize the overall impact of the change for your organization.

HISTORY OF MODIFICATIONS TO ICD

WHO's original intent for ICD was as a statistical tool for the international exchange of mortality data. A subsequent revision was expanded to accommodate data collection for morbidity statistics. An eventual seventh revision, published by WHO in 1955, was clinically modified for use in the United States based upon a joint study on the efficiency of hospital diseases indexing by the American Hospital Association (AHA) and the American Association of Medical Record Librarians (AAMRL). Results of that study led to the 1959 publication of the International Classification of Diseases, Adapted for Indexing Hospital Records (ICDA), by the federal Public Health Service. The ICDA uniformly modified ICD•7, and it gave the United States a way to classify operations and treatments.

Hospitals were initially slow in their acceptance of ICDA, though momentum picked up. An eighth edition of ICD, published by WHO in 1965, lacked the depth of clinical data required for America's emerging healthcare system. In 1968, two widely accepted modifications were published in the United States: the Eighth Revision International Classification of Diseases Adapted for Use in the United States (ICDA-8) and the Hospital Adaptation of ICDA (H-ICDA). Hospitals used either of these two systems through the latter years of the next decade.

ICD•9

The ninth revision by WHO in 1975 prompted the typical American response: clinical modification. This time the impetus flowed from a process initiated in 1977 by NCHS to modify ICD•9 for hospital indexing and retrieving case data for clinical studies. The NCHS and the newly created Council on Clinical Classifications

KEY POINT

Two federal agencies, NCHS and CMS, are responsible for the development of the ICD•9•CM replacement, i.e., ICD•10•CM and ICD•10•PCS.

DEFINITION

Morbidity. The disease rate — or number of cases of a particular disease — in a given age range, gender, occupation, or other relevant population-based grouping.

Mortality. The death rate reflected by the population in a given region, age range, or other relevant statistical grouping.

The Centers for Disease Control in Atlanta publishes a weekly epidemiologic report on the incidence of communicable diseases and deaths (morbidity and mortality) in selected urban areas of the United States.

modified ICD•9 according to U.S. clinical standards, and developed a companion procedural classification. This classification, published as Volume 3 of ICD•9•CM, revised a portion of WHO's International Classification of Procedure Modification (ICPM). In 1978, the three-volume set was published in the United States for use one year later. There were no further changes in the direction to ICD•9•CM until the October 1983 implementation of Diagnosis Related Groups (DRGs), which gave ICD•9•CM a new significance. After almost 30 years since ICD's arrival in the United States, the classification system proves indispensable to hospitals interested in payment schedules for healthcare services.

ICD•10

The evolution of ICD took another turn in 1994 when WHO published ICD•10. Again, the NCHS wanted to modify the latest revision, but with an emphasis on problems that had been identified in the current ICD•9•CM and resolved by the improvements to ICD•10 for classifying mortality and morbidity data. The Center for Health Policy Studies (CHPS) was awarded the NCHS contract to analyze ICD•10 and to develop the appropriate clinical modifications.

ICD•10•CM

Phase I provided the analysis for clinical modification. According to CHPS, ICD•10 must be modified to do the following:

- Return the level of specificity found in ICD•9•CM.
- Facilitate an alphabetic index to assign codes.
- Provide code titles and language that complement accepted clinical practice.
- Remove codes unique to mortality coding.

Phase II followed protocol. CHPS developed modifications based on the analysis, including the following:

- Increasing the five-character structure to six characters
- Incorporating common 4th and 5th digit subclassifications
- Creating laterality
- Combining certain codes
- Adding trimesters to obstetric codes
- Creating combined diagnosis/symptoms codes
- Deactivating procedure codes

In the second phase, CHPS expanded the codes for alcohol/drug abuse, diabetes mellitus, and injuries.

A draft of ICD•10•CM for public comment was released at the conclusion of Phase II. The final version will draw on an analysis of the comments by NCHS and Phase III reviewers.

ICD•10•PCS

ICD•10•PCS was developed to replace ICD•9•CM Volume 3 under a three-year contract with CMS, beginning in 1995. PCS was developed with these CMS objectives in mind: completeness, expandability, uniform structure, and standardized terminology. The contract included: completion of the first draft in year one; training and testing in inpatient and outpatient facilities with revision of the system to accommodate problems revealed in testing; and formal testing in the third year. The

 KEY POINT

WHO's seventh edition of ICD was the first edition modified by the United States. Two versions of a modified ICD•8 were published in 1968. A procedural classification was created by the U.S. government and accompanied the clinical modification of ICD•9, which was published here in 1978.

testing has been completed and results have been reviewed by specialty groups independent of CMS and tested at Clinical Data Abstractions Centers (CDAC). Their work resulted in a final version now standing ready as a replacement for ICD•9•CM Volume 3.

The issue of replacing ICD•9•CM Volume 3 with ICD•10•PCS has become somewhat politicized, and inpatient implementation has been clouded by other issues. In June 1997, the National Center for Vital and Health Statistics recommended a single procedure classification rather than two. Currently CPT is used for physician coding, and Volume 3 for inpatient. NCVHS stated, "We recommend that you advise the industry to build and modify their information systems to accommodate …[a] major change to a unified approach to coding procedures…[We] recommend that you identify and implement an approach for procedure coding that addresses deficiencies in the current systems, including issues of specificity and aggregation, unnecessary redundancy, and incomplete coverage of healthcare providers and settings." It is the concern of some that implementation of ICD•10•PCS could jeopardize the position of the American Medical Association's CPT codes for physician coding.

More recently, the American Health Information Management Association, in testimony at the May 2001 Coordination and Maintenance Committee hearing on ICD•10•PCS, suggested that before ICD•10•PCS is implemented, the issue of one or two procedural coding systems should be decided.

Ingenix Coding Lab: Implementing ICD•10

Chapters and appendixes in the book address these pertinent issues about ICD•10•CM:

- **Chapter 1** describes the major areas that have been clinically modified from the WHO 10th revision of ICD.
- **Chapter 2** reviews the differences and similarities in coding rules and conventions found in ICD•10•CM, as compared to ICD•9•CM.
- **Chapter 3** explores each code family in ICD•10•CM and organizational changes made to disease classification.
- **Chapter 4** addresses a variety of implementation issues surrounding the transition to the 10th revision of ICD.
- **Chapter 5** discusses proposed procedural coding systems, ICD•10•PCS and CPT-5.
- **Chapter 6** describes the impact of national standards under HIPAA on coding systems.
- **Chapter 7** examines documentation issues and considerations for ICD•10•CM.
- **The appendix** provides a complete list of the three-digit categories valid in ICD•10•CM.
- **The Index** facilitates easy lookups

 FOR MORE INFO

NCHS has indicated that the final ICD•10•CM will be posted on the Web at www.cdc.gov/nchswww/about/otheract/ICD9/ICD9HP2.html.

The final draft of ICD•10•PCS is available on the CMS home page (http://www.cms.hhs.gov) under Stats and Data, Public Use Files.

1 Clinical Modifications

OVERVIEW OF CHANGES

Before the clinical modifications to ICD•10 are reviewed and understood, you must first become familiar with the changes made by the World Health Organization when it moved from ICD•9 to ICD•10. The first clue to the revisions is in the full title: International Statistical Classification of Diseases and Related Health Problems. WHO felt this change would not only clarify the classification's content and purpose, but show how the scope of the classification has moved beyond the classification of disease and injuries to the coding of ambulatory care conditions and risk factors frequently encountered in primary care.

Overall, the tenth revision results in an increase in clinical detail and addresses information about previously classified diseases as well as those diseases discovered since the last revision. Conditions are grouped according to the most appropriate for general epidemiological purposes and the evaluation of healthcare. Organizational changes are made and new features added. However, for the most part the format and conventions of the classification remain unchanged.

Keep in mind as you become familiar with ICD•10 and ICD•10•CM that many of the codes considered new in ICD•10 are not necessarily new to users of ICD•9•CM. This is because of the clinical modification of ICD•9 that originally augmented those codes for use in the United States in 1977-1978, and has continued to keep the codes updated annually since 1985. For example, look at the codes available for angina:

ICD•9

413   Angina pectoris

ICD•9•CM

411.1   Intermediate coronary syndrome (includes unstable angina)
413.0   Angina decubitus
413.1   Prinzmetal angina
413.9   Other and unspecified angina pectoris — (includes angina of effort and stenocardia)

ICD•10

All diseases of the circulatory system appear under the letter "I" in ICD•10.

I20.0   Unstable angina
I20.1   Angina pectoris with documented spasm — (includes Prinzmetal angina)
I20.8   Other forms of angina pectoris — (includes angina of effort and stenocardia)
I20.9   Angina pectoris, unspecified

OBJECTIVES

- Provide insight into the purpose of ICD•10•CM.
- Identify the motivations for clinically modifying ICD•10.
- Identify major areas of general clinical modifications made to ICD•10.
- Learn about the many important uses of ICD•10 and ICD•10•CM beyond reimbursement.

No further additions were made to the ICD•10 entries for angina pectoris in ICD•10•CM.

ICD•10 Structure

The WHO published ICD•10 in three volumes. The publication dates for the three volumes are 1992 for Volume 1, 1993 for Volume 2, and 1994 for Volume 3.

Volume 1

Volume 1 contains the listing of alphanumeric codes. The same hierarchical organization of ICD•9 applies to ICD•10: All codes with the same first three digits have common traits. Each digit beyond three adds more specificity. In ICD•10, valid codes can conain anywhere from three to five digits. However, ICD•10•CM for use in the U.S. has been expanded with valid codes containing anywhere from three to seven characters. The extension to seven characters was made with the latest revision. In some instances, the final character may be a lower case letter, known as an alpha extension, and not a number. In some cases, the use of a "reserve" subclassification (identified as an 'x') has been incorporated into codes that continue with greater specificity beyond the fifth digit to allow for built-in expansion within that established level of specificity. Some examples of valid codes in ICD•10 include the following:

E41   **Nutritional marasmus**
  I01.1   **Acute rheumatic endocarditis**
    S32.10   Fracture of sacrum, closed

Valid codes in ICD•10•CM:

E41   **Nutritional marasmus**
  I01.1   **Acute rheumatic endocarditis**
    S32.10   Unspecified fracture of sacrum
      S91.331   Puncture wound without foreign body, right foot
      W22.042q Striking against wall of swimming pool causing other injury, sequelae
    H81.4x1   Vertigo of central origin, right ear

The same ICD•9 hierarchical organization is at work in ICD•10 notes and instructions. When a note appears under a three-character code, it applies to all codes within that rubric. Instructions under a specific four- or five-character code apply only to that single code.

Volume 1 Tabular List

The following is an example of the tabular listing in ICD•10:

Other Disorders of the Skin and Subcutaneous Tissue (L80-L99)
L80   **Vitiligo**
L81   **Other disorders of pigmentation**
      Excludes: birthmark NOS (Q82.5)
          naevus — see Alphabetic Index
          Peutz-Jeghers syndrome (Q85.8)
    L81.0   **Postinflammatory hyperpigmentation**

KEY POINT

When a note appears under a three-digit code, it applies to all codes within that rubric.

L81.1 Chloasma
L81.2 Freckles
L81.3 Café au lait spots
L81.4 Other melanin hyperpigmentation
    Lentigo
L81.5 Leukoderma, not elsewhere classified
L81.6 Other disorders of diminished melanin formation
L81.7 Pigmented purpuric dermatosis
    Angioma serpiginosum
L81.8 Other specified disorders of pigmentation
    Iron pigmentation
    Tattoo pigmentation
L81.9 Disorder of pigmentation, unspecified

L82 **Seborrhoeic keratosis**
    Dermatosis papulosa nigra
    Leser-Trélat disease

L83 **Acanthosis nigricans**
    Confluent and reticulated papillomatosis

L84 **Corns and callosities**
    Callus
    Clavus

This is how the tabular list looks in ICD•10•CM:

Other Disorders of the Skin and Subcutaneous Tissue (L80-L99)

L80 **Vitiligo**

L81 **Other disorders of pigmentation**
    Excludes1: birthmark NOS (Q82.5)
                Peutz-Jeghers syndrome (Q85.8)
    Excludes2: nevus — see Alphabetic Index

L81.2 Freckles
L81.3 Café au lait spots
L81.4 Other melanin hyperpigmentation
    Lentigo
L81.5 Leukoderma, not elsewhere classified
L81.6 Other disorders of diminished melanin formation
L81.7 Pigmented purpuric dermatosis
    Angioma serpiginosum
L81.8 Other specified disorders of pigmentation
    Iron pigmentation
    Tattoo pigmentation
L81.9 Disorder of pigmentation, unspecified

L82 **Seborrheic keratosis**
    Includes: dermatosis papulosa nigra
             Leser-Trélat disease
L82.0 Inflamed seborrheic keratosis
L82.1 Other seborrheic keratosis
    Seborrheic keratosis NOS

L83 **Acanthosis nigricans**
    Includes: confluent and reticulated papillomatosis

L84   Corns and callosities
Includes: callus
clavus

Volume 2 Instruction Manual

In WHO's publication, Volume 2 provides rules and guidelines for mortality and morbidity coding. For ICD•10•CM, it is undecided whether a separate volume will be dedicated to rules, or if these will be organized under a different title. Since NCHS's publication of ICD•10•CM will likely parallel the ICD•9•CM publication and thus be limited to CD-ROM, the issue of a separate volume is unimportant. However, if Volume 2 remains the title of the instructional manual after clinical modification in the United States, coders will need to remember that Volume 2 refers to instructions, and not the index, which is what Volume 2 provides in ICD•9•CM.

CMS and NCHS are modifying the instructions of ICD•10 for use in the United States. These modifications are not yet available. Following is a sample of the ICD•10 instructions:

4.4.1   Guidelines for recording diagnostic information for single-condition analysis of morbidity data

General

The healthcare practitioner responsible for the patient's treatment should select the main condition to be recorded, as well as any other conditions, for each episode of healthcare. This information should be organized systematically by using standard recording methods. A properly completed record is essential for good patient management and is a valuable source of epidemiological and other statistical data on morbidity and other healthcare problems.

Specificity and Detail

Each diagnostic statement should be as informative as possible in order to classify the condition to the most specific ICD category. Examples of such diagnostic statements include:

- Transitional cell carcinoma of trigone of bladder
- Acute appendicitis with perforation
- Diabetic cataract, insulin-dependent
- Meningococcal pericarditis
- Antenatal care for pregnancy-induced hypertension
- Diplopia due to allergic reaction to antihistamine taken as prescribed
- Osteoarthritis of hip due to an old hip fracture
- Fracture of neck of femur following a fall at home
- Third-degree burn of palm of hand

Uncertain Diagnoses or Symptoms

If no definite diagnosis has been established by the end of an episode of care, then the information that permits the greatest degree of and knowledge about the condition that necessitated care or investigation should be recorded. This should be done by stating a symptom, abnormal finding, or problem, rather than qualifying a diagnosis as "possible,"

KEY POINT

NCHS's publication of ICD•10•CM will likely parallel ICD•9•CM, and thus be limited to CD-ROM. Private publishers will produce ICD•10•CM books.

"questionable," or "suspected," when it has been considered but not established.

Volume 3 Alphabetic Index

Volume 3 provides the index to the codes in the Tabular List. As in the ICD•9•CM index, terms in the ICD•10 index are found alphabetically, by diagnosis. This is no different for ICD•10•CM. Therefore, a code for a supernumerary nipple would be accessed by looking under Supernumerary, then nipple. This is how the alphabetic index appears in ICD•10•CM:

Alphabetical Index to Diseases and Nature of Injury

Supernumerary (congenital)
    aortic cusps Q23.8
    auditory ossicles Q16.3
    bone Q79.8
    breast Q83.1
    carpal bones Q74.0
    cusps, heart valve NEC Q24.8
        aortic Q23.8
        mitral Q23.2
        pulmonary Q22.3
    digit(s) Q69.9
    ear (lobule) Q17.0
    fallopian tube Q50.6
    finger Q69.0
    hymen Q52.4
    kidney Q63.0
    lacrimonasal duct Q10.6
    lobule (ear) Q17.0
    mitral cusps Q23.2
    muscle Q79.8
    nipple(s) Q83.3
    organ or site not listed - see Accessory
    ossicles, auditory Q16.3
    ovary Q50.31
    oviduct Q50.6
    pulmonary, pulmonary cusps Q22.3
    rib Q76.6
        cervical or first (syndrome) Q76.5
    roots (of teeth) K00.2
    spleen Q89.09
    tarsal bones Q74.2
    teeth K00.1
        causing crowding M26.3
    testis Q55.29
    thumb Q69.1
    toe Q69.2
    uterus Q51.2
    vagina Q52.1
    vertebra Q76.49

 KEY POINT

Volume 3 in ICD•9•CM is a listing of procedural codes.

Volume 3 in ICD•10 is the index to the diseases listed in the tabular section.

ICD•10 Code Structure

All codes in ICD•10 and ICD•10•CM are alphanumeric, i.e., one letter followed by two numbers at the three-character level, as opposed to three numeric characters in the main classification of ICD•9•CM. Of the 26 available letters, all but the letter U is used, which was reserved for additions and changes that may need to be incorporated in the future or for classification difficulties that may arise between revisions. New codes for terrorism were created after September 11, 2001, within the framework of ICD•10 and ICD•9•CM. They have been incorporated into ICD•9•CM for 2002 and proposed for implementation in ICD•10 as U codes. The new U codes for terrorism have not officially been adopted by WHO yet and will be identified as U.S. codes by an asterisk to distinguish them from official ICD codes.

Some three-character categories have been left vacant for future expansion and revision. A listing of all ICD•10•CM three-digit categories is presented in the appendix to Ingenix Coding Lab: ICD•10 Implementation.

ICD•9•CM

440	Atherosclerosis
441	Aortic aneurysm and dissection
442	Other aneurysm
443	Other peripheral vascular disease
444	Arterial embolism and thrombosis
446	Polyarteritis nodosa and allied conditions
447	Other disorders of arteries and arterioles
448	Disease of capillaries

ICD•10

Diseases of Arteries, Arterioles and Capillaries (I70-I79)

I70	Atherosclerosis
I71	Aortic aneurysm and dissection
I72	Other aneurysm
I73	Other peripheral vascular diseases
I74	Arterial embolism and thrombosis
I77	Other disorders of arteries and arterioles
I78	Diseases of capillaries
I79	Disorders of arteries, arterioles and capillaries in diseases classified elsewhere

There are no further additions within the subchapter, "Diseases of Arteries, Arterioles and Capillaries" (I70-I79) for ICD•10•CM.

Though the use of alpha characters I and O may be confused with numbers 1 and 0, coders should remember that the first character in the ICD•10 system is always a letter, and the following characters are always numerical. Within ICD•10•CM, there is the exception of those codes containing an alpha extension in the final character position or a reserve subclassification, denoted as 'x'.

ICD•10 Category Restructuring

The review of the different diseases and how they are classified in ICD•9 resulted in the restructuring of some of the categories in ICD•10.

ICD•9•CM

In ICD•9•CM, a fifth digit in categories 433 and 434 identifies whether cerebral infarction is mentioned.

433   **Occlusion and stenosis of precerebral arteries**
434   **Occlusion of cerebral arteries**
435   **Transient cerebral ischemia**
436   **Acute, but ill-defined, cerebrovascular disease**

ICD•10

In ICD•10, category I63 includes occlusion and stenosis of cerebral and precerebral arteries, resulting in cerebral infarction.

I63   **Cerebral infarction**
I64   **Stroke, not specified as hemorrhage or infarction**
I65   **Occlusion and stenosis of precerebral arteries, not resulting in cerebral infarction**
I66   **Occlusion and stenosis of cerebral arteries, not resulting in cerebral infarction**

GENERAL ORGANIZATION OF ICD•10

In ICD•10, a chapter may encompass more than one letter and more than one chapter may share a letter.

Chapter 2 – Neoplasms (C00-D48)

Chapter 3 – Diseases of the Blood and Blood-Forming Organs and Certain Disorders Involving the Immune System (D50-D89)

Organizational Changes

The Tabular List is comprised of 21 chapters versus the 17 main chapters and two supplementary classifications (V and E codes) for ICD•9•CM. As in ICD•9•CM, many of the chapters classify diseases of an organ or system. Others are devoted to specific types of conditions grouped according to etiology or nature, e.g., neoplasms, referred to in ICD•10 as "special group" chapters. Three chapters do not fall into either of these categories.

ICD•9•CM

Classification of Diseases and Injuries

1. Infectious and Parasitic Diseases

2. Neoplasms

3. Endocrine, Nutritional and Metabolic Diseases, and Immunity Disorders

4. Diseases of the Blood and Blood-Forming Organs

5. Mental Disorders

6. Diseases of the Nervous System and Sense Organs

7. Diseases of the Circulatory System

8. Diseases of the Respiratory System

 KEY POINT

E codes of ICD•9•CM become V codes, W codes, X codes, and Y codes in ICD•10.

And ICD•9•CM's V codes become Z codes in ICD•10.

ICD•10•CM CODES

V03.10a Pedestrian on foot injured in collision with car, pick-up truck or van in traffic accident, initial encounter

W52.q Crushed, pushed or stepped on by crowd or human stampede, sequelae

X37.0a Hurricane, initial encounter

Y65.2 Failure in suture or ligature during surgical operation

Z80.49 Family history of malignant neoplasm of other genital organs

9. Diseases of the Digestive System

10. Diseases of the Genitourinary System

11. Complications of Pregnancy, Childbirth, and the Puerperium

12. Diseases of the Skin and Subcutaneous Tissue

13. Diseases of the Musculoskeletal System and Connective Tissue

14. Congenital Anomalies

15. Certain Conditions Originating in the Perinatal Period

16. Symptoms, Signs, and Ill-Defined Conditions

17. Injury and Poisoning

18. Classification of Factors Influencing Health Status and Contact with Health Services (V Codes)

19. Classification of External Causes of Injury and Poisoning (E Codes)

ICD•10

1. Certain Infectious and Parasitic Diseases

2. Neoplasms

3. Diseases of the Blood and Blood-Forming Organs and Certain Disorders Involving the Immune Mechanism

4. Endocrine, Nutritional and Metabolic Diseases

5. Mental and Behavioural Disorders

6. Diseases of the Nervous System

7. Diseases of the Eye and Adnexa

8. Diseases of the Ear and Mastoid Process

9. Diseases of the Circulatory System

10. Diseases of the Respiratory System

11. Diseases of the Digestive System

12. Diseases of the Skin and Subcutaneous Tissue

13. Diseases of the Musculoskeletal System and Connective Tissue

14. Diseases of the Genitourinary System

15. Pregnancy, Childbirth, and the Puerperium

16. Certain Conditions Originating in the Perinatal Period

17. Congenital Malformations, Deformations and Chromosomal Abnormalities

18. Symptoms, Signs and Abnormal Clinical and Laboratory Findings, Not Elsewhere Classified

19. Injury, Poisoning and Certain Other Consequences of External Causes

20. External Causes of Morbidity and Mortality

21. Factors Influencing Health Status and Contact with Health Services

 KEY POINT

The three chapters that do not fall into either the body system or the "special groups" are: "Symptoms, Signs and Abnormal Clinical and Laboratory Findings, Not Elsewhere Classified"; "External Causes of Morbidity and Mortality"; and "Factors Influencing Health Status and Contact with Health Services."

The revision of a chapter's title may have occurred for a variety of reasons. For example, the term "Complications of ..." has been removed from the title of the pregnancy chapter as a number of categories in this chapter describe uncomplicated deliveries.

The two new chapters in ICD•10 are "Diseases of the Eye and Adnexa" and "Diseases of the Ear and Mastoid Process." "The External Causes of Morbidity and Mortality and Factors Influencing Health Status" and "Contact with Health Services" chapters are no longer considered to be supplementary, but are a part of the core classification.

Some of the chapter titles are revised in ICD•10. For example, in ICD•9•CM, the title of Chapter 5 is "Mental Disorders." In ICD•10, it is "Mental and Behavioural Disorders." The term "certain" is added to the title of Chapter 1, "Infectious and Parasitic Diseases" to stress the fact that localized infections are classified with the diseases of the pertinent body system. The title of the ICD•9•CM chapter of congenital anomalies is expanded to include "Congenital Malformations, Deformations and Chromosomal Abnormalities."

There also is a rearrangement of the chapter order from ICD•9•CM to ICD•10. This includes expanding the number of categories for disorders of the immune mechanism and placing them with diseases of the blood and blood-forming organs. In ICD•9•CM, these disorders are included with "Endocrine, Nutritional and Metabolic Diseases." The chapters for "Diseases of the Genitourinary System," "Pregnancy, Childbirth and the Puerperium," "Certain Conditions Originating in the Perinatal Period," and "Congenital Malformations, Deformations and Chromosomal Abnormalities" are placed sequentially in ICD•10.

Also, some conditions are reassigned to a different chapter because of new knowledge about those conditions since the last revision. For example, in ICD•9•CM, gout is classified to Chapter 3, "Endocrine, Nutritional, and Metabolic Diseases and Immunity Disorders," and in ICD•10, it is classified to Chapter 13, "Diseases of the Musculoskeletal System and Connective Tissue." See Chapter 3 for more information on disease reclassifications.

NEW FEATURES TO ICD•10

There are a number of new features to ICD•10 with which users will need to become familiar. These additions provide clarity and facilitate proper use of the classification.

More Complete Descriptions

In ICD•9•CM, often the user must review the description of the category in order to determine the complete intent of the subcategory or subclassification. One needs to review the title of the category to understand the meaning of the code. In ICD•10, the subcategory titles are usually complete, with the exception of some codes in the neoplasm and health circumstances sections. In ICD•10•CM, NCHS is striving to make all code descriptions complete.

ICD•9•CM

Typically, in ICD•9•CM, codes are presented in this fashion:

451   **Phlebitis and thrombophlebitis**
      451.0   **of superficial vessels of lower extremities**

 KEY POINT

One major difference in ICD•10•CM is that codes will have complete descriptions rather than relying on the hierarchy.

ICD•10•CM

In ICD•10•CM, most codes have complete descriptions:

I80   **Phlebitis and thrombophlebitis**

      I80.0   **Phlebitis and thrombophlebitis of superficial vessels of lower extremities**

            I80.03   **Phlebitis and thrombophlebitis of superficial vessels of lower extremities, bilateral**

Postprocedural Disorders

New categories for postprocedural disorders specific to a particular body system have been created at the end of each body system chapter. There has been no change to the classification of those situations in which postprocedural conditions are not specific to a particular body system, such as postoperative hemorrhage. However, see page 28 for additional ICD•10•CM changes to these disorders. These can be found in ICD•10 in Chapter 19, "Injury, Poisoning and Certain Other Consequences of External Causes," which is compatible to ICD•9•CM.

ICD•9•CM

In ICD•9•CM, complications specific to the digestive system are not located under one category.

564   **Functional digestive disorders, not elsewhere classified**

      564.2   **Postgastric surgery syndromes**

      564.3   **Vomiting following gastrointestinal surgery**

      564.4   **Other postoperative functional disorders**

569   **Other disorders of intestine**

      569.6   **Colostomy and enterostomy complications**

            569.60 **Colostomy and enterostomy complications, unspecified**

            569.61 **Infection of colostomy or enterostomy**

            569.62 **Mechanical complication of colostomy and enterostomy**

            569.69 **Other complication**

ICD•10•CM

In ICD•10 and ICD•10•CM complications specific to the digestive system are located under the new category for postprocedural disorders.

K91   **Intraoperative and postprocedural complications and disorders of digestive system, not elsewhere classified**

      K91.0   **Vomiting following gastrointestinal surgery**

      K91.1   **Postgastric surgery syndromes**

      K91.2   **Postsurgical malabsorption, not elsewhere classified**

      K91.3   **Postoperative intestinal obstruction**

      K91.5   **Postcholecystectomy syndrome**

      K91.6   **Intraoperative and postprocedural hemorrhage and hematoma complicating a digestive system procedure**

      K91.7   **Accidental puncture or laceration during a digestive system procedure**

DEFINITION

Iatrogenic. Caused by or resulting from medical treatment as in an adverse reaction to a prescribed drug or a postoperative infection. Keep an eye out for this term as physicians may use it to describe a postprocedural disorder.

K91.8   Other postprocedural disorders of digestive system, not
         elsewhere classified

K91.9   Postprocedural disorder of digestive system, unspecified

Notes

The tenth revision contains some changes to the notes as well. At the beginning of
each chapter, "excludes" notes were expanded to provide guidance on the hierarchy of
chapters and to clarify the priority of code assignment.

ICD•10•CM

The following excludes note, found in Chapter 14, indicates the priority of the
"special group" chapters over the genitourinary system chapter.

Diseases of the Genitourinary System (N00-N99)

Excludes2: certain conditions originating in the perinatal period (P04-
             P96)

             certain infectious and parasitic diseases (A00-B99)

             complications of pregnancy, childbirth and the puerperium
              (O00-O99)

             congenital malformations, deformations and chromosomal
              abnormalities (Q00-Q99)

             endocrine, nutritional and metabolic diseases (E00-E90)

             injury, poisoning and certain other consequences of external
              causes (S00-T98)

             neoplasms (C00-D48)

             symptoms, signs and abnormal clinical and laboratory
              findings, not elsewhere classified (R00-R94)

ICD•10 Blocks

After the appropriate includes and excludes notes, each chapter starts with a list of the
subchapters or "blocks" of three-character categories. These blocks provide an
overview of the structure of the chapter.

ICD•10

The blocks for Chapter 14 are:

N00-N08	Glomerular diseases
N10-N16	Renal tubulo-interstitial diseases
N17-N19	Renal failure
N20-N23	Urolithiasis
N25-N29	Other disorders of kidney and ureter
N30-N39	Other diseases of the urinary system
N40-N51	Diseases of male genital organs
N60-N64	Disorders of breast
N70-N77	Inflammatory diseases of female pelvic organs
N80-N98	Noninflammatory disorders of female genital tract
N99	Other disorders of the genitourinary system

These have remained the same for ICD•10•CM.

KEY POINT

"Excludes" notes are expanded in ICD•10
to clarify priority of code assignment and to
provide guidance.

DEFINITION

Special group chapters. "Certain Infectious and Parasitic Diseases," "Neoplasms, Mental and Behavioral Disorders," "Pregnancy, Childbirth and the Puerperium," "Certain Conditions Originating in the Perinatal Period," "Congenital Malformations, Deformations and Chromosomal Abnormalities," and "Injury, Poisoning and Certain Other Consequences of External Causes."

MAJOR CHANGES TO ICD•10

Three chapters in ICD•10 underwent substantial revision. They are:

- Chapter 5 — Mental and Behavioral Disorders
- Chapter 19 — Injury, Poisoning and Certain Other Consequences of External Causes
- Chapter 20 — External Causes of Morbidity

Because major changes were made to these chapters, field-testing took place in a number of countries. In addition, WHO depended on technical support from specific groups in the revision. For example, the Nordic Medical Statistics Committee (NOMESCO) and the WHO Global Steering Committee on the Development of Indicators for Accidents had a major influence on the revision of the classification of injuries and external causes. A more thorough examination of these chapters can be found in Chapter 3 of Ingenix Coding Lab: ICD•10 Implementation.

Chapter 5 — Mental and Behavioral Disorders

Chapter 5 has undergone a number of revisions. First, the title has changed from Mental Disorders in ICD•9•CM to include Mental and Behavioral Disorders in ICD•10. Next, the number of subchapters was expanded from three to eleven.

ICD•9•CM

Chapter 5 — Mental Disorders (290-319)
> **Psychoses (290-299)**
> **Neurotic Disorders, Personality Disorders, and Other Nonpsychotic Mental Disorders (300-316)**
> **Mental Retardation (317-319)**

ICD•10

Chapter 5 — Mental and Behavioural Disorders

F00-F09	Organic, including symptomatic, mental disorders
F10-F19	Mental and behavioural disorders due to psychoactive substance use
F20-F29	Schizophrenia, schizotypal and delusional disorders
F30-F39	Mood [affective] disorders
F40-F48	Neurotic, stress-related and somatoform disorders
F50-F59	Behavioural syndromes associated with physiological disturbances and physical factors
F60-F69	Disorders of adult personality and behaviour
F70-F79	Mental retardation
F80-F89	Disorders of psychological development
F90-F98	Behavioural and emotional disorders with onset usually occurring in childhood and adolescence
F99	Unspecified mental disorder

With this expansion, ICD•10 arranges specific disorders differently than they were in ICD•9•CM, and the clinical detail also is expanded.

ICD•10•CM

Chapter 5 – Mental and Behavioral Disorders

F01-F09	Mental disorders due to known physiological conditions
F10-F19	Mental and behavioral disorders due to psychoactive substance use
F20-F29	Schizophrenia, schizotypal and delusional, and other non-mood psychotic disorders
F30-F39	Mood [affective] disorders
F40-F48	Anxiety, dissociative, stress-related, somatoform and other nonpsychotic mental disorders
F50-F59	Behavioral syndromes associated with physiological disturbances and physical factors
F60-F69	Disorders of adult personality and behavior
F70-F79	Mental retardation
F80-F89	Pervasive and specific developmental disorders
F90-F98	Behavioral and emotional disorders with onset usually occurring in childhood and adolescence
F99	Unspecified mental disorder

As you can see in this example, some of the block titles and ranges within these chapters have been changed in the development of ICD•10•CM.

ICD•9•CM

The ninth revision includes codes for a certain number of conditions that are drug induced.

292	**Drug psychoses**	
	292.0	**Drug withdrawal syndrome**
		292.11 Drug-induced organic delusional syndrome
		292.12 Drug-induced hallucinosis
	292.2	**Pathological drug intoxication**
		292.81 Drug-induced delirium
		292.82 Drug-induced dementia
		292.83 Drug-induced amnestic syndrome
		292.84 Drug-induced organic affective syndrome
		292.89 Other specified drug-induced mental disorders
	292.9	**Unspecified drug-induced mental disorder**

ICD•10

In ICD•10, a number of categories are available to specify the drug causing mental and behavioral disorders due to psychoactive substance use. In addition, there are 10 fourth-character subdivisions to use with these categories to identify the specific mental and behavioral disorder, such as withdrawal state (.3) or withdrawal state with delirium (.4).

Mental and behavioural disorders due to psychoactive substance use (F10-F19)

F10	**Mental and behavioral disorders due to use of alcohol**
F11	**Mental and behavioral disorders due to use of opioids**
F12	**Mental and behavioral disorders due to use of cannabinoids**
F13	**Mental and behavioral disorders due to use of sedatives or hypnotics**

FOR MORE INFO

ICD•10•CM includes additional revisions to the categories for drugs causing the mental and behavioral disorders due to psychoactive substance use.

F14	Mental and behavioral disorders due to use of cocaine
F15	Mental and behavioral disorders due to use of other stimulants, including caffeine
F16	Mental and behavioral disorders due to use of hallucinogens
F17	Mental and behavioral disorders due to use of tobacco
F18	Mental and behavioral disorders due to use of volatile solvents
F19	Mental and behavioral disorders due to multiple drug use and use of other psychoactive substances

ICD•10•CM

ICD•10•CM includes additional revisions to this subchapter: Three other fourth-character subdivisions are used with these categories — excepting F17 — to identify abuse (.1), dependence (.2), or unspecified use (.9). Fifth and sixth-character subdivisions further specify the state of the mental and behavioral disorder, such as intoxication, intoxication with delirium, psychotic disorder with hallucinations, remission, or withdrawal.

Mental and behavioral disorders due to psychoactive substance use (F10-F19)

F10	Alcohol-related disorders
F11	Opioid-related disorders
F12	Cannabis-related disorders
F13	Sedative, hypnotic, or anxiolytic-related disorders
F14	Cocaine-related disorders
F15	Other stimulant-related disorders
F16	Hallucinogen-related disorders
F17	Nicotine dependence
F18	Inhalant-related disorders
F19	Other psychoactive substance-related disorders

Chapter 19 — Injury, Poisoning, and Certain Other Consequences of External Causes

The axis of classification for Chapter 19, "Injury, Poisoning and Certain Other Consequences of External Causes" (Chapter 17, "Injury and Poisoning," in ICD•9•CM) is changed from "type of injury" and then "site of injury" in ICD•9•CM to "body region" and then to "type of injury" in ICD•10.

ICD•9•CM

"Fractures" is the first subchapter in the "Injury and Poisoning" chapter of ICD•9•CM. The breakdown is then by site, e.g., vault of skull, base of skull.

Chapter 17 — Injury and Poisoning
Fractures (800-829)
Fracture of Skull (800-804)

800	Fracture of vault of skull
801	Fracture of base of skull
802	Fracture of face bones
803	Other and unqualified skull fracture
804	Multiple fractures involving skull or face with other bones

ICD•10

Chapter 19 in ICD•10 is a large chapter. It spans two letters, S00-T88. The S codes cover different injury types in relation to a particular, single body region, and the T codes cover injuries to unspecified or multiple body regions, poisonings, burns, frostbite, complications of care, and other consequences of external causes. The chapter, "Injury, Poisoning and Certain Other Consequences of External Causes" describes injuries to the head (the body region) and then breaks down the injury by type, e.g., superficial injury of head, open wound of head.

Chapter 19 – Injury, Poisoning and Certain Other Consequences of External Causes

Injuries to the head (S00-S09)

S00	Superficial injury of head
S01	Open wound of head
S02	Fracture of skull and facial bones
S03	Dislocation, sprain and strain of joints and ligaments of head
S04	Injury of cranial nerves
S05	Injury of eye and orbit
S06	Intracranial injury
S07	Crushing injury of head
S08	Traumatic amputation of part of head
S09	Other and unspecified injuries of head

Categories S03 and S08 have undergone title changes in ICD•10•CM:

S03	Dislocation and sprain of joints and ligaments of head
S08	Avulsion and traumatic amputation of part of head

Chapter 20 – External Causes of Morbidity and Mortality

The chapter for external causes of morbidity and mortality also has been changed in a number of ways. In ICD•9•CM, the supplementary classification of external causes of injury and poisoning (E codes) is found at the end of the Tabular List. In ICD•10, these codes follow Chapter 19, "Injury, Poisoning and Certain Other Consequences of External Causes," and consist of categories V01-Y98. In addition, the transport accidents section of the external causes chapter has been completely revised and extended with blocks of categories identifying the victim's mode of transport.

ICD•9•CM

In ICD•9•CM, the main axis is whether the event was a traffic or non-traffic accident.

Supplementary classification of external causes of injury and poisoning (E800-E999)

Railway accidents (E800-E807)
Motor vehicle traffic accidents (E810-E819)
Motor vehicle nontraffic accidents (E820-E825)
Other road vehicle accidents (E826-E829)

ICD•10

In ICD•10 and ICD•10•CM, the main axis is the injured person's mode of transport. For land transport accidents, categories V01-V89, the vehicle of which the injured person is an occupant, or pedestrian status, is identified in the first two characters since it is perceived as the essential issue for prevention purposes. In ICD•10•CM, an

 DEFINITION

Classification. The systematic arrangement, based on established criteria, of similar entities. ICD•10 is a disease classification. The particular criterion on which the arrangement is based is called the axis of classification. The primary axis of the disease classification as a whole is by anatomy. Other axes have been used, such as etiology and morphology.

additional category, V00, identifies pedestrian conveyance accidents due to falls, collisions with stationary objects, or other accidents not occurring with land transport vehicles.

Chapter 20 — External Causes of Morbidity and Mortality (V01-Y98)

V01-X59	Accidents
V01-V99	Transport accidents
V01-V09	Pedestrian injured in transport accident
V10-V19	Pedal cyclist injured in transport accident
V20-V29	Motorcycle rider injured in transport accident
V30-V39	Occupant of three-wheeled motor vehicle injured in transport accident
V40-V49	Car occupant injured in transport accident
V50-V59	Occupant of pick-up truck or van injured in transport accident
V60-V69	Occupant of heavy transport vehicle injured in transport accident
V70-V79	Bus occupant injured in transport accident
V80-V89	Other land transport accidents
V90-V94	Water transport accidents
V95-V97	Air and space transport accidents
V98-V99	Other and unspecified transport accidents

Another change to this chapter is to the codes for sequelae of external causes. Previously late-effect codes for external causes were located in various subchapters throughout the supplementary classification. In ICD•10, all late effects for each intent, i.e., accidents, suicide, etc., have been brought together in a block (subchapter), "Sequelae of External Causes of Morbidity and Mortality" (Y85-Y89). In ICD•10•CM, these are identified by the use of the alpha extensor for sequelae ('q') added to the code.

ICD•9•CM

E929	Late effects of accidental injury
E959	Late effects of self-inflicted injury
E969	Late effects of injury purposely inflicted by other person
E977	Late effects of injuries due to legal intervention
E989	Late effects of injury, undetermined whether accidentally or purposely inflicted
E999	Late effect of injury due to war operations and terrorism

ICD•10

Sequelae of external causes of morbidity and mortality (Y85-Y89)

Y85	Sequelae of transport accidents
Y86	Sequelae of other accidents
Y87	Sequelae of intentional self-harm, assault and events of undetermined intent
Y88	Sequelae with surgical and medical care as external cause
Y89	Sequelae of other external causes

ICD•10•CM

	T47.7x2q	Poisoning by emetics, intentional self-harm, sequela
	T48.995q	Adverse effect of other agents primarily acting on the respiratory system, sequela
V43.51q		Car driver injured in collision with sport utility vehicle in traffic accident, sequela
V90.02q		Drowning and submersion due to fishing boat overturning, sequela
W55.01q		Bitten by cat, sequela
Y04.0q		Assault by unarmed brawl or fight, sequela

DEFINITION

Late effect. A residual or sequela of a previous disease or injury.

MODIFICATION OF ICD•10

At the International Conference for the Tenth Revision of the International Classification of Diseases, a recommendation was made that "WHO should endorse the concept of an updating process between revisions..." Prior to this time there was no provision for updating the ICD between revisions, i.e., every 10 years. In October 1997, a mechanism was finalized to put an update process into operation. The nine WHO collaborating centers for classification of diseases and an update reference committee have been identified as coordinators and reviewers of proposed updates. With a timeline for issuance of amendments established, one should expect to see modifications to ICD•10 coming from the Secretariat at WHO.

History of the Modification

In May of 1994, the Centers for Disease Control and Prevention published an ICD•10 request for proposal (RFP). The contract sought the answer to the following questions:

1. Is ICD•10 such a significant improvement over ICD•9•CM for morbidity classification that it should be implemented in the United States?

2. Are there any codes or concepts in ICD•9•CM that have not been and should be included in ICD•10?

To answer these questions, the RFP required the contractor to perform an in-depth analysis addressing the following issues and to present recommendations in a report:

*   Strengths and weaknesses of ICD•10 as compared to ICD•9•CM for data collection on:
    — risk factors
    — severity of illness
    — primary care encounters
    — preventive health requirements
    — any other topics important to morbidity, as opposed to mortality, reporting
*   Compatibility of the ICD•10 and ICD•9•CM codes for diagnosis, health status (V codes), and external cause (E codes)
*   Ease of use of the ICD system
*   Adaptability to computerized patient records
*   Identification and review of improvements

FOR MORE INFO

The WHO collaborating center for classification of diseases for the United States is the National Center for Health Statistics, 6525 Belcrest Road, Hyattsville, Maryland 20782.

- Review of and recommendations for change in the tabular notes
- Alternatives to the dagger/asterisk for morbidity application (this system helps identify secondary diagnoses)
- Review of the tabular section and index with an emphasis on whether the category assignments, which are based on mortality, remain appropriate for morbidity
- If the categories are different between ICD•9•CM and ICD•10, determination of what the impact would be on trend analysis

In September 1994, the Center for Health Policy Studies (CHPS) was awarded the contract to perform the in-depth evaluation of ICD•10. Phase One of the contract consisted of describing how significant the modifications to ICD•10 were expected to be and, if made, how such revisions would impact comparability between the two systems. Any problems identified were to be accompanied by solutions. The development of a revised alphabetic index and crosswalk between ICD•9•CM and ICD•10•CM was also a part of Phase One.

Phase One

The contractor formed a Technical Advisory Panel (TAP) to perform the evaluation. The 20 members came from the healthcare and coding community. They included federal members from the Agency for Health Care Policy and Research (CMS and NCHS), nonfederal members from the hospital and physician environment, and classification experts. After evaluating ICD•10, CHPS provided the following goals for a clinical modification of ICD•10:

- Return to the level of specificity implemented in ICD•9•CM
- Facilitate alphabetic index use to assign codes
- Modify code titles and language to enhance consistency with accepted U.S. clinical practice
- Modify the dagger and asterisk codes
- Remove codes unique to mortality coding and those designed for the needs of emerging nations
- Remove procedure codes included with diagnosis codes
- Remove "multiple codes"

In answer to the main questions posed in the evaluation contract, CHPS indicated that ICD•10 is not a significant improvement over ICD•9•CM for morbidity classification, and that a clinical modification should be implemented in the United States that would include the codes or concepts lacking in ICD•10.

Phase Two

Phase Two consisted of further refinement of the clinical modification based on the draft created under the evaluation study. Since WHO holds a copyright on ICD•10, there are specific rules regarding changes. WHO requirements include the following:

- Title changes cannot alter the meaning of the category or code.
- There must be limited modifications to the three and four character codes.

During this phase, ICD•10 was looked at from the standpoint of creating codes for ambulatory and managed-care encounters, clinical decision-making, and outcomes research. This phase also involved a review by physician groups and others to assure clinical accuracy. The reviewers for this phase included the following:

 KEY POINT

In addition to being a member of the TAP, CMS is also responsible for the replacement to Volume 3, the procedure classification of ICD•9•CM. Chapter 5 provides you with the information on ICD•10•PCS.

- American Academy of Pediatrics
- American Academy of Neurology
- American College of Obstetricians and Gynecologists
- American Urological Association
- National Association of Children's Hospitals and Related Institutions
- American Burn Association
- Burn Foundation
- ANSI Z16.2 Workgroup
- American Academy of Dermatology
- CDC Diabetes Program
- National Center for Injury Prevention and Control
- National Center for Infectious Diseases
- National Center for Chronic Disease and Prevention & Health Promotion
- Veterans Administration's National Diabetes Program

During Phase Two, focused reviews were performed. This examination included the evaluation of residual categories to decide if further specificity was needed. An analysis also was made of previous ICD•9•CM coordination and maintenance committee recommendations where adoption was not possible due to ICD•9•CM space limitations.

DEFINITION

Residual category. A place for classifying a specified form of a condition that does not have its own specific subdivision.

Phase Three
The third phase involved a review of the public comments on the proposed ICD•10•CM released to the public in the winter of 1997. More than 1,200 comments from more than 20 organizations were received. Phase Three reviewers included the American Academy of Ophthalmology, American Academy of Orthopedic Surgeons, Johns Hopkins Injury Center, and Pennsylvania Head Injury Center.

As a result of these three phases, there were thousands of clinical modifications made to ICD•10.

Fourth, Fifth, Sixth, and Seventh Character Addition
To be able to have the desired specificity, fifth, sixth, and seventh characters were added throughout the classification. These characters may identify such things as more specificity about a disorder, whether the patient's condition exists on the right or left side, the trimester in which the patient is experiencing problems, and whether the encounter was initial, subsequent, or with sequelae. Here's an example of added specificity at the fifth digit:

ICD•10

    P78.8   Other specified perinatal digestive system disorders

ICD•10•CM

    P78.8   Other specified perinatal digestive system disorders
            P78.81   Congenital cirrhosis (of liver)
            P78.82   Peptic ulcer of newborn
            P78.89   Other specified perinatal digestive system disorders

Here's a sample of the trimester specified with a sixth digit:

ICD•10

O99.0   Anemia complicating pregnancy, childbirth and the puerperium

    O99.01 Anemia complicating pregnancy

ICD•10•CM

O99.0   Anemia complicating pregnancy, childbirth and the puerperium

    O99.01 Anemia complicating pregnancy

        O99.011   Anemia complicating pregnancy, first trimester

        O99.012   Anemia complicating pregnancy, second trimester

        O99.013   Anemia complicating pregnancy, third trimester

        O99.019   Anemia complicating pregnancy, unspecified trimester

The following examples demonstrate laterality at the sixth digit level and the encounter status in the seventh character:

ICD•10

S72   Fracture of femur

    S72.0   Fracture of neck of femur

       S72.00   Closed fracture of neck of femur

ICD•10•CM

S72   Fracture of femur

    S72.0   Fracture of head and neck of femur

       S72.00   Fracture of unspecified part of neck of femurs

           S72.001   Fracture of unspecified part of neck of right femur

               S72.001a   Fracture of unspecified part of neck of right femur, initial encounter for closed fracture

               S72.001b   Fracture of unspecified part of neck of right femur, initial encounter for open fracture type I or II

               S72.001c   Fracture of unspecified part of neck of right femur, initial encounter for open fracture type IIIA, IIIB, or IIIC

               S72.001d   Fracture of unspecified part of neck of right femur, subsequent encounter for closed fracture with routine healing

S72.001e   Fracture of unspecified part of neck of right femur, subsequent encounter for open fracture type I or II with routine healing

S72.001f   Fracture of unspecified part of neck of right femur, subsequent encounter for open fracture type IIIA, IIIB, or IIIC with routine healing

S72.001g   Fracture of unspecified part of neck of right femur, subsequent encounter for closed fracture with delayed healing

S72.001h   Fracture of unspecified part of neck of right femur, subsequent encounter for open fracture type I or II with delayed healing

S72.001i   Fracture of unspecified part of neck of right femur, subsequent encounter for open fracture type IIIA, IIIB, or IIIC with delayed healing

S72.001j   Fracture of unspecified part of neck of right femur, subsequent encounter for closed fracture with nonunion

S72.001k   Fracture of unspecified part of neck of right femur, subsequent encounter for open fracture type I or II with nonunion

S72.001l   Fracture of unspecified part of neck of right femur, subsequent encounter for open fracture type IIIA, IIIB, or IIIC with nonunion

S72.001m   Fracture of unspecified part of neck of right femur, subsequent encounter for closed fracture with malunion

S72.001n   Fracture of unspecified part of neck of right femur, subsequent encounter for open fracture type I or II with malunion

S72.001o   **Fracture of unspecified part of neck of right femur, subsequent encounter for open fracture type IIIA, IIIB, or IIIC with malunion**

S72.001q   **Fracture of unspecified part of neck of right femur, sequela**

INCORPORATION OF COMMON SUBCLASSIFICATIONS

In ICD•10, fourth-digit and fifth-digit subdivisions were often provided for optional use. In ICD•10•CM these subdivisions are incorporated into the code listing thus making them a required component of the code's use. In addition, full code titles are adopted in ICD•10•CM to provide a clear understanding of the code's meaning.

ICD•10

S52   **Fracture of forearm**

The following subdivisions are provided for optional use in a supplementary character position where it is not possible or not desired to use multiple coding to identify fracture and open wound; a fracture not indicated as closed or open should be classified as closed.

    0   closed
    1   open

    Excludes: fracture at wrist and hand level (S62.-)

S52.0   **Fracture of upper end of ulna**
        Coronoid process
        Elbow NOS
        Monteggia's fracture-dislocation
        Olecranon process
        Proximal end

ICD•10•CM

S52   **Fracture of forearm**
    A fracture not identified as displaced or nondisplaced should be coded to displaced.
    Excludes1: traumatic amputation of forearm (S58.-)
    Excludes2: fracture at wrist and hand level (S62.-)
    A fracture not designated as open or closed should be coded to closed.
    Note: the open fracture designations are based on the Gustilo open fracture classification.
    The following extensions are to be added to each code for category S52:
    a   initial encounter for closed fracture
    b   initial encounter for open fracture type I or II
    c   initial encounter for open fracture type IIIA, IIIB, or IIIC
    d   subsequent encounter for closed fracture with routine healing
    e   subsequent encounter for open fracture type I or II with routine healing

 KEY POINT

The modifications to ICD•10 will provide the detail required for morbidity coding in the United States, thereby meeting the goal for more comprehensive and qualitative patient data for all uses and users.

f   subsequent encounter for open fracture type IIIA, IIIB, or IIIC with routine healing

g   subsequent encounter for closed fracture with delayed healing

h   subsequent encounter for open fracture type I or II with delayed healing

i   subsequent encounter for open fracture type IIIA, IIIB, or IIIC with delayed healing

j   subsequent encounter for closed fracture with nonunion

k   subsequent encounter for open fracture type I or II with nonunion

l   subsequent encounter for open fracture type IIIA, IIIB, or IIIC with nonunion

m   subsequent encounter for closed fracture with malunion

n   subsequent encounter for open fracture type I or II with malunion

o   subsequent encounter for open fracture type IIIA, IIIB, or IIIC with malunion

q   sequela

S52.0   Fracture of upper end of ulna

Fracture of proximal end of ulna

Excludes2: fracture of elbow NOS (S42.40-)

Fractures of shaft of ulna (S52.2-)

S52.00   Unspecified fracture of upper end of ulna

S52.001   Unspecified fracture of upper end of right ulna

S52.002   Unspecified fracture of upper end of left ulna

S52.009   Unspecified fracture of upper end of unspecified ulna

S52.01   Torus fracture of upper end of ulna

S52.011   Torus fracture of upper end of right ulna

S52.012   Torus fracture of upper end of left ulna

S52.019   Torus fracture of upper end of unspecified ulna

Laterality

In the past, there have been proposals to the ICD•9•CM coordination and maintenance committee to add laterality codes (i.e., right, left, or bilateral). This has been done in ICD•10•CM; however, ICD•10•CM does not add laterality in all cases. The majority of codes affected by this modification are found in the neoplasm and injury chapters.

ICD•10

C56   Malignant neoplasm of ovary

ICD•10•CM

C56   **Malignant neoplasm of ovary**

C56.0   Malignant neoplasm of right ovary

C56.1   Malignant neoplasm of left ovary

C56.9   Malignant neoplasm of ovary, unspecified side

DEFINITION

Trimester. A period of three months. The first trimester is the period of pregnancy from the first day of the last normal menstrual period through the completion of 13 weeks of gestation. The second trimester is the period of pregnancy from the beginning of the 14th through the 27th completed week of gestation. The third trimester is the period of pregnancy from the beginning of the 28th week until delivery.

Trimester Specificity for Obstetrical Coding

Neither ICD•9 nor ICD•10 expands the codes in the "Pregnancy, Childbirth and the Puerperium" chapter to specify circumstances surrounding the pregnancy. In ICD•9•CM, a fifth-digit subdivision denotes the current episode of care. The episode of care is defined as the encounter in which the patient is receiving care, whether delivery occurred during that encounter, or an antepartum or postpartum condition is being treated without delivery occurring during that episode of care. The fifth digits from ICD•9•CM were not adopted for ICD•10•CM. Instead, the last character in the code reports the patient's trimester. Because certain obstetric conditions or complications occur at only one point in the obstetric period, not all codes will include all three trimesters or a character to describe the trimester at all.

ICD•10

O60   **Preterm delivery**

   Onset (spontaneous) of delivery before 37 completed weeks of gestation.

ICD•10•CM

O60   **Preterm labor Includes: onset (spontaneous) of labor before 37 completed weeks of gestation**
   O60.2   **Preterm labor, second trimester**
   O60.3   **Preterm labor, third trimester**
   O60.9   **Preterm labor, unspecified trimester**

Expansion of Alcohol & Drug Codes

Although ICD•10 had already made major changes to Chapter 5, "Mental and Behavioral Disorders," analysis of the codes for disorders due to alcohol and drug use has resulted in further modifications. The ICD•10 codes were reviewed for ways to better describe these disorders due to psychoactive substance use.

The result is the identification of the effects of use (e.g., abuse and dependence) at the fourth-digit level, the specific aspects to the use (e.g., withdrawal), at the fifth-digit level, and some of the manifestations (e.g., delirium), at the sixth-digit level.

ICD•10

F10.–   **Mental and behavioral disorders due to use of alcohol**
   .0   Acute intoxication
   .1   Harmful use
   .2   Dependence syndrome
   .3   Withdrawal state
   .4   Withdrawal state with delirium
   .5   Psychotic disorder
   .6   Amnesic syndrome
   .7   Residual and late-onset psychotic disorder
   .8   Other mental and behavioral disorders
   .9   Unspecified mental and behavioral disorder

KEY POINT

In ICD•10•CM, sixth-digits will identify:
- trimester
- laterality
- manifestation of drug or alcohol abuse

ICD•10•CM

F10 **Alcohol-related disorders**

Use additional code for blood alcohol level, if applicable (Y90.-)

Excludes1: alcohol use, uncomplicated(Z72.1)

social alcohol use (Z72.1)

F10.1 **Alcohol abuse**

Excludes1: alcohol dependence (F10.2-)

alcohol use, unspecified (F10.9-)

F10.10 **Alcohol abuse, uncomplicated**

F10.12 **Alcohol abuse with intoxication**

F10.120 **Alcohol abuse with intoxication, uncomplicated**

F10.121 **Alcohol abuse with intoxication delirium**

F10.129 **Alcohol abuse with intoxication, unspecified**

F10.14 **Alcohol abuse with alcohol-induced mood disorder**

F10.15 **Alcohol abuse with alcohol-induced psychotic disorder**

F10.150 **Alcohol abuse with alcohol-induced psychotic disorder with delusions**

F10.151 **Alcohol abuse with alcohol-induced psychotic disorder with hallucinations**

F10.159 **Alcohol abuse with alcohol-induced psychotic disorder, unspecified**

F10.18 **Alcohol abuse with other alcohol-induced disorders**

F10.180 **Alcohol abuse with alcohol-induced anxiety disorder**

F10.181 **Alcohol abuse with alcohol-induced sexual dysfunction**

F10.182 **Alcohol abuse with alcohol-induced sleep disorder**

F10.188 **Alcohol abuse with other alcohol-induced disorder**

F10.19 **Alcohol abuse with unspecified alcohol-induced disorder**

Expansion of Injury Codes

To further enhance the restructuring of Chapter 19, "Injury, Poisoning and Certain Other Consequences of External Causes," ICD•10•CM will provide codes to further specify the type and site of the injury. Also, as mentioned previously, subdivisions have been incorporated into the code listing, thus making them a required component of the code's use.

ICD•10

S51   **Open wound of forearm**

         Excludes: open wound of wrist and hand (S61.-)

                     traumatic amputation of forearm (S58.-)

     S51.0   **Open wound of elbow**

ICD•10•CM

S51   **Open wound of elbow and forearm**

         Code also any associated wound infection

         Excludes1: open fracture of elbow and forearm (S52.- with open fracture extensions)

                     traumatic amputation of elbow and forearm (S58.-)

         Excludes2: open wound of wrist and hand (S61.-)

         The following extensions are to be added to each code for category S51

         a   initial encounter

         d   subsequent encounter

         q   sequela

     S51.0   **Open wound of elbow**

        S51.00   **Unspecified open wound of elbow**

            S51.001   Unspecified open wound of right elbow

            S51.002   Unspecified open wound of left elbow

            S51.009   Unspecified open wound of unspecified elbow

        S51.01   **Laceration without foreign body of elbow**

            S51.011   Laceration without foreign body of right elbow

            S51.012   Laceration without foreign body of left elbow

            S51.019   Laceration without foreign body of unspecified elbow

        S51.02   **Laceration with foreign body of elbow**

            S51.021   Laceration with foreign body of right elbow

            S51.022   Laceration with foreign body of left elbow

            S51.029   Laceration with foreign body of unspecified elbow

        S51.03   **Puncture wound without foreign body of elbow**

            S51.031   Puncture wound without foreign body of right elbow

            S51.032   Puncture wound without foreign body of left elbow

            S51.039   Puncture wound without foreign body of unspecified elbow

KEY POINT

Health care providers will need to be educated on the additional details required to be documented in the medical record in order to code injuries. For example, with the reporting of laterality, providers will need to document where the injury occurred.

S51.04   Puncture wound with foreign body of elbow
  S51.041   Puncture wound with foreign body of right elbow
  S51.042   Puncture wound with foreign body of left elbow
  S51.049   Puncture wound with foreign body of unspecified elbow
S51.05   Open bite of elbow
    Bite of elbow NOS
    Excludes1: superficial bite of elbow (S50.36, S50.37)
  S51.051   Open, bite, right elbow
  S51.052   Open bite, left elbow
  S51.059   Open bite, unspecified elbow

S51.8   Open wound of forearm
  Excludes2: open wound of elbow (51.0-)
  S51.80   Unspecified open wound of forearm
    S51.801   Unspecified open wound of right forearm
    S51.802   Unspecified open wound of left elbow
    S51.809   Unspecified open wound of unspecified elbow

Combination Codes

Some common symptoms and complications are added as fifth-digit extensions to certain diagnosis codes. The rationale for combining the diagnosis and manifestation (symptom) or a diagnosis and its complication relates to problems with the assignment of the principal diagnosis. A debate occurs when the patient is admitted for the symptom or complication and it is secondary to a specified disease. The question that often comes up is, Which should be assigned as the principal diagnosis? With the modifications to ICD•10, this problem has been solved.

ICD•10

K50   Crohn's disease [regional enteritis]
    Includes: granulomatous enteritis
    Excludes: ulcerative colitis (K51.-)
  K50.0   Crohn's disease of small intestine
      Crohn's disease [regional enteritis] of:
        duodenum
        ileum
        jejunum
        Ileitis:
        regional
        terminal
      Excludes: with Crohn's disease of large intestine (K50.8)

 Definition

Principal Diagnosis. The Uniform Hospital Discharge Data Set defines as "that condition established after study to be chiefly responsible for occasioning the admission of the patient to the hospital for care." This definition applies only to inpatients in acute, short-term, general hospitals.

ICD•10•CM

K50   Crohn's disease [regional enteritis]

Includes: granulomatous enteritis

Excludes1: ulcerative colitis (K51.-)

Use additional code to identify manifestations, such as:

pyoderma gangrenosum (L88)

K50.0   Crohn's disease of small intestine

Crohn's disease [regional enteritis] of duodenum

Crohn's disease [regional enteritis] of ileum

Crohn's disease [regional enteritis] of jejunum

Regional ileitis

Terminal ileitis

Excludes1: Crohn's disease of both small and large intestine (K50.8)

K50.00   Crohn's disease of small intestine with unspecified complication

K50.01   Crohn's disease of small intestine with rectal bleeding

K50.02   Crohn's disease of small intestine with intestinal obstruction

K50.03   Crohn's disease of small intestine with fistula

K50.04   Crohn's disease of small intestine with abscess

K50.05   Crohn's disease of small intestine without complications

K50.09   Crohn's disease of small intestine with other complication

Combination of Dagger and Asterisk Codes

In ICD•9 and ICD•10, WHO provides a classification scheme in which certain disease entities may be classified twice, once according to etiology or cause of the disease and once according to its manifestations or symptoms. The coder can choose to use one code or the other. In ICD•9•CM and ICD•10•CM, this dual classification was eliminated. In ICD•10•CM the manifestation merged with the etiology codes.

ICD•10

A02.2†   Localized salmonella infections

Salmonella:

arthritis (M01.3*)

meningitis (G01*)

osteomyelitis (M90.2*)

pneumonia (J17.0*)

renal tubulo-interstitial disease (N16.0*)

ICD•10•CM

A02.2   Localized salmonella infections

A02.20   Localized salmonella infection, unspecified

A02.21   Salmonella meningitis

A02.22   Salmonella pneumonia

A02.23   Salmonella arthritis

A02.24   Salmonella osteomyelitis

🕯 **CODING AXIOM**

ICD•9 and ICD•10 provide the dual classification scheme in which certain disease entities may be classified twice, once according to etiology of the disease and once according to its manifestations. This is called the dagger and asterisk system.

A02.25 Salmonella pyelonephritis
Salmonella tubulo-interstitial nephropathy
A02.29 Salmonella with other localized infection

Movement of Categories

The ICD•10•CM reviewers identified the need to move additional disease categories from one chapter to another as the types of conditions grouped under the ICD•10 category were better classified elsewhere.

ICD•10

Diseases of the Digestive System (K00-K93)
K07   Dentofacial anomalies [including malocclusion]
K10   Other diseases of jaw

ICD•10•CM

Diseases of the Musculoskeletal System and Connective Tissue (M00-M99)
M26   Dentofacial anomalies [including malocclusion]
M27   Other diseases of jaws

Expansion of Postoperative Complication Codes

Building on ICD•10's new feature of adding codes for postprocedural disorders to particular body system chapters, NCHS expands ICD•10•CM further by deactivating codes found in Chapter 19, "Injury, Poisoning and Certain Other Consequences of External Causes," and adding these conditions to the body system chapters.

ICD•10

T81.0   Hemorrhage and hematoma complicating a procedure, not elsewhere classified
T81.2   Accidental puncture and laceration during a procedure, not elsewhere classified

ICD•10•CM

Codes T81.0 and T81.2 have been deactivated in ICD•10•CM.

K91.6   Intraoperative and postprocedural hemorrhage and hematoma complicating a digestive system procedure
Excludes1: intraoperative hemorrhage or hematoma due to accidental puncture or laceration during a digestive system procedure (K91.7-)
K91.61 Intraoperative hemorrhage of a digestive system organ or structure during a digestive system procedure
K91.62 Intraoperative hemorrhage of a non-digestive system organ or structure during a digestive system procedure
K91.63 Intraoperative hematoma of a digestive system organ or structure during a digestive system procedure

K91.64 Intraoperative hematoma of a non-digestive system organ or structure during a digestive system procedure

K91.65 Postprocedural hemorrhage of a digestive system organ or structure following a digestive system procedure

K91.66 Postprocedural hemorrhage of a non-digestive system organ or structure following a digestive system procedure

K91.67 Postprocedural hematoma of a digestive system organ or structure following a digestive system procedure

K91.68 Postprocedural hematoma of a non-digestive system organ or structure following a digestive system procedure

Deactived Codes

To meet data-gathering goals desired by the federal government for coding in the United States, some codes that are valid in ICD•10 have been deactivated for ICD•10•CM. These codes fall into several categories: procedure codes, death codes, and some codes that are considered by NCHS and CMS to be highly unspecified. To maintain international data-gathering requirements, deactivated ICD•10 codes cannot be reassigned in ICD•10•CM.

Procedure Codes

Some ICD•10 codes actually identify a procedure, rather than a disease or health status. These codes were reviewed and a determination was made to either deactivate them, or in some instances to revise the category title. For example:

ICD•10

Z23	Need for immunization against single bacterial diseases
Z24	Need for immunization against certain single viral diseases
Z25	Need for immunization against other single viral diseases
Z26	Need for immunization against other single infectious diseases
Z27	Need for immunization against combinations of infectious diseases
Z28	Immunization not carried out
Z29	Need for other prophylactic measures

ICD•10•CM

Z23   Encounter for immunization
> Code first any routine childhood examination
> Note: procedure codes are required to identify the types of immunizations given.

Z24	deactivated
Z25	deactivated
Z26	deactivated
Z27	deactivated
Z28	Immunization not carried out
Z29	deactivated

Categories Z24-Z27 and Z29 have been deactivated and category Z23 has been retitled.

☞ **KEY POINT**

Not all codes in ICD•10 are available in ICD•10•CM. Some are deactivated by NCHS to meet federal data-gathering goals.

Highly Nonspecific Codes

ICD•10 includes codes for "multiple" injuries. In ICD•10•CM, these nonspecific multiple codes have been deactivated. Coders will, instead, be expected to report multiple, individual codes to describe specific injuries.

ICD•10

S30.7	Multiple superficial injuries of abdomen, lower back and pelvis
S49.7	Multiple injuries of shoulder and upper arm

ICD•10•CM

S30.7	deactivated
S49.7	deactivated

Other codes providing overly generalized information have also been deleted:

A16	Respiratory tuberculosis, not confirmed bacteriologically or histologically

For the purpose of tracking disease and health-related issues in the United States, codes associated with conditions in which the death occurs without contact with medical authorities are not appropriate to U.S. reporting. These codes, used in mortality reporting for ICD•10, have been deleted in ICD•10•CM. Some examples include:

R98	Unattended death
S18	Traumatic amputation at neck level
R95	Sudden infant death syndrome

Notes

In addition to the analysis of the codes themselves, the notes in ICD•10 were reviewed. Many of the clinical modifications reflect the addendum to ICD•9•CM published over the years, while others were added as new codes to ICD•10•CM.

ICD•10

C34	Malignant neoplasm of bronchus and lung

ICD•10•CM

This excludes note was added because of the addition of codes C46.50-C46.52 for Kaposi's sarcoma of the lung.

C34	Malignant neoplasm of bronchus and lung
	Excludes1: Kaposi's sarcoma of lung (C46.5-)

ICD•10

D05	Carcinoma in situ of breast
	Excludes1: carcinoma in situ of skin of breast (D04.5)
	melanoma in situ of breast (skin) (D03.5)

 DEFINITION

Deactivation. Tthe code will not be available for use in coding. This helps maintain international data-gathering goals.

ICD•10•CM

The note for Paget's disease is found in ICD•9•CM.

D05   Carcinoma in situ of breast

Excludes1: carcinoma in situ of skin of breast (D04.5)

melanoma in situ of breast (skin) (D03.5)

Paget's disease of breast or nipple (C50.-)

DISCUSSION QUESTIONS

1. What are some reasons for clinically modifying ICD•10 in the United States?

_____

_____

_____

2. Iatrogenic illnesses have been relocated in ICD•10•CM. Where do they occur?

_____

_____

_____

3. How are dagger and asterisk codes handled in ICD•10•CM?

_____

_____

_____

4. What are three reasons why ICD•10 codes would be deactivated in ICD•10•CM?

_____

_____

_____

2 Coding Conventions

Now that you have an understanding of the overall clinical modifications made to ICD•10, it is time to build on that knowledge and examine the conventions of the ICD•10•CM system. While many of the rules have not changed, there are others that are new, expanded, or deleted. The rules must be understood to accurately apply them and to assign a correct code from ICD•10•CM.

Both the Tabular List, Volume 1, and the Alphabetic Index, Volume 3, contain conventions. Some of the rules are unique to one volume or the other. For example, the "excludes" note is found only in the Tabular List. Other conventions are found in both volumes, such as the use of the term "with" to indicate certain codes that have been provided for diseases in combination.

Prior to reviewing these various conventions, this chapter provides an explanation of the overall arrangement of ICD•10•CM. Chapter 1 introduced you to the contents of ICD•10•CM, while this chapter gives the general order of each volume to help you become more comfortable with the classification system. As you will see, ICD•10•CM is not so foreign. Much of what we are familiar with as users of ICD•9•CM remains a part of ICD•10•CM.

OBJECTIVES

- Learn the general arrangement of ICD•10•CM.
- Identify the conventions in the Tabular List and Alphabetic Index of ICD•10•CM.
- Describe how these conventions compare and contrast to ICD•9•CM.
- Learn how to use these conventions for assigning an ICD•10•CM code.

AXIS OF CLASSIFICATION

The ICD•10•CM is an arrangement of similar entities, diseases, and other conditions on the basis of specific criteria. Diseases can be arranged in a variety of ways: according to etiology, anatomy, or severity. The particular criterion chosen is called the axis of classification.

Anatomy is the primary axis of classification of ICD•10•CM. Thus, there are chapters entitled "Diseases of the Circulatory System" and "Diseases of the Genitourinary System." ICD•10•CM employs other axes as well, such as etiology, as in the chapter, "Certain Infectious and Parasitic Diseases."

Different axes are used in classifying different diseases within the same chapters. The choice is based upon the most important aspects of the disease from both a statistical and clinical point of view. For example:

- Pneumonia: etiology or cause of the pneumonia
- Malignant neoplasm: site
- Cardiac arrhythmia: type
- Leukemia: morphology

ARRANGEMENT OF THE TABULAR LIST

The Tabular List consists of chapters, subchapters, three character categories, four character subcategories, and five, six, and seven character subdivisions.

DEFINITION

Rubric. A grouping of similar conditions. In ICD•10•CM, rubric denotes either a three-character category or a four-character subcategory.

Chapters and Subchapters

As mentioned, the chapter order in ICD•10•CM is not always the same as in lCD•9•CM. Disorders of the immune mechanism in ICD•10•CM are found with diseases of the blood and blood-forming organs. In ICD•9•CM these disorders are included with endocrine, nutritional, and metabolic diseases. Chapters for diseases of the genitourinary system; pregnancy, childbirth and the puerperium; certain conditions originating in the perinatal period; and congenital malformations, deformations and chromosomal abnormalities are placed consecutively in ICD•10. This chapter arrangement is the same in ICD•10•CM.

The ICD•10•CM classification is divided into 21 chapters. The chapter title describes the general content of the chapter. The code range describes the extent of the chapter; for example, Chapter 7, "Diseases of the Eye and Adnexa" (H00–H59).

Chapters are subdivided into subchapters or "blocks" containing rubrics that identify closely related conditions. Each chapter begins with a summary of its subchapters to provide an overview of the classification structure at that level.

The title describes the content of the subchapter. The code range describes the extent of the subchapter; for example, "Disorders of Vitreous Body and Globe" (H43–H45).

Three-character Category

Three-character categories are the essential subdivisions of the disease classification. The disease classification begins with category A00 and ends with Z99. Not all letters of the alphabet or all numbers at the second and third positions have been used.

Three-character categories may represent a single disease entity or may represent a group of homogenous or closely related conditions. The three-character category title describes the exact content of the category. For example: Category K55 provides codes for a number of vascular disorders, while category R64 is very specific to the condition, cachexia.

K55   Vascular disorders of intestine
R64   Cachexia

Generally the sequence of the categories within a block begins with categories that have specific titles, and progresses to categories with less specific titles. The next-to-the-last three-character category in a series is called the "residual" three-character category. This is the one used for "other specified disease." For example:

Hernia (K40–K46)
K40   Inguinal hernia
K41   Femoral hernia
K42   Umbilical hernia
K43   Ventral hernia
K44   Diaphragmatic hernia
K45   Other abdominal hernia
K46   Unspecified abdominal hernia

Three-character category K45 is the residual category for abdominal hernias.

There are three-character categories that have not been subdivided. These unsubdivided three-character categories describe a disease that needs no further specificity. For example:

I64 **Stroke, not specified as hemorrhage or infarction**
Includes: cerebrovascular accident NOS
Excludes1: any condition classifiable to I60–I63
sequelae of stroke (I69.4)

The majority of three-character categories are subdivided into four-character subcategories. Whenever a three-character category has been subdivided, the three-character category rubric is considered an invalid code and cannot be used. A fourth-digit subcategory (and perhaps a fifth-, sixth-, or seventh-digit subdivision) is required for a valid code. For example, the rubric K35 cannot stand alone as the code for acute appendicitis. A fourth-digit, 0, 1, or 9, must be used, as shown:

K35 **Acute appendicitis**
K35.0 **Acute appendicitis with generalized peritonitis**
K35.1 **Acute appendicitis with peritoneal abscess**
K35.9 **Acute appendicitis without peritonitis**

Four-character Subcategory

Four-character subcategories are the subdivisions of three-character categories, and define the axis of classification by describing the site, etiology, manifestation, or stage of the disease classified to the three-character category. The four-character subcategory rubric is comprised of the three-character category rubric plus a decimal digit and an additional number.

The axes of the subdivisions vary according to the nature of the condition or conditions included within the three-character category. For example, the subdivisions may describe the stages of the disease (acute, subacute, chronic), the sites of the disease (upper end, shaft, etc.), or the causes of the disease (Streptococcus, rhinovirus, etc.). For example:

N70 **Salpingitis and oophoritis**
N70.0 **Acute salpingitis and oophoritis**
N70.01 **Acute salpingitis**
N70.02 **Acute oophoritis**
N70.03 **Acute salpingitis and oophoritis**
N70.1 **Chronic salpingitis and oophoritis**
Hydrosalpinx
N70.11 **Chronic salpingitis**
N70.12 **Chronic oophoritis**
N70.13 **Chronic salpingitis and oophoritis**
N70.9 **Salpingitis and oophoritis, unspecified**
N70.91 **Salpingitis, unspecified**
N70.92 **Oophoritis, unspecified**
N70.93 **Salpingitis and oophoritis, unspecified**

Four-character subcategories within a three-character category progress in terms of specificity. Often the next-to-the-last four-character subdivision, identified by the

KEY POINT

Some three-character rubrics stand alone as the valid code for the condition. Do not "zero fill" these codes, as that makes them invalid. Valid codes in ICD•10•CM may have three, four, five, six, or seven characters.

KEY POINT

Decimals and digits .8 and .9 may be used to create the subdivision needed despite nonapplication of rubrics from 0–7.

fourth digit .8, is the residual category ("other specified") and is the place to classify a specified form of a condition that does not have its own subdivision.

The last four-character subcategory is used for coding the unspecified form (site, cause, etc.) of the condition. Generally this four-character subcategory is identified by the fourth digit .9. For example:

G50 **Disorders of trigeminal nerve**
        Includes: disorders of 5th cranial nerve
    G50.0 **Trigeminal neuralgia**
          Syndrome on paroxysmal facial pain
          Tic douloureux
        G50.1 **Atypical facial pain**
        G50.8 **Other disorders of trigeminal nerve**
        G50.9 **Disorder of trigeminal nerve, unspecified**

Often four-character subcategories are themselves further subdivided to provide even greater specificity. Whenever a four-character subcategory has been subdivided, that four-character rubric cannot stand alone as the code for the disease to be encoded. The following example of an unsubdivided four-character subcategory shows that code O15.1 can be assigned as the code for eclampsia in labor. The subdivided four-character subcategory O15.0, however, cannot be used as the code for eclampsia in pregnancy. A fifth digit must be used.

O15 **Eclampsia**
        Includes: convulsions following conditions in O10-14 and O16
    O15.0 **Eclampsia in pregnancy**
        O15.00 **Eclampsia in pregnancy, unspecified trimester**
        O15.02 **Eclampsia in pregnancy, second trimester**
        O15.03 **Eclampsia in pregnancy, third trimester**
    O15.1 **Eclampsia in labor**
    O15.2 **Eclampsia is the puerperium**
    O15.9 **Eclampsia, unspecified as to time period**
        Eclampsia NOS

To retain the same degree of specificity present in ICD•10•CM, manifestations of diseases are identified in the same fashion as in ICD•9•CM. Following are the two ways to identify the diseases, each followed separately by an example:

1.   As individual five-character subdivisions of the four-character subcategories to represent the etiology of the disease.

        A02.2 **Localized salmonella infections**
            A02.20 **Localized salmonella infection, unspecified**
            A02.21 **Salmonella meningitis**
            A02.22 **Salmonella pneumonia**
            A02.23 **Salmonella arthritis**
            A02.24 **Salmonella osteomyelitis**
            A02.25 **Salmonella pyelonephritis**

2. As an additional code assigned whenever a three-character category or four-character subcategory is followed by an instructional note to "code first underlying condition." The code for the condition first represents the etiology of the diseases, while the secondary code represents the manifestation of the disease.

The World Health Organization (WHO) did not want manifestations in the primary tabulation of causes for morbidity and mortality. Consequently, the manifestation code never appears as a first diagnosis. For example:

DEFINITION

Manifestation. The display or disclosure of characteristic signs or symptoms of an illness, as applied to medicine.

H42   **Glaucoma in diseases classified elsewhere**
Code first underlying condition, such as:
amyloidosis (E85)
aniridia (Q13.1)
Lowe's syndrome (E72.03)
Reiger's anomaly (Q13.81)
specified metabolic disorder (E70-E90)
Excludes1: glaucoma (in):
Diabetes mellitus (E08.39, E09.39, E10.39, E11.39, E13.39, E14.39)
onchocerciasis (B73.02)
syphilis (A52.71)
tuberculous (A18.59)

Five-, Six-, and Seven-character Subclassifications

In ICD•9•CM, there are never more than five digits to a code. In ICD•10•CM, there are five-, six-, and seven-character codes. For example:

ICD•9•CM

882   **Open wound of hand except finger(s) alone**
    882.0   **Without mention of complication**
    882.1   **Complicated**
    882.2   **With tendon involvement**

ICD•10•CM

S61.4   **Open wound of hand**
    S61.40   **Unspecified open wound of hand**
        S61.401   **Unspecified open wound of right hand**
        S61.402   **Unspecified open wound of left hand**
        S61.409   **Unspecified open wound of unspecified hand**
    S61.41   **Laceration without foreign body of hand**
        S61.411   **Laceration without foreign body of right hand**
        S61.412   **Laceration without foreign body of left hand**
        S61.419   **Laceration without foreign body of unspecified hand**

Five-character and six-character subdivisions are used in two ways: first, to provide specific codes for individual inclusion terms within a single four-character subcategory; second, to provide a second axis of classification for an entire three-character category or series of three-character categories. This second axis permits a different cross section of the condition than is provided by the four-character category.

Five- and six-character subclassifications are presented in their natural sequence. When they occur, seventh digits in ICD•10•CM are always presented as an alpha-extension table and referenced in the instructions for that code.

Alpha Extensions

ICD•10•CM has incorporated the use of extension characters to specify the encounter status for that episode of care, or to identify the status of the current condition under care for that specific encounter.

The extensor is a lowercase letter, called an alpha extension or alpha kicker, which may create valid codes that extend to the seventh-character subdivision level. Alpha extensors are not found solely at the seventh-character position; however, they are always the final character in a code, and may be found as the fourth, fifth, sixth, or seventh character in a code:

> X75.q **Intentional self-harm by explosive material, sequelae**
>> X73.1a **Intentional self-harm by hunting rifle discharge, initial encounter**
>>> X95.01a **Assault by airgun discharge, initial encounter**
>>>> W22.042q **Striking against wall of swimming pool causing other injury, sequelae**

Where applicable, an instructional note appears under the three-digit category, or further divided subcategory, directing the coder to add an extension to each code within the category or subcategory. Every code must have one of these alpha extensions to be valid. The valid codes created by these mandatory alpha extensions are not found listed individually within the tabular list under each subclassification level to which they apply. Instead, the coder must refer to the instructional note and add the appropriate extensor to the available code at its highest specification level within the category:

S59   **Other and unspecified injuries of elbow and forearm**
> Excludes2: other and unspecified injuries of wrist and hand (S69.-)
> The following extensions are to be added to each code for subcategories S59.0, S59.1, and S59.2
> a   initial encounter for fracture
> d   subsequent encounter for fracture with routine healing
> g   subsequent encounter for fracture with delayed healing
> j   subsequent encounter for fracture with nonunion
> m   subsequent encounter for fracture with malunion
> q   sequela

> **S59.0**   **Physeal fracture of lower end on ulna**
>> **S59.00**   **Unspecified physeal fracture of lower end of ulna**
>>> **S59.001**   **Unspecified physeal fracture of lower end of ulna, right arm**

KEY POINT

Use of the fifth, sixth, or seventh digit is not optional. If five-digit subclassifications appear in ICD•9•CM, they must be used. If five-, six-, or seven-digit subclassifications appear in ICD•10•CM, they must be used.

	S59.002	Unspecified physeal fracture of lower end of ulna, left arm

S59.002 Unspecified physeal fracture of lower end of ulna, left arm

S59.009 Unspecified physeal fracture of lower end of ulna, unspecified arm

Coma Extensions

The convention of using alpha extensors in ICD•10•CM for more granularity in coding has been implemented in a unique way within the coma subcategory to denote the time. These are the alpha extensors to be used when reporting the coma scale codes:

a in the field [EMT or ambulance]
b at arrival to emergency department
c at hospital admission
d 24 hours after hospital admission
e unspecified time

R40.212a Coma scale, eyes open, to pain, in the field

R40.222b Coma scale, best verbal response, incomprehensible words, at arrival to emergency department

R40.233d Coma scale, best motor response, abnormal,24 hours after hospital admission

Fetus Identification in Multiple Gestation

ICD•10•CM provides a very specialized group of extensions to be used in the subchapter, "Maternal care related to the fetus and amniotic cavity and possible delivery problems," in the category for complications specific to multiple gestation. These extensions are the capital letters A-H. They denote fetus A, fetus B, fetus C and so on, and are used in conjunction with the applicable complication code to identify which fetus is involved.

Place holding X

There are many ways that the hierarchal coding system of ICD•9•CM and ICD•10•CM provides an advantage over other types of coding systems. For collating data and statistical analysis, the hierarchal codes allow disease groups to be monitored easily. Coders using the system become familiar with these hierarchies so code lookup is easy. But despite the system's many advantages, there are disadvantages. Chief among the intrinsic disadvantages is the fixed space within each classification: there can be only 10 divisions of each code at the next level. The creation of an alpha first-character relieved much of the space problems for ICD•10•CM, providing 26 characters instead of 10, but there is still concern that medical advances could outstrip the room left in the coding system. In an effort to plan for these medical advances, some "place-holders" have been added to ICD•10•CM, so that in the future additional detail can be added to the classification. For example:

O45.8 Other premature separation of placenta

O45.8x Other premature separation of placenta

O45.8x1	Other premature separation of placenta, first trimester
O45.8x2	Other premature separation of placenta, second trimester
O45.8x3	Other premature separation of placenta, third trimester
O45.8x9	Other premature separation of placenta, unspecified trimester

Note that the definition of O45.8 and O45.8x are exactly the same. It is the intention of the creators of ICD•10•CM that if, in the future, there are causes of premature separation of the placenta that should be assigned unique codes, these causes would be assigned numbers that replace the x "place holder." Until then, coders are required to use the x as a place holder. It is not acceptable to drop the x.

TABULAR LIST CONVENTIONS

The ICD•10•CM Tabular List employs certain abbreviations, punctuations, symbols, and other conventions that must be clearly understood to use the classification appropriately.

NEC and NOS

Two abbreviations are found in the Tabular List: NEC and NOS. The abbreviation NEC means "not elsewhere classified" or "not elsewhere classifiable." NOS means "not otherwise specified."

Exercise caution when using the NEC category. NEC tells you that certain specified forms are classified elsewhere.

In the Tabular List, the phrase "not elsewhere classified" is applied to residual categories that do not appear in sequence with (i.e., immediately following) the pertinent specific categories. These residual categories are entitled "other specified." For example, K73 is the residual category for chronic hepatitis. This category is not immediate to the specific categories for forms of chronic hepatitis. The forms of the disease are assigned to various categories throughout the classification. An exclusion note in an NEC category lets you know that the condition is elsewhere classified.

K70	Alcoholic liver disease
K71	Toxic liver disease
K72	Hepatic failure, not elsewhere classified
K73	Chronic hepatitis, not elsewhere classified

Excludes1: alcoholic hepatitis (chronic) (K70.1–)
drug-induced hepatitis (chronic) (K71.–)
granulomatous hepatitis (chronic) NEC (K75.3)
reactive, nonspecific hepatitis (chronic) (K75.2)
viral hepatitis (chronic) (B15–B19)

The abbreviation NOS is equivalent to "unspecified." The term is assigned when the documentation does not provide the detail for a specific code. Double check the medical record for information about the condition before selecting an NOS code.

The term "bronchitis" alone means the same as "bronchitis, unspecified" or "bronchitis NOS."

J40   Bronchitis, not specified as acute or chronic
         Includes: bronchitis NOS
                      catarrhal bronchitis
                      bronchitis with tracheitis NOS
                      tracheobronchitis NOS

A term without an essential modifier is the unspecified form of the condition, though there are exceptions. Unqualified terms can be classified to a three-character category for a more specific type of condition. For example: Mitral stenosis is a common descriptor used as a diagnosis. ICD•10•CM assumes the cause to be rheumatic, whether or not "rheumatic" is included in the diagnosis.

I05   Rheumatic mitral valve diseases
         Includes: conditions classifiable to both I05.0 and I05.2-I05.9, whether specified as rheumatic or not
I05.0   Rheumatic mitral stenosis

} Braces
ICD•9•CM uses braces to enclose a series of terms, each of which is modified by the word(s) following the brace. This is not so in ICD•10•CM; no braces are used. For example:

ICD•9•CM
Code 560.9 includes obstruction, occlusion, stenosis, or stricture of intestine or colon.

560.9   Unspecified intestinal obstruction
           Enterostenosis

           Obstruction
           Occlusion   } of intestine
           Stenosis   or colon
           Stricture

ICD•10•CM
K56.6   Other and unspecified intestinal obstruction
           Enterostenosis
           Obstructive ileus NOS
           Occlusion of colon or intestine
           Stenosis of colon or intestine
           Stricture of colon or intestine

Note that no braces were used to list the inclusion terms in K56.9.

[ ] Brackets
Brackets enclose synonyms, alternative wordings, or explanatory phrases in ICD•9•CM and ICD•10•CM. For example: Crohn's disease is defined by the phrase in brackets as regional enteritis.

K50   Crohn's disease [regional enteritis]

KEY POINT

Code to the highest level of specificity allowed by the medical record documentation.

KEY POINT

Incorporating all common subclassifications and including full titles clarify a code's meaning even when the code contains six characters.

In ICD•9•CM, brackets are also used to enclose the fifth digits available for the fourth-digit subcategory. Since ICD•10•CM presents the five- and six-character subclassifications in their natural sequence, this use of brackets is not necessary in ICD•10•CM.

: Colon

ICD•9•CM and ICD•10•CM employ colons similarly. In the Tabular List, a colon follows an incomplete term that needs one or more modifiers to assign the term to a given code. The colon is applied rather than a comma for a term that has more than one essential modifier. For example: The terms "exudative," "nonsuppurative NOS," "seromucinous," and "with effusion (nonpurulent)" are essential modifiers. One of these terms must be present in the diagnostic statement in order to use H65.49.

> **H65.49 Other chronic nonsuppurative otitis media**
> Chronic exudative otitis media
> Chronic nonsuppurative otitis media NOS
> Chronic otitis media with effusion (nonpurulent)
> Chronic seromucinous otitis media

, Comma

Commas are found in both ICD•10•CM and ICD•9•CM for the same reasons. Words following a comma are essential modifiers. The terms in the inclusion note must be present in the diagnostic statement to qualify for that particular code. For example, the term "postpartum" is an essential modifier and must be present in the statement for deep-vein thrombosis or pelvic thrombophlebitis to assign code O87.1.

> **O87.1   Deep phlebothrombosis in the puerperium**
> Deep-vein thrombosis, postpartum
> Pelvic thrombophlebitis, postpartum

( ) Parentheses

In ICD•9•CM, parentheses enclose supplementary words that may be present or absent in the statement of a disease or procedure, but do not affect the code. Parentheses also enclose the categories included in a subchapter, and a code or code range listed in an excludes note. The same rules for parentheses apply to ICD•10•CM.

Nonessential modifiers usually appear in the three-character category that has been assigned the unspecified form of the disease modified. For example: The nonessential modifiers in the example below are: (acute), (chronic), (nonpuerperal), and (subacute).

> **N61   Inflammatory disorders of breast**
> Includes: abscess (acute) (chronic) (nonpuerperal) of areola
>   abscess (acute) (chronic) (nonpuerperal) of breast
>   carbuncle of breast
>   infective mastitis (acute) (subacute) (nonpuerperal)
>   mastitis (acute) (subacute) (nonpuerperal) NOS

§ Section Mark

The section mark symbol in some versions of ICD•9•CM precedes a code to denote the placement of a footnote at the bottom of the page. The footnote applies to all

---

 KEY POINT

Parentheses enclose terms that are called "nonessential modifiers." A patient's condition need not match the nonessential modifiers for that code to be selected.

---

subdivisions within that code. This symbol is not found in ICD•10•CM; rather, the subdivisions are listed in their natural sequence. For example:

ICD•9•CM

789   **Other symptoms involving abdomen and pelvis**

The following fifth-digit subclassification is to be used for codes 789.0, 789.3, 789.4, and 789.6:

0   unspecified site
1   right upper quadrant
2   left upper quadrant
3   right lower quadrant
4   right lower quadrant
5   periumbilic
6   epigastric
7   generalized
9   other specified site
      multiple sites

§789.0   **Abdominal pain**

§ Requires fifth-digit. See above for codes and definitions.

ICD•10•CM

R10.1   **Pain localized to upper abdomen**

R10.10   **Upper abdominal pain, unspecified**
R10.11   **Right upper quadrant pain**
R10.12   **Left upper quadrant pain**
R10.13   **Epigastric pain**

Inclusion term, Includes note

Inclusion terms and includes notes carry the same meaning in ICD•10•CM as they do in ICD•9•CM.

Since titles are not always self-explanatory, the Tabular List contains inclusion terms to clarify the content (intent) of the chapter, subchapter, category, or subdivision to which the terms apply. These "inclusion" terms are listed below the code title and describe other conditions classified to that code, such as synonyms of the condition listed in the code title, or an entirely different condition. For example:

R72.0   **Elevated white blood cell count**

Leukocytosis
Lymphocytosis
Monocytosis
Plasmacytosis

Inclusion notes appearing under chapter and subchapter titles provide general definitions to the content of that section. These notes apply to each category within the chapter or subchapter. For example:

Chapter XVI Certain Conditions Originating in the Perinatal Period (P00–P96)

Note: Codes from this chapter are for use on newborn records only, never on maternal records

 KEY POINT

Many of the alternative names found in the Alphabetic Index are not listed as inclusion terms in the Tabular List. To code accurately, consult the Index and then verify the code found in the Tabular List.

Includes: conditions that have their origin in the perinatal period (the first 28 days of life) even though morbidity occurs later

Infections specific to the perinatal period (P35-P39)

Includes: infections acquired in utero or during birth

Inclusion notes appearing under three-, four-, and five-character codes may define or provide a list of specific terms applicable to that category, and, if subdivided, to each subdivision.

The inclusion note appearing under the three-character category Q60 applies to all codes beneath it:

Q60 **Renal agenesis and other reduction defects of kidney**
Includes: congenital absence of kidney
congenital atrophy of kidney
infantile atrophy of kidney
Q60.0 **Renal agenesis, unilateral**
Q60.1 **Renal agenesis, bilateral**
Q60.2 **Renal agenesis, unspecified**
Q60.3 **Renal hypoplasia, unilateral**
Q60.4 **Renal hypoplasia, bilateral**
Q60.5 **Renal hypoplasia, unspecified**
Q60.6 **Potter's syndrome**

Notes

Throughout the Tabular List in ICD•9•CM, notes describe the general content of the succeeding categories and provide instructions for using the codes. The same holds true for ICD•10•CM. For example:

Encounters for other specific health care (Z40–Z53)

Note: Categories Z40–Z53 are intended for use to indicate a reason for care. They may be used for patients who have already been treated for a disease or injury, but who are receiving aftercare or prophylactic care, convalescent care, or care to consolidate the treatment, or to deal with a residual state.

Excludes2: Follow-up examination for medical surveillance after treatment (Z08–Z09)

Excludes Notes

Exclusion notes always appear with the word "excludes."

The purpose of excludes notes is to guide readers to proper application of codes. In ICD•9•CM, there has been significant confusion regarding excludes notes. In ICD•9•CM, an excludes note may indicate that two codes are mutually exclusive, and are not to be reported together. For example, the excludes note with the code for male stress incontinence of urine excludes the code for female stress incontinence. These codes are mutually exclusive and would never be reported correctly together. However, the excludes note for 304.6 Other specified drug dependence has a different role. This excludes note excludes tobacco from the drugs identified by 304.6. It would be appropriate and correct to report both codes for a patient with a tobacco habit and a glue-sniffing habit.

KEY POINT

The placement of instructional notes is important. Notes appearing at the beginning of chapters apply to all categories within the chapter. Notes appearing at the beginning of subchapters apply to all codes within the subchapter. Notes appearing at three-character categories apply to all four-, five-, six-, and seven-character codes within the various subdivisions.

KEY POINT

The excludes notes in ICD•10•CM are labeled as a type 1,2, or 3 excludes note:

An "excludes1" note indicates codes listed elsewhere that would never be used together. The two conditions are not the same, and are, in fact, mutually exclusive.

An "excludes2" note indicates codes that may be reported together with the listed codes, if appropriate. This excludes note is clarifying that the excluded condition is not considered part of the main code, and can be reported in addition to the main code.

An "excludes3" note identifies a code that describes both the etiology and the manifestation. The combination code should be used in place of the main code, if appropriate.

The excludes notes have been expanded in ICD•10•CM so there is no confusion over the intent of the codes. The excludes notes in ICD•10•CM are labeled as a type 1,2, or 3 excludes note:

An "excludes1" note indicates codes listed elsewhere that would never be used together. The two conditions are not the same, and are, in fact, mutually exclusive.

An "excludes2" note indicates codes that may be reported together with the listed codes, if appropriate. This excludes note is clarifying that the excluded condition is not considered part of the main code, and could be reported in addition to the main code.

An "excludes3" note identifies a code that describes both the etiology and the manifestation. Many disease codes have been expanded in ICD•10•CM so that there is a specific code for the disease and manifestation. The combination code should be used in place of the main code, and this excludes note reminds readers to use the dual code if appropriate.

General exclusions are found at the beginning of a chapter, block, or category title. For example:

Chapter V Mental and Behavioral Disorders (F01-F09)
Includes: disorders of psychological development
Excludes2: symptoms, signs and abnormal clinical laboratory findings, not elsewhere classified (R00–R99)

An excludes note is a warning that you may be in the wrong category, so read it carefully when checking a code listed in the Tabular List. Some excludes notes are warning that the two conditions are not the same and do not occur together. For example, the excludes note for three-character category Q16 shows that this is not the code for congenital deafness. That code is found in category H90.

Q16   Congenital malformations of ear causing impairment of hearing
Excludes1: congenital deafness (H90.-)

Some excludes notes are warning that the codes in that section do not include that particular condition and you will need to look elsewhere. The codes may or may not be appropriately used together. For example, the excludes note for three-character category T83 shows that this code does not include, or specify, the failure or rejection of a transplanted organ. The correct code can be found in category T86.

T83   Complications of genitourinary prosthetic devices, implants and grafts
Excludes2: failure and rejection of transplanted organs and tissues (T86.–)

Certain categories represent diseases in combination, or the specific manifestation in combination with the etiology. Exclusion notes in these cases instruct you not to use the code if the condition mentioned in the exclusion note is also present. Using both codes is inaccurate, redundant, and confusing. Examples: if the patient had cholecystitis and cholelithiasis, choose the appropriate code under category K80.

K81   Cholecystitis
Excludes1: cholecystitis with cholelithiasis (K80.–)

If the patient has a mycobacterium infection of tuberculosis, choose the correct code from A15-A19 and not A31.

A31   Infection due to other mycobacteria
        Excludes3: leprosy (A30.-)
                 Tuberculosis (A15-19)

Exclusion notes may reference the condition excluded. Sometimes, however, a condition may be so general that coding instructions are provided instead of a code reference. The absence of a code reference or coding instruction tells you that this is a "normal" condition, not to be coded at all. For example, this excludes note directs you to the Alphabetic Index.

Z39.0   Encounter for care and examination immediately after delivery
        Care and observation in uncomplicated cases when the delivery occurs outside a healthcare facility
        Excludes1: care for postpartum complication — see Alphabetic Index

"Code First" Note
The ICD•10•CM "code first" note tells you that two codes are necessary to describe the condition. The code first note appears in a category to describe the manifestation of a condition. The additional code, i.e., the one used first, describes the etiology of the condition. Code first notes may identify the added code—or examples of the added code—required, a range of codes, or instructions to code the underlying disease. Review the medical record prior to coding the underlying disease.

K87   Disorders of gallbladder, biliary tract and pancreas in diseases classified elsewhere
        Code first underlying disease
        Excludes1: cytomegaloviral pancreatitis (B25.2)
                 mumps pancreatitis (B26.3)
                 syphilitic gallbladder (A52.74)
                 syphilitic pancreas (A52.74)
                 tuberculosis of gallbladder (A18.83)
                 tuberculosis of pancreas (A18.83)

"Use" Note
"Use" notes common to both ICD•9•CM and ICD•10•CM carry the same meaning: a specific instruction to use an additional code to completely describe a condition. For example:

G25.3   Myoclonus
        Drug-induced myoclonus
        Use additional external cause code (Chapter XX) to identify drug
        Excludes1: facial myokymia (G51.4)
                 myoclonic epilepsy (G40.–)

The additional code may identify the following:

- An external cause such as a drug:

  L23   Allergic contact dermatitis
  > Use additional external cause code (Chapter XX), to identify drug or substance

- The cause of the disease:

  J02.8   Acute pharyngitis due to other specified organisms
  > Use additional code (B95–B97) to identify infectious agent

- An associated condition:

  F94.1   Reactive attachment disorder of childhood
  > Use additional code to identify any associated failure to thrive or growth retardation

- The nature of the condition:

  O91   Infections of breast associated with pregnancy, the puerperium and lactation
  > Use additional code to identify infection

Depending upon the additional information to be encoded, a use note may give a specific code, a range of codes, or examples of the codes to be applied. In some instances no codes may be specified, though the note describes the information to be encoded. For example: note that this list is incomplete in its representation:

K50   Crohn's disease [regional enteritis]
> Includes: granulomatous enteritis
> Excludes1: ulcerative colitis (K51.–)

Note that the term "as" indicates that this list is incomplete:

> Use additional code to identify manifestations, such as:
> pyoderma gangrenosum (L88)

Type Face
Chapter and subchapter titles, 3-digit categories, and all valid codes and their titles, including those requiring the alpha extension, are in bold typeface in the Tabular List. Main terms in the Alphabetic Index are also in bold typeface.

Excludes, includes, use, and code first underlying notes, as well as all rubrics not used for primary tabulations of disease, are not bolded.

Terminology
The connective "and" can be interpreted to mean "and/or" in the Tabular List and the Alphabetic Index. The connective "also" may indicate that the sites or conditions are included in the code (i.e., a combination code).

The preposition "with" in the Alphabetic Index references the code for diseases in combination. A "with" reference always follows the main term (or subterm) of reference (e.g., "with" appears as a subterm but not in strict alphabetical sequence).

 KEY POINT

The additional code requested by the "code first" note is never optional. The additional code requested must always precede, on any coding document, the code containing the code first note.

 KEY POINT

"Use" notes are not optional. Information requested by the use note must be coded if the associated condition or cause is present in the source document.

.– Point Dash

A point dash (.–) replaces the list of options available at a level of specificity past the three-character category. It instructs you to turn to the category or subcategory referenced to review the subdivisions available for coding.

In ICD•10•CM, the following excludes note indicates the category J02 for a patient who has an acute sore throat. The point dash indicates the code is incomplete. An additional digit completes the code.

J03   Acute tonsillitis
Excludes1: acute sore throat (J02.–)
              hypertrophy of tonsils (J35.1)
              peritonsillar abscess (J36)
              sore throat NOS (J02.9)
              streptococcal sore throat (J02.2)
Excludes2: chronic tonsillitis (J35.0)

ARRANGEMENT OF THE ALPHABETIC INDEX

The Alphabetic Index in ICD•10•CM is divided into three sections, similar to ICD•9•CM. It consists of the main alphabetic index to disease and injury, an external cause index, and a table of drugs and chemicals.

The main section in the Alphabetic Index of ICD•10•CM contains alphabetically sequenced terms pertaining to diseases, syndromes, pathological conditions, injuries, and signs and symptoms as reasons to contact the healthcare provider. The Alphabetic Index is organized by main terms, printed in bold type for easy reference. Main terms identify disease conditions. For example, chronic tonsillitis is found under the main term "tonsillitis."

Adjectives, such as "chronic" and "hereditary," and references to anatomic sites, such as "foot" and "kidney," appear as main terms with cross references to "see condition." For example, "Chronic — see condition; Kidney — see condition."

Neoplasms are listed in the Alphabetic Index in two ways: by anatomic site and morphology. The list of anatomic sites is found in a table under the main term entry "neoplasm, neoplastic." The table contains six columns: "malignant primary," "malignant secondary," "malignant ca in situ," "benign, uncertain behavior," and "unspecified."

Histological terms for neoplasms, such as "carcinoma," and "adenoma," are listed as main terms in the Alphabetic Index with cross references to the neoplasm table. Each morphological term appears with its morphology code from ICD•Oncology (ICD•O). For example:

ICD•10•CM

Adenoma (M8140/0) — *see also* Neoplasm, benign

The alphabetically-listed terms in the External Cause Index describe the circumstances of an accident or act of violence (the underlying cause or means of injury). The main terms represent the type of accident or violent encounter (e.g., "assault," "collision"). The Index includes terms for codes classified to V00–Y98, excluding drugs and chemicals.

The Table of Drugs and Chemicals is an extensive, but not exhaustive (new products are developed every day) resource containing a list of drugs, industrial solvents, corrosives, metals, gases, noxious plants, household cleaning products, pesticides, and other toxic agents that can be harmful. The table provides the diagnostic codes for poisoning by and adverse effect of these products—whether the poisoning is accidental (unintentional), an assault, self-inflicted, or undetermined whether accidental or intentional.

ALPHABETIC INDEX CONVENTIONS

The extensive amount of information in ICD•10•CM requires the complete understanding of the conventions and rules established to accurately assign a code.

The National Center for Health Statistics (NCHS) has clinically modified the ICD•10 index developed by the WHO. These modifications include adding entries for new fifth- and sixth-digit subclassifications, and deleting entries for codes that do not apply to the clinical modification.

Main Term

The Alphabetic Index is organized by main terms printed in bold typeface for easy reference. Main terms describe disease conditions. For example, acute bronchitis is found under the main term "bronchitis," and congestive heart failure is found under "failure."

There are exceptions to the rule. Obstetric conditions are found under "delivery," "pregnancy," and "puerperal," and under main terms for specific conditions "labor" and "vomiting."

Complications of medical and surgical procedures are indexed under "complications" and under the terms relating to specific conditions "dehiscence," and "infection."

Late effects of certain conditions (e.g., cerebral infections, injuries, infectious diseases) are found under "sequelae" with a note to "see also condition."

The Z codes from Chapter 21, "Factors Influencing Health Status and Contact with Health Services," are found under main terms such as "examination," "history," "observation," "problem," "screening," "status," or "vaccination."

Modifiers

Main terms in the Alphabetic Index may be followed by nouns or adjectives that further describe them. These descriptors are called modifiers, and there are two types: essential modifiers and nonessential modifiers.

Essential modifiers are descriptors that affect code selection for a given diagnosis, due to the axis of classification. For coding purposes, these modifiers describe essential differences in the site, etiology, or clinical type of disease. All terms must be present in the diagnosis to code according to the category modified.

ICD•10•CM

In ICD•10•CM the axis of classification for pneumonia is etiology or cause. "Aspiration," "pneumococcal," and "viral" are essential modifiers of pneumonia. Each term describes a different cause that requires a different code. The modifiers must be present in the diagnosis to use these codes. For example:

DEFINITION

Eponyms. Namesakes for certain diseases or syndromes. They are listed as main terms in alphabetic sequence.

KEY POINT

If a term describing a condition can be expressed in more than one form, all forms will appear in the main term entry. For example, "excess," "excessive," and "excessively" are listed together in the Alphabetic Index.

KEY POINT

An essential modifier that is the sole essential modifier for a main term appears in the Alphabetic Index on the same line as the main term, separated by a comma. For example: Insufflation, fallopian Z31.41. "Fallopian" is an essential modifier, and the only essential modifier of the main term "insufflation."

Pneumonia J18.9
Aspiration pneumonia J69.0
Pneumococcal pneumonia J13
Viral pneumonia J12.9

Main terms with multiple essential modifiers present each modifier on a separate line in a list indented below the main term. These multiple essential modifiers are called "subterms." For example, "allergic," "cluster," and "drug-induced" are essential modifiers for the main term "headache." Each appears as a subterm under "headache."

Headache R51
    allergic NEC G44.8
    cluster (chronic) (episodic) G44.0
    drug-induced NEC G44.4

Subterms may also be modified by other essential modifiers. In the Alphabetic Index they are further indented. For example, "visual" is an essential modifier of the main term "disorder." "Cortex" is an essential modifier of the subterm "visual," and "blindness" is an essential modifier of the complete subterm "visual cortex disorder."

Disorder
  visual
    cortex
    blindness H47.619
    left brain H47.612
    right brain H47.611

Nonessential modifiers do not affect code selection for a given diagnosis, due to the axis of classification. Nonessential modifiers appear as parenthetical terms following the words they modify. For example: Etiology is the axis of classification for pneumonia. The terms "acute," "double," and "septic" are nonessential modifiers since they describe conditions other than the cause of pneumonia. The code for "pneumonia" is J18.9 despite the absence or presence of any of the nonessential modifiers.

Pneumonia (acute) (Alpenstich) (benign) (bilateral) (brain) (cerebral) (circumscribed) (congestive) (creeping) (delayed resolution) (double) (epidemic) (fever) (flash) (fulminant) (fungoid) (granulomatous) (hemorrhagic) (incipient) (infantile) (infectious) (infiltration) (insular) (intermittent) (latent) (migratory) (organized) (overwhelming) (primary (atypical)) (progressive) (pseudolobar) (purulent) (resolved) (secondary) (senile) (septic) (suppurative) (terminal) (true) (unresolved) (vesicular) J18.9

Nonessential modifiers may follow subterms in the Alphabetic Index. For example:

Murmur (cardiac) (heart) (organic) R01.1
    aortic (valve) — *see* Endocarditis, aortic

Abbreviations

In the Alphabetic Index the abbreviation NEC, "not elsewhere classified," serves as a warning with ill-defined terms. The code is assigned only if a review of the code choices does not yield an appropriate code for the condition.

KEY POINT

Nonessential modifiers may be present or absent for the diagnosis to be coded. Either way, the code remains the same.

NEC following "Granuloma, foreign body (in soft tissue)" indicates that M60.20 may not be the correct code or subcategory for classifying a foreign body granuloma. Before assigning the NEC code for a given diagnosis, you must first scan all the available subterms to determine whether there is another entry that is more specific. This ensures that the most appropriate code is assigned.

In this case, NEC references the residual category for a condition, e.g., the category for "other specified" forms of soft tissue foreign body granulomas. As you scan the subterms in the index, you may be directed to a specified subcategory, such as for skin or subcutaneous tissue, L92.3, or to a more appropriate code within the NEC subcategory.

An index entry may also appear as "specified NEC." This convention ensures that the correct code will be chosen although the term to be coded does not appear in the index.

Granuloma
    foreign body (in soft tissue) NEC M60.20
        shoulder region M60.219
          left M60.212
          right M60.211
        skin L92.3
        specified site NEC M60.28
        subcutaneous tissue L92.3

Cross References

Cross references in the Alphabetic Index point to all the possible information for a term or its synonyms.

There are two types of cross references: "— see" and "— see also."

In ICD•10•CM, "see" directs you to another term in the index that provides more complete information. It is also used with anatomical site main entries to remind you that the index is organized by condition. For example, the cross reference "see" indicates that the term "hardening of arteries" is coded to "arteriosclerosis."

Hardening
    artery — *see* Arteriosclerosis

Or, you are directed to the condition affecting the heart.

Heart — *see* condition

The cross reference "see also" directs you to another main term if you need more information than what is listed under the first term selected. For example:

Necrosis, necrotic (ischemic) — *see also* Gangrene

Modifiers under "necrosis" are not definitive. Modifiers applying to "necrosis" are the same as those for "gangrene." If the modifier cannot be found under "necrosis," the cross reference instructs you to "— see also Gangrene."

CODING AXIOM

In ICD•10•CM, as in ICD•9•CM, you should always seek your code first in the index and then verify your selection in the tabular section.

KEY POINT

Review the Alphabetic Index for cross references and notes prior to referring to the Tabular List. Notes at the beginning of main terms may not be repeated.

Notes

New to the ICD•10•CM index is the omission of the notes that were common in ICD•9•CM. Because the information in the notes section of the ICD•9•CM index is repeated in the tabular section of ICD•9•CM, it may have been considered redundant. Editors may also have felt that to retain the notes in the index encouraged coders to code from the index — a practice considered taboo by experienced coders.

Etiology and Manifestation of Disease

You must code both the etiology and the manifestation of the disease for certain conditions. A single five-digit code, such as A54.31 Gonococcal conjunctivitis may accomplish the task. Specific fifth-digit subclassifications, however, are not always available. In these latter cases, code the two facets individually and in the same sequence, as found in the Alphabetic Index.

Gonococcus, gonococcal (disease) (infection) (see also condition) A54.9
  conjunctiva, conjunctivitis (neonatorum) A54.31

Ring(s)
  Fleischer's (cornea) E83.01 [H18.049]

DISCUSSION QUESTIONS

1. What do we mean by "axis of classification?" Please give examples of some axes.

   _____

   _____

   _____

2. Explain the rules surrounding use of parentheses in the Tabular Section and Index to Diseases.

   _____

   _____

   _____

3. Why should you use caution in coding with a code designated as NEC or NOS?

   _____

   _____

   _____

4. What are alpha extensions and how are they used?

   _____

   _____

   _____

5. Discuss the three types of excludes notes and how each is different.

_____

_____

_____

3 Code Families

This chapter provides a detailed review and analysis of the changes to individual chapters and the code "families," i.e., the block of three-character categories the chapters contain. While not every single revision has been identified in every chapter, the highlights given here should help you feel assured that coding correctly with ICD•10•CM, even though it is not the way you are accustomed to under ICD•9•CM, is not so drastically different in most cases.

With any revision to a classification, changes are made for specific reasons. Overall, as mentioned in chapter 1, conditions have been grouped in a way that is most appropriate for general epidemiological purposes and the evaluation of healthcare.

Specific reasons for changes to the contents of the chapters include the desire to do the following:

- Increase clinical detail about a specific disorder
- Reclassify diseases because of recent scientific information
- Identify recently discovered diseases, i.e., since the last revision
- Accommodate all the required detail of a group of diseases
- Make effective use of available space

In general, conditions were moved as a group or individual conditions were reclassified. For example, the number of categories for disorders of the immune mechanism was expanded and the category group was moved to "Diseases of the Blood and Blood-forming Organs." In ICD•9•CM, these disorders are included with "Endocrine, Nutritional, and Metabolic Diseases."

OBJECTIVES

- Identify each code family
- Gain a better understanding of the structural changes to ICD•10•CM at the three-character category level
- Learn the organizational adjustments that have occurred to individual diseases

CHAPTER 1

Chapter 1, Certain Infectious and Parasitic Diseases, contains 21 code families depicted by the code's first character of "A" and "B." They are:

A00-A09	Intestinal infectious diseases
A15-A19	Tuberculosis
A20-A28	Certain zoonotic bacterial diseases
A30-A49	Other bacterial diseases
A50-A64	Infections with a predominantly sexual mode of transmission
A65-A69	Other spirochetal diseases
A70-A74	Other diseases caused by chlamydiae
A75-A79	Rickettsioses
A80-A89	Viral infections of the central nervous system
A90-A99	Arthropod-borne viral fevers and viral hemorrhagic fevers
B00-B09	Viral infections characterized by skin and mucous membrane lesions

B15-B19	Viral hepatitis
B20	Human immunodeficiency virus [HIV] disease
B25-B34	Other viral diseases
B35-B49	Mycoses
B50-B64	Protozoal diseases
B65-B83	Helminthiases
B85-B89	Pediculosis, acariasis and other infestations
B90-B94	Sequelae of infectious and parasitic diseases
B95-B97	Bacterial, viral and other infectious agents
B99	Other infectious diseases

ICD•10•CM Subchapter Restructuring

After reviewing different disease categories, the developers of ICD•10 restructured some of their groupings to bring together those groups that were related by cause. For example, the ICD•9•CM subchapter "Syphilis and Other Venereal Diseases" has been rearranged, and the subchapter "Rickettsioses and Other Arthropod-borne Diseases" has been split into two separate subchapters in ICD•10•CM.

ICD•9•CM

Rickettsioses and Other Arthropod-borne Diseases (080-088)

Syphilis and Other Venereal Diseases (090-099)

Other Spirochetal Diseases (100-104).

ICD•10•CM

Infections with a predominantly sexual mode of transmission (A50-A64)

Other spirochetal diseases (A65-A69)

Rickettsioses (A75-A79)

Arthropod-borne viral fevers and hemorrhagic fevers (A90-A99)

Category Title Changes

As the examples above illustrate, a number of category and subchapter titles have been revised in chapter I. Titles were changed to better reflect the content, which was often necessary when specific types of diseases were given their own block, a new category was created, or an existing category was redefined.

ICD•9•CM

046   Slow virus infection of central nervous system

ICD•10•CM

A81   Atypical virus infections of central nervous systems

Organizational adjustments

When comparing ICD•9•CM to ICD•10•CM, some codes have been added, deleted, combined, and moved.

The code for human immunodeficiency virus disease followed the subchapter, "Other Bacterial Diseases" in ICD•9•CM. The code for human immunodeficiency virus disease has been moved in ICD•10•CM to follow the subchapter for viral hepatitis.

 KEY POINT

In some cases, the codes in ICD•10 and ICD•10•CM closely resemble those in ICD•9•CM. For example:

ICD•9•CM
021.2   Pulmonary tularemia

ICD•10•CM
A21.2   Pulmonary tularemia

In other cases, the codes and nomenclature are quite different:

ICD•9•CM
233.0   Carcinoma in situ of breast

ICD•10•CM
There are 24 codes for carcinoma in situ of breast, including:

D05.12   Intraductal carcinoma in situ of left female breast

 KEY POINT

The term "certain" has been added to the title of chapter 1, "Infectious and Parasitic Diseases," to stress the fact that localized infections are classified with the diseases of the pertinent body system.

ICD•9•CM

042   Human immunodeficiency virus [HIV] disease

ICD•10•CM

B20   Human immunodeficiency virus [HIV] disease

The ICD•10 code for opportunistic mycoses, B48.7, has been deleted in ICD•10•CM. The conditions that would have been classified to this code have been moved to B48.8.

ICD•9•CM

118   Opportunistic mycoses

ICD•10•CM

B48.8   Other specified mycoses
            Adiaspiromycosis
            Infection of tissue and organs by alternaria
            Infection of tissue and organs by dreschlera
            Infection of tissue and organs by fusarium
            Infection of tissue and organs by saprophytic fungi NEC

There was no specific code in ICD•9•CM for septicemia due to enterococcus. A code has been added to the ICD•10•CM to classify this disorder.

ICD•10•CM

A41.81 Septicemia due to enterococcus

CHAPTER 2

Chapter 2, "Neoplasms," contains 17 code families depicted by the code's first character of "C" and "D." The letter D is also shared with the next chapter, "Diseases of the Blood and Blood-Forming Organs and Certain Disorders Involving the Immune System." C and D code families for this chapter are:

C00-C75	Malignant neoplasms, stated or presumed to be primary, of specified sites, except of lymphoid, hematopoietic and related tissue
C00-C14	Lip, oral cavity and pharynx
C15-C26	Digestive organs
C30-C39	Respiratory and intrathoracic organs
C40-C41	Bone and articular cartilage
C43-C44	Skin
C45-C49	Mesothelial and soft tissue
C50	Breast
C51-C58	Female genital organs
C60-C63	Male genital organs
C64-C68	Urinary tract
C69-C72	Eye, brain and other parts of central nervous system
C73-C75	Thyroid and other endocrine glands
C76-C80	Malignant neoplasms of ill-defined, secondary and unspecified sites

C81-C96	Malignant neoplasms, stated or presumed to be primary, of lymphoid, hematopoietic and related tissue
D00-D09	In situ neoplasms
D10-D36	Benign neoplasms
D37-D48	Neoplasms of uncertain behavior

D49 Neoplasms of unspecified behavior

Category Title Changes

A number of category titles have been revised in chapter 2. Titles were changed to better reflect the category's content, which was often necessary when specific types of diseases were given their own block, a new category was created, or an existing category was redefined.

ICD•9•CM

141   Malignant neoplasm of tongue

ICD•10•CM

C01   Malignant neoplasm of base of tongue

C02   Malignant neoplasm of other and unspecified parts of tongue

Organizational Adjustments

When comparing ICD•9•CM to ICD•10•CM, some codes have been added, deleted, combined, and moved.

The codes for malignant neoplasm of retroperitoneum and peritoneum were in the subchapter, "Malignant Neoplasm of the Digestive Organs and Peritoneum" in ICD•9•CM. These codes have been moved in ICD•10•CM to the subchapter, "Malignant neoplasms of mesothelial and soft tissue."

ICD•9•CM

Malignant Neoplasm of Digestive Organs and Peritoneum (150-159)

150   Malignant neoplasm of esophagus

151   Malignant neoplasm of stomach

152   Malignant neoplasm of small intestine, including duodenum

153   Malignant neoplasm of colon

154   Malignant neoplasm of rectum, rectosigmoid junction, and anus

156   Malignant neoplasm of gallbladder and extrahepatic bile ducts

157   Malignant neoplasm of pancreas

158   Malignant neoplasm of retroperitoneum and peritoneum

159   Malignant neoplasm of other and ill-defined sites within the digestive organs and peritoneum

ICD•10•CM

Malignant Neoplasms of Mesothelial and Soft Tissue (C45-C49)

C45   Mesothelioma

C46   Kaposi's sarcoma

C47   Malignant neoplasm of peripheral nerves and autonomic nervous system

C48   Malignant neoplasm of retroperitoneum and peritoneum

C49   Malignant neoplasm of other connective and soft tissue

CODING AXIOM

One of ICD's specialty-based adaptations is the International Classification of Diseases for Oncology (ICD•O). This dual-axis classification is used in cancer registries and in pathology and other departments specializing in cancer.

The codes for the cervical, thoracic, and abdominal sites for malignant neoplasm of the esophagus have been deleted in ICD•10•CM. The conditions that would have been classified to these codes should be classified to codes C15.3-C15.8 as appropriate.

ICD•9•CM

150		Malignant neoplasm of esophagus
	150.0	Cervical esophagus
	150.1	Thoracic esophagus
	150.2	Abdominal esophagus
	150.3	Upper third of esophagus
	150.4	Middle third of esophagus
	150.5	Lower third of esophagus
	150.8	Other specified part
	150.9	Esophagus, unspecified

ICD•10•CM

C15		Malignant neoplasm of esophagus
	C15.3	Malignant neoplasm of upper third of esophagus
	C15.4	Malignant neoplasm of middle third of esophagus
	C15.5	Malignant neoplasm of lower third of esophagus
	C15.8	Malignant neoplasm of overlapping sites of esophagus
	C15.9	Malignant neoplasm of esophagus, unspecified

KEY POINT

While all codes beginning with C report neoplasms, codes beginning with D are divided between neoplasms and diseases of the blood-forming organs and immune disorders.

In ICD•9•CM, 199.1 was used to classify a malignant neoplasm without specification as to site for either a primary or secondary site. In ICD•10•CM, category C80 reports malignancy without a site specification.

ICD•10•CM

C80		Malignant neoplasm without specification of site
	Includes:	Cancer unspecified site (primary)(secondary)
		Carcinoma unspecified site (primary)(secondary)
		Carcinomatosis unspecified site (primary)(secondary)
		Generalized cancer unspecified site (primary)(secondary)
		Malignancy unspecified site (primary)(secondary)
		Malignant cachexia
		Multiple cancer unspecified site (primary)(secondary)
		Primary site unknown

CHAPTER 3

Chapter 3, "Diseases of the Blood and Blood-forming Organs and Certain Disorders Involving the Immune Mechanism," contains six code families depicted by the code's first character of "D," which is also shared with the previous chapter, "Neoplasms." The coding families in this chapter are:

D50-D53	Nutritional anemias
D55-D59	Hemolytic anemias
D60-D64	Aplastic and other anemias
D65-D69	Coagulation defects, purpura and other hemorrhagic conditions

D70-D78   Other diseases of blood and blood-forming organs

D80-D89   Certain disorders involving the immune mechanism

KEY POINT

In ICD•10•CM, the contents of chapter 3 and chapter 4 are different than in ICD•9•CM. First, the number of categories for disorders of the immune mechanism was expanded. Then, they were put with diseases of the blood and blood-forming organs. Finally, this combination of disorders was moved before the chapter on endocrine, nutritional and metabolic diseases.

ICD•10•CM Category Restructuring

In ICD•9•CM, there were no subchapters in the chapter for diseases of blood and blood-forming organs. Blocks have been added to this restructured chapter for ICD•10•CM. The arrangement of the various disorders, given the addition of these new blocks, has resulted in restructuring of the categories.

ICD•9•CM

280	Iron deficiency anemias
281	Other deficiency anemias
282	Hereditary hemolytic anemias
283	Acquired hemolytic anemias
284	Aplastic anemia
285	Other and unspecified anemias
286	Coagulation defects
287	Purpura and other hemorrhagic conditions
288	Diseases of white blood cells
289	Other diseases of blood and blood-forming organs

ICD•10•CM

Nutritional anemias (D50-D53)

D50	Iron deficiency anemia
D51	Vitamin B12 deficiency anemia
D52	Folate deficiency anemia
D53	Other nutritional anemias

Category Title Changes

A number of category title revisions were made in chapter 3. Titles were changed to better reflect the category's content. This was often necessary when specific types of diseases were given their own block, a new category was created, or an existing category was redefined.

ICD•9•CM

281		Other deficiency anemias
	281.0	Pernicious anemia
	281.1	Other vitamin B12 deficiency anemia
	281.2	Folate-deficiency anemia
	281.3	Other specified megaloblastic anemias not elsewhere classified
	281.4	Protein-deficiency anemia
	281.8	Anemia associated with other specified nutritional deficiency
	281.9	Unspecified deficiency anemia

ICD•10•CM

D50		Iron deficiency anemia
D51		Vitamin B12 deficiency anemia
D52		Folate deficiency anemia
D53		Other nutritional anemias
	D53.0	Protein deficiency anemia

D53.1   Other megaloblastic anemias, not elsewhere classified

D53.2   Scorbutic anemia

D53.8   Other specified nutritional anemias

Organizational Adjustments

When comparing ICD•9•CM to ICD•10•CM, some codes have been added, deleted, combined, and moved.

The code for chronic lymphadenitis, nonspecific mesenteric lymphadenitis, and unspecified lymphadenitis in ICD•9•CM were classified to the chapter on diseases of the blood and blood-forming organs. These conditions have been moved in ICD•10 to the chapter for diseases of the circulatory system where they are best classified with other disorders of the lymphatic vessels and lymph nodes.

ICD•9•CM

289.1   Chronic lymphadenitis

289.2   Nonspecific mesenteric lymphadenitis

289.3   Lymphadenitis, unspecified, except mesenteric

ICD•10•CM

I88   Nonspecific lymphadenitis

I88.0   Nonspecific mesenteric lymphadenitis

I88.1   Chronic lymphadenitis, except mesenteric

I88.8   Other nonspecific lymphadenitis

I88.9   Nonspecific lymphadenitis, unspecified

The specific code for iron deficiency anemia secondary to inadequate dietary iron intake that was available in ICD•9•CM is deleted in ICD•10. The condition that would have been classified to this code will now be coded to the residual subcategory.

ICD•9•CM

280.1   Iron deficiency anemia secondary to inadequate dietary iron intake

ICD•10•CM

D50.8   Other iron deficiency anemias

Iron deficiency anemia due to inadequate dietary iron intake

There was no specific code in ICD•9•CM for agranulocytosis secondary to cancer chemotherapy. A new code has been added to the ICD•10•CM to classify this disorder.

ICD•10•CM

D70.1   Agranulocytosis secondary to cancer chemotherapy

CHAPTER 4

Chapter 4, "Endocrine, Nutritional and Metabolic Diseases," contains eight code families depicted by the code's first character of "E." They are:

E00-E07   Disorders of thyroid gland

E08-E14   Diabetes mellitus

 KEY POINT

In addition to chapter 3 being restructured, the "excludes" note was greatly expanded, referring you to nine other chapters in ICD•10•CM. Be sure and review this note found at the beginning of the chapter to ensure you are in the right place.

E15-E16	Other disorders of glucose regulation and pancreatic internal secretion
E20-E36	Disorders of other endocrine glands
E40-E46	Malnutrition
E50-E64	Other nutritional deficiencies
E65-E68	Obesity and other hyperalimentation
E70-E90	Metabolic disorders

ICD•10•CM Category Restructuring

The review of the different disease categories resulted in the restructuring of some of them by the developers of ICD•10. This was done to separate out certain disorders and to give them a specific three-character category range. For example, in ICD•9•CM there is a subchapter for nutritional deficiencies (260-269), which includes malnutrition and other nutritional deficiencies. In ICD•10•CM, malnutrition has been given its own separate subchapter (E40-E46) and so has other nutritional deficiencies (E50-E64).

ICD•9•CM

Nutritional Deficiencies (260-269)

260	Kwashiorkor
261	Nutritional marasmus
262	Other severe, protein-calorie malnutrition
263	Other and unspecified protein-calorie malnutrition
264	Vitamin A deficiency
265	Thiamin and niacin deficiency states
266	Deficiency of B-complex components
267	Ascorbic acid deficiency
268	Vitamin D deficiency
269	Other nutritional deficiencies

ICD•10•CM

Malnutrition (E40-E46)

E40	Kwashiorkor
E41	Nutritional marasmus
E42	Marasmic kwashiorkor
E43	Unspecified severe protein-calorie malnutrition
E45	Retarded development following protein-calorie malnutrition
E46	Unspcified protein-calorie malnutrition

Other nutritional deficiencies (E50-E64)

E50	Vitamin A deficiency
E51	Thiamine deficiency
E52	Niacin deficiency [pellagra]
E53	Deficiency of other B group vitamins
E54	Ascorbic acid deficiency
E55	Vitamin D deficiency
E56	Other vitamin deficiencies

Category Title Changes

A number of category title revisions were made in chapter 4. Titles were changed to better reflect the category's content, which was often necessary when specific types of diseases were given their own block, a new category was created, or an existing category was redefined.

ICD•9•CM

265   Thiamin and niacin deficiency states
266   Deficiency of B-complex components

ICD•10•CM

E51   Thiamine deficiency
E52   Niacin deficiency [pellagra]
E53   Deficiency of other B group vitamins

Organizational Adjustments

When comparing ICD•9•CM to ICD•10•CM, some codes have been added, deleted, combined, or moved.

The code for osteomalacia was a subcategory code of Vitamin D deficiency in ICD•9•CM. This condition has been moved in ICD•10•CM to its own three-character category for adult osteomalacia in the "Diseases of the Musculoskeletal System and Connective Tissues" chapter .

ICD•9•CM

268   Vitamin D deficiency
    268.2   Osteomalacia, unspecified

ICD•10•CM

M83   Adult osteomalacia
    M83.0   Puerperal osteomalacia
    M83.1   Senile osteomalacia
    M83.2   Adult osteomalacia due to malabsorption
    M83.3   Adult osteomalacia due to malnutrition
    M83.4   Aluminum bone disease
    M83.5   Other drug-induced osteomalacia in adults
    M83.8   Other adult osteomalacia
    M83.9   Adult osteomalacia, unspecified

The specific code for thyroid cyst that was available in ICD•9•CM is deleted in ICD•10. The condition that is currently classified to code 246.2 will now be coded to the residual subcategory.

ICD•9•CM

    246.2   Cyst of thyroid

ICD•10•CM

    E07.89   Other specified disorders of thyroid

There was no separate code in ICD•9•CM for dehydration or hypovolemia. They were grouped together as inclusion terms under code 276.5 Volume depletion. Codes have been added to ICD•10•CM to classify each of these conditions independently.

WORTH NOTING

Although their alpha placement is purely coincidental, it may help you remember code families to consider the following:

- Most neoplasm codes begin with "C," as in cancer.
- Diabetes and other endocrine disorders begin with "E," as in endocrinology.
- Nephrology codes can be found under "N."
- Obstetrical codes begin with the letter "O."
- Perinatal codes begin with the letter "P."

KEY POINT

There are many reasons for changes to the contents of the chapters, including the need for increased clinical detail about a specific disorder, and the reclassification of diseases due to increased knowledge of their causes.

ICD•10•CM

E86	**Volume depletion**	
	E86.0	**Dehydration**
	E86.1	**Hypovolemia**
		Depletion of volume of plasma or extracellular fluid
	E86.9	**Volume depletion, unspecified**

CHAPTER 5

Chapter 5, "Mental and Behavioral Disorders," contains 11 code families depicted by the code's first character of "F." They are:

F01-F09	Mental disorders due to known physiological conditions
F10-F19	Mental and behavioral disorders due to psychoactive substance use
F20-F29	Schizophrenia, schizotypal and delusional, and other non-mood psychotic disorders
F30-F39	Mood [affective] disorders
F40-F48	Anxiety, dissociative, stress-related, somatoform and other nonpsychotic mental disorders
F50-F59	Behavioral syndromes associated with physiological disturbances and physical factors
F60-F69	Disorders of adult personality and behavior
F70-F79	Mental retardation
F80-F89	Pervasive and specific developmental disorders
F90-F98	Behavioral and emotional disorders with onset usually occurring in childhood and adolescence
F99	Unspecified mental disorder

ICD•10•CM Subchapter Restructuring

Chapter 5 underwent a number of revisions, including the expansion of the number of subchapters from three to eleven. With this increase, ICD•10 arranges specific disorders differently than they are in ICD•9•CM and broadens the clinical detail. Based on the ICD•10 arrangement of chapter 5, ICD•10•CM has made further modifications to these expanded subchapter divisions and titles.

ICD•9•CM

Chapter 5 — Mental Disorders (290-319)

Psychoses (290-299)

Organic Psychotic Conditions (290-294)

Other Psychoses (295-299)

Neurotic Disorders, Personality Disorders, and Other Nonpsychotic Mental Disorders (300-316)

Mental Retardation (317-319)

☞ **KEY POINT**

Three chapters in ICD•10 underwent substantial review and revision: chapters 5, 19, and 20. Be sure you understand the changes made to these chapters so that you can code correctly from them.

ICD•10

Chapter 5 Mental and Behavioral Disorders (F00-F99)

F00-F09	Organic, including symptomatic, mental disorders
F10-F19	Mental and behavioral disorders due to psychoactive substance use
F20-F29	Schizophrenia, schizotypal and delusional disorders
F30-F39	Mood [affective] disorders
F40-F48	Neurotic, stress-related and somatoform disorders
F50-F59	Behavioral syndromes associated with physiological disturbances and physical factors
F60-F69	Disorders of adult personality and behavior
F70-F79	Mental retardation
F80-F89	Disorders of psychological development
F90-F98	Behavioral and emotional disorders with onset usually occurring in childhood and adolescence
F99	Unspecified mental disorder

Subchapter Title Changes

There have been a number of subchapter title revisions in chapter 5. Titles were changed to better reflect the block's content, which was often necessary when specific types of diseases were given their own block or defined differently.

ICD•9•CM

Organic Psychotic Conditions (290-294)

Other Psychoses (295-299)

Neurotic Disorders, Personality Disorders, and Other Nonpsychotic Mental Disorders (300-316)

Mental Retardation (317-319)

ICD•10

F00-F09	Organic, including symptomatic, mental disorders
F20-F29	Schizophrenia, schizotypal and delusional disorders
F40-F48	Neurotic, stress-related and somatoform disorders
F80-F89	Disorders of psychological development

ICD•10•CM

F01-F09	Mental disorders due to known physiological conditions
F20-F29	Schizophrenia, schizotypal and delusional, and other non-mood psychotic disorders
F40-F48	Anxiety, dissociative, stress-related, somatoform and other nonpsychotic mental disorders
F80-F89	Pervasive and specific developmental disorders

Organizational Adjustments

When comparing ICD•9•CM to ICD•10•CM, some codes have been added, deleted, combined, or moved.

The code for tension headache was found in ICD•9•CM chapter 5 under the subchapter "Neurotic Disorders, Personality Disorders, and Other Nonpsychotic Mental Disorders." The code for this condition has been moved in ICD•10•CM and is found in chapter 6, "Diseases of the Nervous System."

ICD•9•CM

307   **Special symptoms or syndromes, not elsewhere classified**
     307.8   **Psychalgia**
          307.81   **Tension headache**

ICD•10•CM

G44   **Other headache syndromes**
     G44.2   **Tension-type headache**

The specific code for psychogenic dysmenorrhea has been deleted in ICD•10•CM. This condition that is currently classified to code 306.52 will now be coded to the residual subcategory.

ICD•9•CM

         306.52   **Psychogenic dysmenorrhea**

ICD•10•CM

     F45.8   **Other somatoform disorders**
          Psychogenic dysmenorrhea
          Psychogenic dysphagia, including "globus hystericus"
          Psychogenic pruritus
          Psychogenic torticollis
          Somatoform autonomic dysfunction
          Teeth-grinding

There were no codes in ICD•9•CM for denoting specific types of anorexia nervosa. New codes have been added to ICD•10•CM to classify the two types.

ICD•10•CM

     F50.0   **Anorexia nervosa**
          F50.00   Anorexia nervosa, unspecified
          F50.01   Anorexia nervosa, restricting type
          F50.02   Anorexia nervosa, binge eating/purging type

CHAPTER 6

Chapter 6, "Diseases of the Nervous System," contains 11 code families depicted by the code's first character of "G." They are:

G00-G09	Inflammatory diseases of the central nervous system
G10-G13	Systemic atrophies primarily affecting the central nervous system
G20-G26	Extrapyramidal and movement disorders
G30-G32	Other degenerative diseases of the nervous system
G35-G37	Demyelinating diseases of the central nervous system
G40-G47	Episodic and paroxysmal disorders
G50-G59	Nerve, nerve root and plexus disorders

📖 **DEFINITION**

Somatoform disorder. A chronic, but fluctuating, neurotic disorder that begins early in life and is characterized by recurrent and multiple somatic complaints for which medical attention is sought but which are not apparently due to any physical illness.

G60-G64   Polyneuropathies and other disorders of the peripheral
nervous system

G70-G73   Diseases of myoneural junction and muscle

G80-G83   Cerebral palsy and other paralytic syndromes

G90-G99   Other disorders of the nervous system

ICD•10•CM Category Restructuring

After reviewing the different disease categories, the developers of ICD•10 restructured some of them to bring together those groups that are somehow related. For example, toward the end of chapter 6, new categories for intraoperative complications and postprocedural disorders specific to the nervous system were created.

ICD•9•CM

349.0   **Reaction to spinal or lumbar puncture**

349.1   **Nervous system complications from surgically implanted device**

    997.00   **Nervous system complication, unspecified**

    997.01   **Central nervous system complication**

    997.09   **Other nervous system complications**

    998.11   **Hemorrhage complicating a procedure**

    998.12   **Hematoma complicating a procedure**

998.2   **Accidental puncture or laceration during a procedure**

ICD•10•CM

G97   **Intraoperative and postprocedural complications and disorders of nervous system, not elsewhere classified**

    G97.0   **Cerebrospinal fluid leak from spinal puncture**

    G97.1   **Other reaction to spinal and lumbar puncture**

    G97.2   **Intracranial hypotension following ventricular shunting**

    G97.3   **Intraoperative and postprocedural hemorrhage or hematoma complicating a nervous system procedure**

      G97.31   **Intraoperative hemorrhage of a nervous system organ during a nervous system procedure**

      G97.32   **Intraoperative hemorrhage of other organ during a nervous system procedure**

      G97.33   **Intraoperative hematoma of a nervous system organ during a nervous system procedure**

      G97.34   **Intraoperative hematoma of other organ during a nervous system procedure**

      G97.35   **Postprocedural hemorrhage of a nervous system organ following a nervous system procedure**

      G97.36   **Postprocedural hemorrhage of other organ following a nervous system procedure**

      G97.37   **Postprocedural hematoma of a nervous system organ following a nervous system procedure**

      G97.38   **Postprocedural hematoma of other organ following a nervous system procedure**

    G97.4   **Accidental puncture or laceration during a nervous system procedure**

 KEY POINT

No change was made to the classification of those situations where postprocedural conditions are not specific to a particular body system. They can be found in ICD•10•CM in chapter 19, "Injury, Poisoning and Certain Other Consequences of External Causes," compatible with where you would find them in ICD•9•CM.

G97.41　Accidental puncture or laceration of a nervous system structure during a nervous system procedure

G97.42　Accidental puncture or laceration of other organs or structure during a nervous system procedure

G97.8　Other intraoperative and postprocedural complications and disorders of nervous system

G97.81　Other intraoperative complications of nervous system procedure

G97.82　Other postprocedural complications and disorders of nervous system procedure

G97.9　Intraoperative and postprocedural complication and disorder of the nervous system, unspecified

Category Title Changes

A number of category title revisions were made in chapter 6. Titles were changed to better reflect the category's content, which was often necessary when specific types of diseases were given their own block, a new category was created, or an existing category was redefined.

ICD•9•CM

354　Mononeuritis of upper limb and mononeuritis multiplex

ICD•10•CM

G56　Mononeuropathies of upper limb

Organizational Adjustments

When comparing ICD•9•CM to ICD•10•CM, some codes have been added, deleted, combined, and moved.

The code for Tay-Sachs disease, which includes gangliosidosis, found in the nervous system and sense organs chapter in ICD•9•CM, has been moved in ICD•10•CM. Specific codes were created for Tay-Sachs and the different types of gangliosidosis in ICD•10•CM and are found in chapter 4, "Endocrine, Nutritional and Metabolic Disorders."

ICD•9•CM

330.1　Cerebral lipidoses

Amaurotic (familial) idiocy

Disease:

Batten

Jansky-Bielschowsky

Kufs'

Spielmeyer-Vogt

Tay-Sachs

Gangliosidosis

ICD•10•CM

E75.0　GM2 gangliosidosis

E75.00　GM2 gangliosidosis, unspecified

E75.01　Sandhoff disease

E75.02　Tay-Sachs disease

E75.09 Other GM2 gangliosidosis
E75.1 Other and unspecified gangliosidosis
E75.10 Unspecified gangliosidosis
E75.11 Mucolipidosis IV
E75.19 Other gangliosidosis

The code for eosinophilic meningitis has been deleted in ICD•10•CM and is now coded to the residual code.

ICD•9•CM

322.1 Eosinophilic meningitis

ICD•10•CM

G03.8 Meningitis due to other specified causes

While ICD•9•CM does have code 331.0 Alzheimer's disease, it provides no further detail about the disorder. Alzheimer's has been assigned its own category in ICD•10•CM, with eight new valid five-digit codes to classify this disorder based on onset and whether a behavioral disturbance is present.

ICD•10•CM

G30 Alzheimer's disease
G30.0 Alzheimer's disease with early onset
G30.00 Alzheimer's disease with early onset without behavioral disturbance
G30.01 Alzheimer's disease with early onset with behavioral disturbance
G30.1 Alzheimer's disease with late onset
G30.10 Alzheimer's disease with late onset without behavioral disturbance
G30.11 Alzheimer's disease with late onset with behavioral disturbance
G30.8 Other Alzheimer's disease
G30.80 Other Alzheimer's disease without behavioral disturbance
G30.81 Other Alzheimer's disease with behavioral disturbance
G30.9 Alzheimer's disease, unspecified
G30.90 Alzheimer's disease, unspecified without behavioral disturbance
G30.91 Alzheimer's disease unspecified with behavioral disturbance

CHAPTER 7

Chapter 7, "Diseases of the Eye and Adnexa," contains 11 code families depicted by the code's first character of "H," which is also shared with the next chapter, "Diseases of the Ear and Mastoid Process." The coding families in this chapter are:

Diseases of the Eye and Adnexa (H00–H59)

H00-H05 Disorders of eyelid, lacrimal system and orbit

 KEY POINT

Diseases of the eye and ear are no longer grouped with nervous system diseases. In ICD•10•CM, eye and ear diseases are found in two chapters, sharing the letter "H."

 KEY POINT

Some codes specific to certain disorders are being further subclassified in ICD•10•CM, to specify which side of the body is affected by that condition in a single code.

For example:

371.70	Corneal deformity
371.71	Corneal ectasia
371.72	Descemetocele
371.73	Corneal staphyloma
H18.70	Unspecified corneal deformity
H18.71	Corneal ectasia
H18.711	Corneal ectasia, right eye
H18.712	Corneal ectasia, left eye
H18.713	Corneal ectasia, bilateral
H18.719	Corneal ectasia, unspecified eye
H18.72	Corneal staphyloma
H18.721	Corneal staphyloma, right eye
H18.722	Corneal staphyloma, left eye
H18.723	Corneal staphyloma, bilateral
H18.729	Corneal staphyloma, uspecified eye
H18.73	Descemetocele
H18.731	Descemetocele, right eye
H18.732	Descemetocele, left eye
H18.733	Descemetocele, bilateral
H18.739	Descemetocele, unspecified eye

H10-H13	Disorders of conjunctiva
H15-H21	Disorders of sclera, cornea, iris and ciliary body
H25-H28	Disorders of lens
H30-H36	Disorders of choroid and retina
H40-H42	Glaucoma
H43-H45	Disorders of vitreous body and globe
H46-H47	Disorders of optic nerve and visual pathways
H49-H52	Disorders of ocular muscles, binocular movement, accommodation and refraction
H53-H54	Visual disturbances and blindness
H55-H59	Other disorders of eye and adnexa

ICD•10•CM Category Restructuring

The ICD•9•CM has only one subchapter for disorders of the eye and adnexa under the chapter for diseases of the nervous system. ICD•10•CM has reclassified these diseases into their own chapter, according to the blocks described above. For example, diseases of the eyelids fall into the middle in ICD•9•CM's subchapter. In ICD•10•CM, it is the first block.

Category Title Changes

A number of category title revisions were made in chapter 7. Titles were changed to better reflect the category's content, which was often necessary when specific types of diseases were given their own block, a new category was created, or an existing category was redefined.

ICD•9•CM

366.0	**Infantile, juvenile, and presenile cataract**
366.1	**Senile cataract**

ICD•10•CM

H25	**Age-related cataract**
H26	**Other cataract**
H26.0	**Infantile and juvenile cataract**

Organizational adjustments

When comparing ICD•9•CM to ICD•10•CM, some codes have been added, deleted, combined, or moved.

In ICD•9•CM, the code for amaurosis fugax is an inclusion term under code 362.34. The code for this disease has been moved in ICD•10•CM. It now has its own code and is found in the chapter for diseases of the nervous system.

ICD•9•CM

362.34	**Transient arterial occlusion**
	Amaurosis fugax

ICD•10•CM

G45.3   Amaurosis fugax

Up until the latest revision for 2002, there was no specific code in ICD•9•CM for aqueous misdirection (or malignant glaucoma). A new set of codes has been added to ICD•10•CM to classify this disorder by specified eye.

KEY POINT

"Diseases of the Eye and Adnexa" is a new chapter, as is "Diseases of the Ear and Mastoid Process." In ICD•9•CM, the codes for these diseases were included within chapter 6, "Diseases of the Nervous System and Sense Organs."

ICD•9•CM

365.83 Aqueous misdirection

ICD•10•CM

H40.83 Aqueous misdirection
Malignant glaucoma
H40.831 Aqueous misdirection, right eye
H40.832 Aqueous misdirection, left eye
H40.833 Aqueous misdirection, bilateral
H40.839 Aqueous misdirection, unspecified eye

CHAPTER 8

Chapter 8, "Diseases of the Ear and Mastoid Process," contains four code families depicted by the code's first character of "H," which is also shared with the previous chapter, "Diseases of the Eye and Adnexa." These are the coding families:

H60-H62	Diseases of external ear
H65-H75	Diseases of middle ear and mastoid
H80-H83	Diseases of inner ear
H90-H95	Other disorders of ear

ICD•10•CM Category Restructuring

"Diseases of the Ear and Mastoid Process" is a new chapter. In ICD•9•CM, the codes for these diseases were included within chapter 6, "Diseases of the Nervous System and Sense Organs." In addition, the ICD•9•CM has only one subchapter for disorders of the ear and mastoid process. ICD•10•CM reclassified these diseases according to the blocks described above.

Category Title Changes

A number of category title revisions were made in chapter 8. Titles were changed to better reflect the category's content, which was often necessary when specific types of diseases were given their own block, a new category was created, or an existing category was redefined.

ICD•9•CM

381 Nonsuppurative otitis media and Eustachian tube disorders
382 Suppurative and unspecified otitis media

ICD•10•CM

H65 Nonsuppurative otitis media
H66 Suppurative and unspecified otitis media
H67 Otitis media in diseases classified elsewhere
H68 Eustachian salpingitis and obstruction
H69 Other and unspecified disorders of the Eustachian tube

Organizational Adjustments

When comparing ICD•9•CM to ICD•10•CM, some codes have been added, deleted, combined, or moved.

The code for cerebrospinal fluid otorrhea, found under the subchapter for diseases of the ear and mastoid process in the nervous system and sense organs chapter in

---

 KEY POINT

Some codes specific to certain disorders are being further subclassified in ICD•10•CM, to specify which side of the body is affected by that condition in a single code. For Instance:

380.31 Hematoma of auricle or pinna

This disorder is reported using one of four codes in ICD•10•CM:

H61.12 Hematoma of pinna
Hematoma of auricle
H61.121 Hematoma of pinna, right ear
H61.122 Hematoma of pinna, left ear
H61.123 Hematoma of pinna, bilateral
H61.129 Hematoma of pinna, unspecified ear

ICD•9•CM, has not been included in the new chapter for diseases of the ear and mastoid process in ICD•10•CM, but is found in chapter 6, "Diseases of the Nervous System."

ICD•9•CM

388.61 Cerebrospinal fluid otorrhea

ICD•10•CM

G96.0 Cerebrospinal fluid leak

The codes for the specific types of tinnitus have not been completely developed in ICD•10•CM. The conditions that are classified to these codes in ICD•9•CM are now all under a single grouping of codes, with the reserved fifth digit for future expansion.

ICD•9•CM

388.30 Tinnitus, unspecified
388.31 Subjective tinnitus
388.32 Objective tinnitus

ICD•10•CM

H93.1x Tinnitus
    H93.1x1 Tinnitus, right ear
    H93.1x2 Tinnitus, left ear
    H93.1x3 Tinnitus, bilateral
    H93.1x9 Tinnitus, unspecified ear

There is no specific code in ICD•9•CM for acute recurrent otitis media. There are several codes available under two subcategories in ICD•10•CM to code this condition by type and laterality in ICD•10•CM.

H65.04 Acute serous otitis media, recurrent, right ear
H65.05 Acute serous otitis media, recurrent, left ear
H65.06 Acute serous otitis media, recurrent, bilateral
H65.07 Acute serous otitis media, recurrent, unspecified ear

and

H65.114 Acute and subacute allergic otitis media (mucoid) (sanguinous) (serous), recurrent, right ear
H65.115 Acute and subacute allergic otitis media (mucoid) (sanguinous) (serous), recurrent, left ear
H65.116 Acute and subacute allergic otitis media (mucoid) (sanguinous) (serous), recurrent, bilateral
H65.117 Acute and subacute allergic otitis media (mucoid) (sanguinous) (serous), recurrent, unspecified ear

---

DEFINITION

Tinnitus. Another name for a noise in the ears, as in ringing, buzzing, or roaring.

Chapter 9

Chapter 9, "Diseases of the Circulatory System," contains 10 code families, depicted by the code's first character of "I." They are:

I00-I02	Acute rheumatic fever
I05-I09	Chronic rheumatic heart diseases
I10-I15	Hypertensive diseases
I20-I25	Ischemic heart diseases
I26-I28	Pulmonary heart disease and diseases of pulmonary circulation
I30-I52	Other forms of heart disease
I60-I69	Cerebrovascular diseases
I70-I79	Diseases of arteries, arterioles and capillaries
I80-I89	Diseases of veins, lymphatic vessels and lymph nodes, not elsewhere classified
I95-I99	Other and unspecified disorders of the circulatory system

ICD•10•CM Category Restructuring

After reviewing the different disease categories, developers of ICD•10 restructured some of them to bring together those groups that are related in some way. For example, in ICD•10•CM, the final block includes the following: gangrene, not elsewhere classified, intraoperative and postprocedural complications and disorders of the circulatory system, not elsewhere classified, and other and unspecified disorders of the circulatory system.

Category Title Changes

A number of category title revisions were made in chapter 9. Titles were changed to better reflect the category's content, which was often necessary when specific types of diseases were given their own block, a new category was created, or an existing category was redefined.

ICD•9•CM

394	**Diseases of mitral valve**
395	**Diseases of aortic valve**
396	**Diseases of mitral and aortic valves**
397	**Diseases of other endocardial structures**

ICD•10•CM

I05	**Rheumatic mitral valve diseases**
I06	**Rheumatic aortic valve diseases**
I07	**Rheumatic tricuspid valve diseases**
I08	**Multiple valve diseases**

Organizational Adjustments

When comparing ICD•9•CM to ICD•10•CM, some codes have been added, deleted, combined, or moved.

The codes for transient cerebral ischemia are included in ICD•9•CM's "Disease of the Circulatory System" chapter. These codes have been moved in ICD•10•CM. They are now classified under "Diseases of the Nervous System."

KEY POINT

The codes in this chapter, I00-I99, and those in the chapter on pregnancy, childbirth and the puerperium O00-O99, represent a challenge in accurate reporting as the alpha character I and O can be recorded incorrectly as 1 and 0 if great care is not taken.

WORTH NOTING

Documentation requirements for circulatory disorders are greater with ICD•10•CM than under ICD•9•CM. For instance, in subdermal hemorrhage, ICD•10•CM codes available for this condition specify acute, subacute, or chronic.

ICD•9•CM

435   Transient cerebral ischemia

      435.0   Basilar artery syndrome

      435.1   Vertebral artery syndrome

      435.2   Subclavial steal syndrome

      435.3   Vertebrobasilar artery syndrome

      435.8   Other specified transient cerebral ischemias

      435.9   Unspecified transient cerebral ischemia

ICD•10•CM

G45   Transient cerebral ischemic attacks and related syndromes

      G45.0   Vertebro-basilar artery syndrome

      G45.1   Carotid artery syndrome (hemispheric)

      G45.2   Multiple and bilateral precerebral artery syndromes

      G45.3   Amaurosis fugax

      G45.4   Transient global amnesia

      G45.8   Other transient cerebral ischemic attacks and related syndromes

      G45.9   Transient cerebral ischemic attack, unspecified

The codes that specified the type of hypertension — malignant, benign, or unspecified — have been deleted in ICD•10•CM. Hypertension no longer uses type as an axis of classification.

ICD•9•CM

      401.0   Essential hypertension, malignant

      401.1   Essential hypertension, benign

      401.9   Essential hypertension, unspecified

ICD•10•CM

I10   Essential (primary) hypertension

      Includes: high blood pressure

                    Hypertension (arterial) (benign) (essential) (malignant) (primary) (systemic)

      Excludes2: essential (primary) hypertension involving vessels of brain (I60-I69)

                    essential (primary) hypertension involving vessels of eye (H35.0)

There is no single code in ICD•9•CM for arteriosclerotic heart disease with angina. Codes have been added to the ICD•10•CM to classify the combination of the underlying disease and the symptom.

ICD•10•CM

      I25.10   Atherosclerotic heart disease without angina

      I25.11   Atherosclerotic heart disease with unspecified angina pectoris

      I25.12   Atherosclerotic heart disease with unstable angina

      I25.13   Atherosclerotic heart disease with angina pectoris with documented spasm

I25.19   Atherosclerotic heart disease with other forms of angina pectoris

CHAPTER 10

Chapter 10, "Diseases of the Respiratory System," contains 10 code families depicted by the code's first character of "J." They are:

J00-J06	Acute upper respiratory infections
J10-J18	Influenza and pneumonia
J20-J22	Other acute lower respiratory infections
J30-J39	Other diseases of upper respiratory tract
J40-J47	Chronic lower respiratory diseases
J60-J70	Lung diseases due to external agents
J80-J84	Other respiratory diseases principally affecting the interstitium
J85-J86	Suppurative and necrotic conditions of the lower respiratory tract
J90-J94	Other diseases of the pleura
J95-J99	Other diseases of the respiratory system

ICD•10•CM Category Restructuring

After reviewing the different disease categories, developers of ICD•10 restructured some of them to bring together those groups that are related in some way. For example, in ICD•9•CM, "Pneumonia and influenza" falls directly after "Acute respiratory infections" and "Other diseases of the upper respiratory tract." In ICD•10•CM, "Influenza and pneumonia" is followed by a new family for other acute lower respiratory infections.

ICD•9•CM

460-466	Acute respiratory infections
470-478	Other diseases of the upper respiratory tract
480-487	Pneumonia and influenza
490-496	Chronic obstructive pulmonary disease and allied conditions

ICD•10•CM

J00-J06	Acute upper respiratory infections
J10-J18	Influenza and pneumonia
J20-J22	Other acute lower respiratory infections
J30-J39	Other diseases of upper respiratory tract
J40-J47	Chronic lower respiratory diseases

Category Title Changes

A number of category title revisions were made in chapter 10. Titles were changed to better reflect the category's content, which was often necessary when specific types of diseases were given their own block, a new category was created, or an existing category was redefined.

ICD•9•CM

490   **Bronchitis, not specified as acute or chronic**

☞ **KEY POINT**

Some common symptoms and complications were added as fifth-digit extensions to certain diagnosis codes in ICD•10•CM. The rationale for combining a diagnosis and its manifestation (symptom) or a diagnosis and its complication relates to problems with the assignment of the principal diagnosis. A debate occurs when the patient is admitted for the symptom or complication and it is secondary to a specified disease. The question that often comes up is, Which should be assigned the principal diagnosis? With the modifications to ICD•10, this problem won't come up, as one combination code is available.

---

491   Chronic bronchitis
492   Emphysema
493   Asthma
494   Bronchiectasis
495   Extrinsic allergic alveolitis
496   Chronic airway obstruction, not elsewhere classified

ICD•10•CM

J40   Bronchitis, not specified as acute or chronic
J41   Simple and mucopurulent chronic bronchitis
J42   Unspecified chronic bronchitis
J43   Emphysema
J44   Other chronic obstructive pulmonary disease
J45   Asthma
J47   Bronchiectasis

Organizational Adjustments

When comparing ICD•9•CM to ICD•10•CM, some codes have been added, deleted, combined, or moved.

Lobar pneumonia is listed as an inclusion term under code 481. This condition has been moved in ICD•10•CM and is now classified in the three-character category J18 Pneumonia, unspecified organism.

ICD•9•CM

481   Pneumococcal pneumonia [Streptococcus pneumoniae pneumonia]
        Lobar pneumonia, organism unspecified

ICD•10•CM

J18.1   Lobar pneumonia, unspecified organism

The code for "pneumonia due to gram-negative anaerobes" has been deleted in ICD•10•CM. This condition is now classified to the residual subcategory for bacterial pneumonia.

ICD•9•CM

482.81   Pneumonia due to other specified bacteria, anaerobes

ICD•10•CM

J15.8   Pneumonia due to other specified bacteria

There is no specific code in ICD•9•CM for acute recurrent sinusitis. Seven codes have been added to the ICD•10•CM to classify this disorder by type.

ICD•10•CM

J01.01   Acute recurrent maxillary sinusitis
J01.11   Acute recurrent frontal sinusitis
J01.21   Acute recurrent ethmoidal sinusitis
J01.31   Acute recurrent sphenoidal sinusitis
J01.41   Acute recurrent pansinusitis
J01.81   Other acute recurrent sinusitis
J01.91   Acute recurrent sinusitis, unspecified

 KEY POINT

While many conditions are getting their own specific code in ICD•10•CM, some codes specific to certain disorders are being classified to the residual subcategory in ICD•10•CM.

For example:

519.2   Mediastinitis

In ICD•10•CM, this disorder is reported as:

J98.5   Diseases of mediastinum, not elsewhere classified

The asthma codes in ICD•9•CM are classified as extrinsic, intrinsic, chronic obstructive, and unspecified. In ICD•10•CM, this organizational method of classifying asthma has been totally restructured.

ICD•9•CM

493.0   Extrinsic asthma
Asthma:
  allergic with stated cause
  atopic
  childhood
  hay
  platinum
  hay fever with asthma

493.1   Intrinsic asthma
Late-onset asthma

493.2   Chronic obstructive asthma
Asthma with COPD
Chronic asthmatic bronchitis

493.9   Asthma, unspecified
Asthma (bronchial) (allergic NOS)
Bronchitis:
  Allergic
  asthmatic

ICD•10•CM

J45.0   Predominantly allergic asthma
Allergic bronchitis NOS
Allergic rhinitis with asthma
Atopic asthma
Extrinsic allergic asthma
Hay fever with asthma

J45.1   Nonallergic asthma
Idiosyncratic asthma
Intrinsic nonallergic asthma

J45.8   Mixed asthma
Combination of conditions listed in J45.0 and J45.1

J45.9   Asthma, unspecified
Asthmatic bronchitis NOS
Late onset asthma

CHAPTER 11

Chapter 11, "Diseases of the Digestive System," contains 10 code families, depicted by the code's first character of "K." They are:

K00-K14	Diseases of oral cavity and salivary glands
K20-K31	Diseases of esophagus, stomach and duodenum
K35-K38	Diseases of appendix
K40-K46	Hernia
K50-K52	Noninfective enteritis and colitis

 WORTH NOTING

In ICD•9•CM, two codes were required for acute bronchitis and its cause. In ICD•10•CM, only one code will be necessary. For example, "acute bronchitis due to streptococcus" is coded J20.2.

K55-K63	Other diseases of intestines
K65-K68	Diseases of peritoneum and retroperitoneum
K70-K77	Diseases of liver
K80-K87	Disorders of gallbladder, biliary tract and pancreas
K90-K94	Other diseases of the digestive system

ICD•10•CM Category Restructuring

After reviewing the different disease categories, developers of ICD•10 restructured some of them to bring together those groups that are related in some way. In chapter 11, the new blocks are K70-K77, "Diseases of liver," and K80-K87, "Disorders of gallbladder, biliary tract and pancreas."

Category Title Changes

A number of category title revisions were made in chapter 11. Titles were changed to better reflect the category's content, which was often necessary when specific types of diseases were given their own block, a new category was created, or an existing category was redefined.

ICD•9•CM

565   Anal fissure and fistula

ICD•10•CM

K60   Fissure and fistula of anal and rectal regions

Organizational Adjustments

When comparing ICD•9•CM to ICD•10•CM, some codes have been added, deleted, combined, or moved.

Jaw disorders were deleted from the chapter, "Diseases of the Digestive System" and added to the chapter, "Musculoskeletal and Connective Tissue Disorders" in ICD•10•CM.

ICD•9•CM

Diseases of the Digestive System
524   Dentofacial anomalies, including malocclusion
526   Diseases of jaws

ICD•10•CM

Diseases of the Musculoskeletal System and Connective Tissue
M26   Dentofacial anomalies [including malocclusion]
M27   Other diseases of jaws

The codes that specified whether obstruction was mentioned in conjunction with a gastric, duodenal, peptic, or gastrojejunal ulcer have been deleted in ICD•10•CM. Obstruction is no longer an axis of classification for ulcers. For example:

ICD•9•CM

531.00   Acute gastric ulcer with hemorrhage without mention of obstruction
531.01   Acute gastric ulcer with hemorrhage with obstruction

☞ **KEY POINT**

Another condition in which ICD•9•CM and ICD•10•CM differ in specificity is for inguinal and femoral hernias. In ICD•9•CM, you can identify whether the hernia was recurrent or not. In ICD•10•CM, this axis is gone.

ICD•10•CM

> **K25.0** **Acute gastric ulcer with hemorrhage**

There was no single code in ICD•9•CM for alcoholic hepatitis with ascites. A new code has been added to the ICD•10•CM to classify this disorder.

ICD•10•CM

> **K70.10** **Alcoholic hepatitis without ascites**
> **K70.11** **Alcoholic hepatitis with ascites**

CHAPTER 12

Chapter 12, "Diseases of the Skin and Subcutaneous Tissue," contains nine code families, depicted by the code's first character of "L." They are:

L00-L08	Infections of the skin and subcutaneous tissue
L10-L14	Bullous disorders
L20-L30	Dermatitis and eczema
L40-L45	Papulosquamous disorders
L50-L54	Urticaria and erythema
L55-L59	Radiation-related disorders of the skin and subcutaneous tissue
L60-L75	Disorders of skin appendages
L76	Intraoperative and postprocedural complications of dermatologic procedures
L80-L99	Other disorders of the skin and subcutaneous tissue

ICD•10•CM Category Restructuring

After reviewing the different disease categories, developers of ICD•10 restructured some of them to bring together those groups that are related in some way. In ICD•9•CM, there are only three subchapters for diseases of the skin and subcutaneous tissue. They are, "Infections of Skin and Subcutaneous Tissue," "Other Inflammatory Conditions of Skin and Subcutaneous Tissue," and "Other Diseases of Skin and Subcutaneous Tissue." In ICD•10•CM, these disorders have been rearranged to fit into the new blocks shown above.

Category Title Changes

A number of category title revisions were made in chapter 12. Titles were changed to better reflect the category's content, which was often necessary when specific types of diseases were given their own block, a new category was created, or an existing category was redefined.

ICD•9•CM

681 **Cellulitis and abscess of finger and toe**
682 **Other cellulitis and abscess**

ICD•10•CM

L03 **Cellulitis and acute lymphangitis**

Organizational Adjustments

When comparing ICD•9•CM to ICD•10•CM, some codes have been added, deleted, combined, or moved.

 KEY POINT

Many conditions have been assigned their own codes in ICD•10•CM, and then are further subclassified to specify which side of the body is affected by that condition in a single code.

For example:

680.3	Carbuncle and furuncle of upper arm and forearm
680.4	Carbuncle and furuncle of hand
680.6	Carbuncle and furuncle of leg, except foot
680.7	Carbuncle and furuncle of foot

Carbuncle and furuncle each have their own subclassifications by body area with laterality included:

L02.423	Furuncle of right upper limb
L02.424	Furuncle of left upper limb
L02.435	Carbuncle of right lower limb
L02.436	Carbuncle of left lower limb
L02.521	Furuncle of right hand
L02.522	Furuncle of left hand
L02.631	Carbuncle of right foot
L02.632	Carbuncle of left foot

The code for carbuncle and furuncle of the breast is listed as an inclusion site under code 680.2 in ICD•9•CM. The code for this condition has been moved in ICD•10•CM and is found in the chapter, "Diseases of the Genitourinary System."

ICD•9•CM

680.2   **Carbuncle and furuncle, trunk**

ICD•10•CM

N61   Inflammatory disorders of breast

The code for seborrhea has been deleted in ICD•10•CM. This condition is now classified to the residual subcategory under "Other disorders of skin and subcutaneous tissue."

ICD•9•CM

706.3   **Seborrhea**

ICD•10•CM

L98.8   **Other specified disorders of the skin and subcutaneous tissue**

In ICD•9•CM, code 707.0 reports decubitus ulcer. New codes have been added to the ICD•10•CM to further classify this disorder.

ICD•10•CM

L89   Decubitus ulcer
  L89.0   Decubitus ulcer of the back
    L89.04   Decubitus ulcer of left lower back
      L89.041   Decubitus ulcer of left lower back limited to breakdown of the skin
      L89.042   Decubitus ulcer of left lower back with fat layer exposed
      L89.043   Decubitus ulcer of left lower back with necrosis of muscle
      L89.044   Decubitus ulcer of left lower back with necrosis of bone
      L89.049   Decubitus ulcer of left lower back with unspecified severity

CHAPTER 13

Chapter 13, "Diseases of the Musculoskeletal System and Connective Tissue," contains 16 code families, depicted by the code's first character of "M." They are:

M00-M02	Infectious arthropathies
M05-M14	Inflammatory polyarthropathies
M15-M19	Osteoarthritis
M20-M25	Other joint disorders
M26-M27	Dentofacial anomalies [including malocclusion] and other disorders of jaw
M30-M36	Systemic connective tissue disorders
M40-M43	Deforming dorsopathies
M45-M49	Spondylopathies

M50-M54	Other dorsopathies
M60-M63	Disorders of muscles
M65-M67	Disorders of synovium and tendon
M70-M79	Other soft tissue disorders
M80-M85	Disorders of bone density and structure
M86-M90	Other osteopathies
M91-M94	Chondropathies
M95-M99	Other disorders of the musculoskeletal system and connective tissue

ICD•10•CM Category Restructuring

After reviewing the different disease categories, developers of ICD•10 restructured some of them to bring together those groups that are related in some way. For example, in ICD•9•CM, the category for arthropathy associated with infections is included in the first subchapter, "Arthropathies and Related Disorders." In ICD•10•CM, "Infectious arthropathies" is an entire block containing separate three-character categories based on: the type of etiological relationship, whether it is a direct or indirect infection, and whether it is reactive and postinfective.

Category Title Changes

A number of category title revisions were made in chapter 13. Titles were changed to better reflect the category's content, which was often necessary when specific types of diseases were given their own block, a new category was created, or an existing category was redefined.

ICD•9•CM

714   **Rheumatoid arthritis and other inflammatory polyarthropathies**

ICD•10•CM

M05   **Rheumatoid arthritis with rheumatoid factor**
M06   **Other rheumatoid arthritis**
M07   **Enteropathic arthropathies**
M08   **Juvenile arthritis**

Organizational Adjustments

When comparing ICD•9•CM to ICD•10•CM, some codes have been added, deleted, combined, or moved.

In ICD•9•CM, gout is classified to chapter 3, "Endocrine, Nutritional, and Metabolic Diseases and Immunity Disorders," and in ICD•10•CM, to chapter 13, "Diseases of the Musculoskeletal System and Connective Tissue."

ICD•9•CM

274   **Gout**

ICD•10•CM

M10   **Gout**

The code for swelling of limb has been deleted in ICD•10•CM. This condition is now classified to the residual three-character category for other soft tissue disorders not elsewhere classified.

KEY POINT

Another condition that has moved from chapter 12 is clubbing of fingers. This condition is found in the chapter, "Symptoms, Signs and Abnormal Clinical and Laboratory Findings, Not Elsewhere Classified" in ICD•10•CM.

ICD•9•CM

729.81   Swelling of limb

ICD•10•CM

M79.8   Other specified soft tissue disorders

There was no single code in ICD•9•CM for osteoporosis with pathological fracture. Codes have been added to the ICD•10•CM to classify the combination of these two conditions and to further describe additional types of osteoporosis, i.e., more than what was in ICD•9•CM.

ICD•10•CM

M80   Osteoporosis with current pathological fracture
  M80.0   Postmenopausal osteoporosis with current pathological fracture
  M80.8   Other osteoporosis with current pathological fracture
        Drug-induced osteoporosis with current pathological fracture
        Idiopathic osteoporosis with current pathological fracture
        Osteoporosis of disuse with current pathological fracture
        Postsurgical malabsorption osteoporosis with current pathological fracture

CHAPTER 14

Chapter 14, "Diseases of the Genitourinary System," contains 11 code families, depicted by the code's first character of "N." They are:

N00-N08	Glomerular diseases
N10-N16	Renal tubulo-interstitial diseases
N17-N19	Renal failure
N20-N23	Urolithiasis
N25-N29	Other disorders of kidney and ureter
N30-N39	Other diseases of the urinary system
N40-N51	Diseases of male genital organs
N60-N64	Disorders of breast
N70-N77	Inflammatory diseases of female pelvic organs
N80-N98	Noninflammatory disorders of female genital tract
N99	Other disorders of genitourinary system

ICD•10•CM Category Restructuring

After reviewing the different disease categories, developers of ICD•10 restructured some of them to bring together those groups that are related by cause. For example, in ICD•9•CM, there is no separate subchapter for urolithiasis, and the various sites where a calculus may occur are not grouped together. In ICD•10•CM, this condition has its own block and sites as listed below:

ICD•9•CM

Other Diseases of Urinary System (590-599)
592   Calculus of kidney and ureter
593   Other disorders of kidney and ureter

DEFINITION

Direct infection of a joint. Occurs when organisms invade synovial tissue and microbial antigen is present in the joint.

☞   **KEY POINT**

While many conditions are getting their own specific code in ICD•10•CM, some codes specific to certain disorders are being classified to the residual subcategory in ICD•10•CM.

For example:

602.2   Atrophy of prostate

This disorder is reported with one code in ICD•10•CM:

N42.89   Other specified disorders of the prostate

594   Calculus of lower urinary tract

ICD•10•CM

Urolithiasis (N20-N23)
N20   Calculus of kidney and ureter
N21   Calculus of lower urinary tract
N22   Calculus of urinary tract in diseases classified elsewhere

Category Title Changes

A number of category title revisions were made chapter 14. Titles were changed to better reflect the category's content, which was often necessary when specific types of diseases were given their own block, a new category was created, or an existing category was redefined.

ICD•9•CM
599   Other disorders of urethra and urinary tract

ICD•10•CM
N39   Other disorders of urinary system

Organizational Adjustments

When comparing ICD•9•CM to ICD•10•CM, some codes have been added, deleted, combined, or moved.

The code for galactocele has been deleted in ICD•10•CM. This condition is coded in the residual three-character category for other disorders of breast.

ICD•9•CM
611.5   Galactocele

ICD•10•CM
N64.8   Other specified disorders of breast
           Galactocele

There is no specific code in ICD•9•CM to specify the grade of cervical dysplasia. Codes have been added to the ICD•10•CM to specify whether the dysplasia is grade I, II, or III.

ICD•10•CM
N87.0   Mild cervical dysplasia
N87.1   Moderate cervical dysplasia
N87.2   Severe cervical dysplasia, not elsewhere classified
N87.9   Dysplasia of cervix uteri, unspecified

CHAPTER 15

Chapter 15, "Pregnancy, Childbirth, and the Puerperium," contains nine code families, depicted by the code's first character of "O." They are:

          O00-O08   Pregnancy with abortive outcome
          O09   Supervision of high-risk pregnancy

O10-O16	Edema, proteinuria and hypertensive disorders in pregnancy, childbirth and the puerperium
O20-O29	Other maternal disorders predominantly related to pregnancy
O30-O48	Maternal care related to the fetus and amniotic cavity and possible delivery problems
O60-O77	Complications of labor and delivery
O80	Encounter for full-term uncomplicated delivery
O85-O92	Complications predominantly related to the puerperium
O93	Sequelae of complication of pregnancy, childbirth, and the puerperium
O94-O99	Other obstetric conditions, not elsewhere classified

KEY POINT

The codes in chapter 15 should only be used on the mother's record and not on the newborn's record. There may be instances, however, where a record is created for a developing fetus still in the womb and codes from category O37, "Fetal care for fetal abnormality and damage," may be applied in such cases.

ICD•10•CM Category Restructuring

After reviewing the different disease categories, developers of ICD•10 restructured some of them to bring together those groups that are related in some way. For example, in ICD•9•CM, the codes for encounter for supervision of high-risk pregnancy are found in the V codes. These codes have been moved to their own block added to the ICD•10•CM chapter for pregnancy, childbirth and the puerperium.

Category Title Changes

A number of category title revisions were made in chapter 15. Titles were changed to better reflect the category's content, which was often necessary when specific types of diseases are given their own block, a new category was created, or an existing category was redefined.

ICD•9•CM

652   Malposition and malpresentation of fetus

ICD•10•CM

O32   Maternal care for malpresentation of fetus

Organizational Adjustments

When comparing ICD•9•CM to ICD•10•CM, some codes have been added, deleted, combined, or moved.

The codes for complete legally and illegally induced abortions without complications are classified with the abortion codes in ICD•9•CM. These have been moved to chapter 21 in ICD•10•CM under "Elective termination of pregnancy."

ICD•9•CM

635.92   Legally induced abortion without mention of complication, complete

636.92   Illegally induced abortion without mention of complication, complete

ICD•10•CM

Z33.12   Encounter for elective termination of pregnancy

The code for breech or other malpresentation successfully converted to cephalic presentation has been deleted in ICD•10•CM. This condition is now classified to the residual category under three-character rubric O32.

ICD•9•CM

    652.1   **Breech or other malpresentation successfully converted to cephalic presentation**

ICD•10•CM

O32   **Maternal care for malpresentation of fetus**

There is no specific code in ICD•9•CM for a malignant neoplasm complicating pregnancy, childbirth, and the puerperium. A new category has been added to the ICD•10•CM to classify maternal malignant neoplasms and other harm or injury, confirmed or suspected, that affects any trimester, delivery, or the puerperium.

ICD•10•CM

O94   **Maternal malignant neoplasms, traumatic injuries and abuse classifiable elsewhere but complicating pregnancy, childbirth and the puerperium**

CHAPTER 16

Chapter 16, "Certain Conditions Originating in the Perinatal Period," contains 11 code families, depicted by the code's first character of "P." They are:

P00-P04	Newborn affected by maternal factors and by complications of pregnancy, labor, and delivery
P05-P08	Disorders related to length of gestation and fetal growth
P10-P15	Birth trauma
P19-P29	Respiratory and cardiovascular disorders specific to the perinatal period
P35-P39	Infections specific to the perinatal period
P50-P61	Hemorrhagic and hematological disorders of newborn
P70-P74	Transitory endocrine and metabolic disorders specific to newborn
P75-P78	Digestive system disorders of newborn
P80-P83	Conditions involving the integument and temperature regulation of newborn
P84	Other problems with newborn
P90-P96	Other disorders originating in the perinatal period

ICD•10•CM Category Restructuring

After reviewing the different disease categories, developers of ICD•10 restructured some of them to bring together those groups that are related by type of condition. For example, in ICD•9•CM, there are only two subchapters, "Maternal Causes of Perinatal Morbidity and Mortality," and "Other Conditions Originating in the Perinatal Period." In ICD•10•CM, the conditions have been reorganized into the blocks described above.

Category Title Changes

A number of category title revisions were made in chapter 16. Titles were changed to better reflect the category's content, which was often necessary when specific types of diseases were given their own block, a new category was created, or an existing category was redefined.

ICD•9•CM

769   Respiratory distress syndrome

770   Other respiratory conditions of fetus and newborn

ICD•10•CM

Respiratory and cardiovascular disorders specific to the perinatal period (P19-P29)

P19   Metabolic academia in newborn

P22   Respiratory distress of newborn

P23   Congenital pneumonia

P24   Neonatal aspiration syndromes

P25   Interstitial emphysema and related conditions originating in the perinatal period

P26   Pulmonary hemorrhage originating in the perinatal period

P27   Chronic respiratory disease originating in the perinatal period

P28   Other respiratory conditions originating in the perinatal period

Organizational Adjustments

When comparing ICD•9•CM to ICD•10•CM, some codes have been added, deleted, combined, or moved.

The code for fetal alcohol syndrome is found in the chapter, "Certain Conditions Originating in the Perinatal Period" in ICD•9•CM. This code has been moved to the chapter, "Congenital Malformations, Deformations and Chromosomal Abnormalities" in ICD•10•CM.

ICD•9•CM

760.71   Noxious influences affecting fetus via placenta or breast milk, alcohol

ICD•10•CM

Q86.0   Fetal alcohol syndrome (dysmorphic)

There is no specific code in ICD•9•CM for exposure to tobacco smoke in the perinatal period. A new code has been added to the ICD•10•CM to classify this disorder.

ICD•10•CM

P96.6   Exposure to (parental)(environmental) tobacco smoke in the perinatal period

Chapter 17

Chapter 17, "Congenital Malformations, Deformations and Chromosomal Abnormalities," contains 11 code families, depicted by the code's first character of "Q." They are:

Q00-Q07	Congenital malformations of the nervous system
Q10-Q18	Congenital malformations of eye, ear, face and neck
Q20-Q28	Congenital malformations of the circulatory system
Q30-Q34	Congenital malformations of the respiratory system
Q35-Q37	Cleft lip and cleft palate

> **KEY POINT**
>
> The fifth digits for maternity codes in ICD•9•CM were not adopted for ICD•10•CM. Instead, the last character in the code represents the patient's trimester. Because certain obstetric conditions or complications occur at only one point in the obstetric period, not all codes include all three trimesters or a character to describe the trimester at all.

> **KEY POINT**
>
> The chapters, "Diseases of the Genitourinary System," "Pregnancy, Childbirth and the Puerperium," "Certain Conditions Originating in the Perinatal Period," and "Congenital Malformations, Deformations and Chromosomal Abnormalities" are placed sequentially in ICD•10•CM.

Q38-Q45	Other congenital malformations of the digestive system
Q50-Q56	Congenital malformations of genital organs
Q60-Q64	Congenital malformations of the urinary system
Q65-Q79	Congenital malformations and deformations of the musculoskeletal system
Q80-Q89	Other congenital malformations
Q90-Q99	Chromosomal abnormalities, not elsewhere classified

ICD•10•CM Category Restructuring

After reviewing the different disease categories, developers of ICD•10 restructured some of them to bring together those groups that are related in some way. For example, ICD•9•CM has no subchapters for the above conditions. In ICD•10•CM, 11 blocks have been created.

Category Title Changes

A number of category title revisions were made in chapter 17. Titles were changed to better reflect the category's content, which was often necessary when specific types of diseases were given their own block, a new category was created, or an existing category was redefined.

ICD•9•CM

| 741 | Spina bifida |
| 742 | Other congenital anomalies of nervous system |

ICD•10•CM

Congenital malformations of the nervous system (Q00-Q07)

Q00	Anencephaly and similar malformations
Q01	Encephalocele
Q02	Microcephaly
Q03	Congenital hydrocephalus
Q04	Other congenital malformations of brain
Q05	Spina bifida
Q06	Other congenital malformations of spinal cord
Q07	Other congenital malformations of nervous system

Organizational Adjustments

When comparing ICD•9•CM to ICD•10•CM, some codes have been added, deleted, combined, or moved.

The code for persistent fetal circulation is classified to code 747.83 in ICD•9•CM. This condition has been moved in ICD•10•CM to the chapter, "Certain Conditions Originating in the Perinatal Period."

ICD•9•CM

| 747.83 | Persistent fetal circulation |

ICD•10•CM

| P29.3 | Persistent fetal circulation |

CODING AXIOM

The title of the ICD•9•CM chapter, "Congenital Anomalies," has been expanded to include "Deformations and Chromosomal Abnormalities."

The code for congenital chorioretinal degeneration has been deleted in ICD•10•CM. This condition is now classified to the residual category, "Other congenital malformations of posterior segment of eye."

ICD•9•CM

> 743.53 Chorioretinal degeneration, congenital

ICD•10•CM

> Q14.8 Other congenital malformations of posterior segment of eye

There is no specific code in ICD•9•CM for peripheral arteriovenous aneurysm. Six codes have been added to the ICD•10•CM to classify this disorder according to site.

ICD•10•CM

> Q27.3 Arteriovenous malformation (peripheral)
> Q27.30 Arteriovenous malformation, site unspecified
> Q27.31 Arteriovenous malformation of vessel of upper limb
> Q27.32 Arteriovenous malformation of vessel of lower limb
> Q27.33 Arteriovenous malformation of digestive system vessel
> Q27.34 Arteriovenous malformation of renal vessel
> Q27.39 Arteriovenous malformation, other site

CHAPTER 18

Chapter 18, "Symptoms, Signs and Abnormal Clinical and Laboratory Findings, Not Elsewhere Classified," contains 13 code families, depicted by the code's first character of "R." They are:

R00-R09	Symptoms and signs involving the circulatory and respiratory systems
R10-R19	Symptoms and signs involving the digestive system and abdomen
R20-R23	Symptoms and signs involving the skin and subcutaneous tissue
R25-R29	Symptoms and signs involving the nervous and musculoskeletal systems
R30-R39	Symptoms and signs involving the urinary system
R40-R46	Symptoms and signs involving cognition, perception, emotional state and behavior
R47-R49	Symptoms and signs involving speech and voice
R50-R69	General symptoms and signs
R70-R79	Abnormal findings on examination of blood, without diagnosis
R80-R82	Abnormal findings on examination of urine, without diagnosis
R83-R89	Abnormal findings on examination of other body fluids, substances and tissues, without diagnosis
R90-R94	Abnormal findings on diagnostic imaging and in function studies, without diagnosis
R99	Ill-defined and unknown cause of mortality

☞ KEY POINT

The arrangement of the conditions classified to chapter 17, "Congenital Malformations, Deformations and Chromosomal Abnormalities," is, for the most part, by body system.

☞ KEY POINT

Many more codes are available in ICD•10•CM to describe pain. Among the choices are acute, intractable, or postoperative pain, or pain resulting from neoplastic disease.

ICD•10•CM Category Restructuring

After reviewing the different disease categories, developers of ICD•10 restructured some of them to bring together those groups that are related in some way. For example, in ICD•9•CM, all symptoms are grouped together under one subchapter. In ICD•10•CM, 13 blocks have been created and the disorders placed, for the most part, according to body system.

Category Title Changes

A number of category title revisions were made in chapter 18. Titles were changed to better reflect the category's content, which was often necessary when specific types of diseases were given their own block, a new category was created, or an existing category was redefined.

ICD•9•CM

786   **Symptoms involving respiratory system and other chest symptoms**

ICD•10•CM

R05   **Cough**
R06   **Abnormalities of breathing**
R07   **Pain in throat and chest**
R09   **Other symptoms and signs involving the circulatory and respiratory system**

Organizational Adjustments

When comparing ICD•9•CM to ICD•10•CM, some codes have been added, deleted, combined, or moved.

The code for gangrene is listed in the chapter for symptoms in ICD•9•CM. This condition has been moved in ICD•10•CM to the chapter, "Diseases of the Circulatory System."

ICD•9•CM

785.4   **Gangrene**

ICD•10•CM

I96   **Gangrene, not elsewhere classified**

The code for elevated prostate specific antigen (PSA) has been moved in ICD•10•CM. This condition is now classified to the category for other abnormal immunological findings in serum.

ICD•9•CM

790.93   **Elevated prostate specific antigen (PSA)**

ICD•10•CM

R76.81   **Elevated prostate specific antigen (PSA)**

Generalized pain is coded to 780.9 Other general symptoms in ICD•9•CM. Thirteen codes have been added to the ICD•10•CM to classify this disorder more specifically.

ICD•10•CM

Pain, not elsewhere classified

 KEY POINT

Not all signs and symptoms are classified to this chapter. Those that point rather definitely to a given diagnosis have been assigned to a category in other chapters of the classification. For example, a mass or lump in the breast is coded to the chapter, "Diseases of the Genitourinary System."

R52.00 Acute pain, unspecified
R52.01 Acute postoperative pain
R52.02 Acute pain in neoplastic disease
R52.09 Other acute pain
R52.10 Chronic intractable pain, unspecified
R52.11 Chronic intractable postoperative pain
R52.12 Chronic intractable pain in neoplastic disease
R52.19 Other chronic intractable pain
R52.20 Other chronic pain, unspecified
R52.21 Other chronic postoperative pain
R52.22 Other chronic pain in neoplastic disease
R52.29 Other chronic pain
R52.9 Pain, unspecified

CHAPTER 19

Chapter 19, "Injury, Poisoning and Certain Other Consequences of External Causes," contains 20 code families, depicted by the code's first character of either "S" or "T." The code families are:

S00-S09	Injuries to the head
S10-S19	Injuries to the neck
S20-S29	Injuries to the thorax
S30-S39	Injuries to the abdomen, lower back, lumbar spine and pelvis
S40-S49	Injuries to the shoulder and upper arm
S50-S59	Injuries to the elbow and forearm
S60-S69	Injuries to the wrist and hand
S70-S79	Injuries to the hip and thigh
S80-S89	Injuries to the knee and lower leg
S90-S99	Injuries to the ankle and foot
T07	Unspecified multiple injuries
T14	Injury of unspecified body region
T15-T19	Effects of foreign body entering through natural orifice
T20-T32	Bums and corrosions
T33-T34	Frostbite
T36-T50	Poisoning by drugs, medicaments and biological substances
T51-T65	Toxic effects of substances chiefly nonmedicinal as to source
T66-T78	Other and unspecified effects of external causes
T79	Certain early complications of trauma
T80-T88	Complications of surgical and medical care, not elsewhere classified

ICD•10•CM Category Restructuring

The axis of classification for chapter 19, "Injury, Poisoning and Certain Other Consequences of External Causes" (chapter 17, "Injury and Poisoning," in ICD•9•CM), has been changed from type of injury and then site of injury in ICD•9•CM to body region and then to type of injury in ICD•10. ICD•10•CM further enhances this restructuring by adding codes for laterality and alpha extensor

©2002 Ingenix, Inc.

characters for sequelae and status of the encounter. For example, "Fractures" is the first subchapter in the injury and poisoning chapter of ICD•9•CM. The breakdown is then by site, e.g., vault of skull, base of skull. For ICD•10, the first subchapter in "Injury, Poisoning and Certain Other Consequences of External Causes" describes injuries to the head (the body region), and then a breakdown by type of injury, e.g., superficial injury of head, open wound of head.

ICD•9•CM

Chapter 17 Injury and Poisoning

Fractures (800-829)

Fracture of Skull (800-804)

800	Fracture of vault of skull
801	Fracture of base of skull
802	Fracture of face bones
803	Other and unqualified skull fractures
804	Multiple fractures involving skull or face with other bones

ICD•10•CM

Chapter 19 Injury, Poisoning and Certain Other Consequences of External Causes

Injuries to the head (S00-S09)

S00	Superficial injury of head
S01	Open wound of head
S02	Fracture of skull and facial bones
S03	Dislocation and sprain of joints and ligaments of head
S04	Injury of cranial nerve
S05	Injury of eye and orbit
S06	Intracranial injury
S07	Crushing injury of head
S08	Avulsion and traumatic amputation of part of head
S09	Other and unspecified injuries of head

Category Title Changes

A number of category title revisions were made in chapter 19 due to the restructuring described above. Titles were changed to better reflect the category's content, which was often necessary when specific types of diseases were given their own block, a new category was created, or an existing category was redefined. For example, frostbite has its own block of three-character categories, T33-T34.

Organizational Adjustments

When comparing ICD•9•CM to ICD•10•CM, some codes have been added, deleted, combined, or moved.

The code for cataract fragments in the eye following cataract surgery is found in the chapter for injury and poisoning in ICD•9•CM. The condition has been moved to the chapter, "Diseases of the Eye and Adnexa" in ICD•10•CM.

 KEY POINT

Chapter 19 uses the S-section for coding different types of injuries related to single body regions, and the T-section to cover injuries to unspecified and multiple body regions, as well as poisoning, burns, and certain other consequences of external causes.

ICD•9•CM

> 998.82 Cataract fragments in eye following cataract surgery

ICD•10•CM

> H59.10 Cataract (lens) fragments in eye following cataract surgery, unspecified eye
>
> H59.11 Cataract (lens) fragments in eye following cataract surgery, right eye
>
> H59.12 Cataract (lens) fragments in eye following cataract surgery, left eye
>
> H59.13 Cataract (lens) fragments in eye following cataract surgery, bilateral

The code for non-healing surgical wound has been deleted in ICD•10•CM. This condition is now classified to the residual subcategory for other complications of procedures not elsewhere classified.

ICD•9•CM

> 998.83 Non-healing surgical wound

ICD•10•CM

> T81.89 Other complications of procedures, not elsewhere classified

There is no specific code in ICD•9•CM for strain of muscle at the neck level. A new code has been added to the ICD•10•CM to classify this disorder.

ICD•10•CM

> S16.1   Strain of muscle and tendon at neck level

CHAPTER 20

Chapter 20, "External Causes of Morbidity," contains 30 code families depicted by the code's first character of "V," "W," and "X." They are:

V00-V09	Pedestrian injured in transport accident
V10-V19	Pedal cyclist injured in transport accident
V20-V29	Motorcycle rider injured in transport accident
V30-V39	Occupant of three-wheeled motor vehicle injured in transport accident
V40-V49	Car occupant injured in transport accident
V50-V59	Occupant of pick-up truck or van injured in transport accident
V60-V69	Occupant of heavy transport vehicle injured in transport accident
V70-V79	Bus occupant injured in transport accident
V80-V89	Other land transport accidents
V90-V94	Water transport accidents
V95-V97	Air and space transport accidents
V98-V99	Other and unspecified transport accidents
W00-W19	Falls

 KEY POINT

Where multiple sites of injury are specified in the titles, the word "with" indicates involvement of both sites, and the word "and" indicates involvement of either or both sites.

W20-W49	Exposure to inanimate mechanical forces
W50-W64	Exposure to animate mechanical forces
W65-W74	Accidental drowning and submersion
W85-W99	Exposure to electric current, radiation and extreme ambient air temperature and pressure
X00-X09	Exposure to smoke, fire and flames
X10-X19	Contact with heat and hot substances
X30-X39	Exposure to forces of nature
X50-X57	Overexertion, travel and privation
X58	Accidental exposure to other specified factors
X71-X83	Intentional self-harm
X92-Y08	Assault
Y21-Y33	Event of undetermined intent
Y35-Y38	Legal intervention, operations of war, military operation, and terrorism
Y62-Y69	Misadventures to patients during surgical and medical
Y70-Y82	Medical devices associated with adverse incidents in diagnostic and therapeutic use
Y83-Y84	Surgical and other medical procedures as the cause of abnormal reaction of the patient, or of later complication, without mention of misadventure at the time of the procedure
Y90-Y98	Supplementary factors related to causes of morbidity classified elsewhere

ICD•10•CM Category Restructuring

After reviewing the different disease categories, developers of ICD•10 restructured some of them to bring together those groups that are related in some way. For example, in ICD•9•CM, the supplementary classification of external causes of injury and poisoning (E codes) is found at the end of the Tabular List. In ICD•10•CM, these codes follow chapter 19, "Injury, Poisoning and Certain Other Consequences of External Causes." In addition, the transport accident section has been completely revised and extended, with blocks of categories identifying the victim's mode of transport.

It is also important to note that after the events of September 11, 2001, the National Center for Health Statistics (NCHS) recognized a definite need for accurate statistical classifications to characterize deaths and illnesses related to acts of terrorism. The NCHS has developed a new set of codes within the framework of ICD•10, the classification presently used for mortality reporting, and ICD•9•CM, used for morbidity, to allow these identifications to be reported.

The new codes for terrorism were implemented into ICD•9•CM for 2002 within the existing chapter for external causes.

Since the ICD•10 classification system is not under U.S. maintenance, implementing new codes into ICD•10 requires international deliberation under the World Health Organization's (WHO's) sanction and can take much longer. The codes have been presented and will be placed in the "U" chapter, reserved for future additions and changes. Although not adopted by WHO at the time of publication of this book, these U.S. codes will be distinguished by an asterisk to separate them from official WHO ICD•10 codes.

ICD•9•CM

In ICD•9•CM, the main axis is whether the event is a traffic or non-traffic accident.

Supplementary Classification of External Causes of Injury and Poisoning (E800-E999)

E800-E807	Railway Accidents
E810-E819	Motor Vehicle Traffic Accidents
E820-E825	Motor Vehicle Nontraffic Accidents
E826-E829	Other Road Vehicle Accidents

ICD•10•CM

In ICD•10, the main axis is the injured person's mode of transport. For land transport accidents, categories V01-V89, the vehicle of which the injured person is an occupant is identified in the first two characters since it is perceived as the essential issue for prevention purposes.

External Causes of Morbidity (V00-Y98)

V00-X58	Accidents
V00-V99	Transport accidents
V00-V09	Pedestrian injured in transport accident
V10-V19	Pedal cyclist injured in transport accident
V20-V29	Motorcycle rider injured in transport accident
V30-V39	Occupant of three-wheeled motor vehicle injured in transport accident
V40-V49	Car occupant injured in transport accident
V50-V59	Occupant of pick-up truck or van injured in transport accident
V60-V69	Occupant of heavy transport vehicle injured in transport accident
V70-V79	Bus occupant injured in transport accident
V80-V89	Other land transport accidents
V90-V94	Water transport accidents
V95-V97	Air and space transport accidents
V98-V99	Other and unspecified transport accidents

Category Title Changes

A number of category title revisions were made in chapter 20. Titles were changed to better reflect the category's content, which was often necessary when specific types of diseases were given their own block, a new category was created, or an existing category was redefined.

ICD•9•CM

E917	**Striking against or struck accidentally by objects or persons**

ICD•10•CM

W21	**Striking against or struck by sports equipment**
W22	**Striking against or struck by other objects**
W50	**Accidental hit, strick, kick, twist, bite or scratch by another person**
W51	**Accidental striking against or bumped into by another person**

> **☞ KEY POINT**
>
> The late effect codes are scattered throughout this chapter in ICD•9•CM. In ICD•10•CM, sequalae of external cause is indicated by using extension "q":
>
> V95.01q Helicopter crash injuring occupant, sequelae
>
> W23.0q Caught, crushed, jammed, or pinched between moving objects, sequelae
>
> X15.0q Contact with hot stove (kitchen), sequelae
>
> X76.q Intentional self-harm by smoke, fire and flames, sequelae
>
> Y28.0q Contact with sharp glass, undetermined intent, sequelae

W52   Crushed, pushed or stepped on by crowd or human stampede

Organizational Adjustments

When comparing ICD•9•CM to ICD•10•CM, some codes have been added, deleted, combined, or moved.

The late effect codes for external causes are located in various subchapters throughout the supplementary classification in ICD•9•CM. In ICD•10•CM, all late effects for each intent, i.e., accidents, suicide, etc., can be denoted by adding the sequela extension (q) to the code itself, where appropriately identified.

ICD•9•CM

E929	Late effects of accidental injury
E959	Late effects of self-inflicted injury
E969	Late effects of injury purposely inflicted by other person
E977	Late effects of injuries due to legal intervention
E989	Late effects of injury, undetermined whether accidentally or purposely inflicted
E999	Late effect of injury due to war operations

ICD•10•CM

	V00.02q Pedestrian on foot injured in collision with skateboarder, sequelae
	W50.4q Accidental scratch by another person, sequelae
	X71.0q Intentional self-harm by drowning and submersion while in bathtub, sequelae
Y02.q	Assault by pushing or placing victim before moving object, sequelae
	Y24.8q Other firearm discharge, undetermined intent, sequelae

The codes for accidental poisoning by drugs, medicinal substances, and biologicals (E850.0-E869.9) and by other solid and liquid substances, gases, and vapors (E860-E869) have been moved in ICD•10•CM. The specific substance is identified with a code from the T36-T50 range for poisoning by and adverse effects of drugs, medicaments, and biological substances, or the T51-T65 range for toxic effects of substances chiefly nonmedicinal, using the code identified as accidental (unintentional).

ICD•9•CM

E856	Accidental poisoning by antibiotics
	E860.4 Accidental poisoning by fusel oil

ICD•10•CM

	T36.0x1 Poisoning by penicillins, accidental (unintentional)
	T51.3x1 Toxic effect of fusel oil, accidental (unintentional)

There is no specific code in ICD•9•CM for exposure to radon. A new code has been added to ICD•10•CM to classify this health risk factor.

KEY POINT

Contents of this chapter were often referred to as the "E codes" chapter in ICD•9•CM and constituted the end of the classification. With ICD•10•CM, there are four alphabetic characters, V, W, X, and Y, that make up the next-to-last chapter of the classification.

ICD•10•CM

X39.01   Exposure to radon

CHAPTER 21

Chapter 21, "Factors Influencing Health Status and Contact with Health Services," contains nine code families, depicted by the code's first character of "Z." They are:

Z00-Z13	Persons encountering health services for examination and investigation
Z20-Z28	Persons with potential health hazards related to communicable diseases
Z30-Z39	Persons encountering health services in circumstances related to reproduction
Z40-Z53	Persons encountering health services for specific procedures and health care
Z55-Z65	Persons with potential health hazards related to socioeconomic and psychosocial circumstances
Z66	Do not resuscitate [DNR] status
Z67	Blood type
Z69-Z76	Persons encountering health services in other circumstances
Z79-Z99	Persons with potential health hazards related to family and personal history and certain conditions influencing health status

ICD•10•CM Category Restructuring

After reviewing the different disease categories, developers of ICD•10 restructured some of them to bring together those groups that are related in some way. For example, in ICD•9•CM, the categories for problems related to household, economic, family, and other psychosocial circumstances are classified under the subchapter for persons encountering health services in other circumstances. The categories for these types of problems have been moved to their own subchapter for persons with potential health hazards related to socioeconomic and psychosocial circumstances in ICD•10•CM. There is also a new, stand-alone category to denote a DNR order.

Category Title Changes

A number of category title revisions were made in chapter 21. Titles were changed to better reflect the category's content, which was often necessary when specific types of diseases were given their own block, a new category was created, or an existing category was redefined.

ICD•9•CM

V60	Housing, household, and economic circumstances
V61	Other family circumstances
V62	Other psychosocial circumstances

ICD•10•CM

Z59	Problems related to housing and economic circumstance
Z60	Problems related to social environment
Z61	Problems related to negative life events in childhood

☞ **KEY POINT**

This chapter, which in previous revisions of ICD constituted a supplementary classification, permits the classification of environmental events and circumstances as the cause of injury, poisoning, and other adverse effects. Where a code from this section is applicable, it is intended that it shall be used in addition to a code from another chapter of the classification indicating the nature of the condition.

 DEFINITION

Z codes. Used to report reasons for encounters. A corresponding procedure should accompany a Z code if a procedure is performed.

Z62 Other problems related to upbringing

Z63 Other problems related to primary support group, including family circumstances

Z64 Problems related to certain psychosocial circumstances

Z65 Problems related to other psychosocial circumstances

When comparing ICD•9•CM to ICD•10•CM, some codes have been added, deleted, combined, or moved.

The codes for supervision of high-risk pregnancy, category V23, are found in the V code chapter in ICD•9•CM. These situations have been moved in ICD•10•CM to a new category in the chapter, "Pregnancy, Childbirth and the Puerperium." For example:

ICD•9•CM

V23.0 Pregnancy with a history of infertility

ICD•10•CM

O09.00 Supervision of pregnancy with history of infertility, unspecified trimester

O09.01 Supervision of pregnancy with history of infertility, first trimester

O09.02 Supervision of pregnancy with history of infertility, second trimester

O09.03 Supervision of pregnancy with history of infertility, third trimester

The codes for orthopedic aftercare, V54.0-V54.9, have been consolidated into a single code in ICD•10•CM. No longer will there be a code for such things as change of plaster cast (V54.8) or removal of pins (V54.0).

ICD•9•CM

V54.0 Aftercare involving removal of fracture plate or other internal fixation device

V54.8 Other orthopedic aftercare

V54.9 Unspecified orthopedic aftercare

ICD•10•CM

Z48.08 Encounter for other specified surgical aftercare

There is no specific code in ICD•9•CM for an encounter for paternity testing. A new code has been added to ICD•10•CM to classify encounters for this purpose.

ICD•10•CM

Z02.81 Encounter for paternity testing

DISCUSSION QUESTIONS

1. Why was the term, "certain" added to the title of chapter 1, "Certain Infectious and Parasitic Diseases?" Give examples.

    _____

    _____

    _____

2. How has the classification of conditions as sequelae changed in ICD•10•CM? Give examples.

    _____

    _____

    _____

3. Can you think of any reasons for some changes that render ICD•10•CM less specific than ICD•9•CM?

    _____

    _____

    _____

4. Where can codes for signs and symptoms be found in ICD•10•CM?

    _____

    _____

    _____

5. Identify the chapter(s) where codes for external causes relative to the E codes are found in ICD•10•CM.

    _____

    _____

    _____

4 Implementation Issues

It has been more than 20 years since the United States adopted a new medical coding system. Since that time, payment systems have shifted from a system in which physicians and facilities were paid based upon what they charged, to one in which payments are standardized and based upon what is coded. The reliance upon codes for reimbursement has greatly increased the importance of medical coding for everyone in American health care — more than 500,000 physicians and more than 6,000 hospitals. Preparing all professionals at your facility—not just the coders—for the impact of the new coding system is key to the successful implementation of ICD•10•CM. Now is the time to begin baseline training. A heightened awareness of the issues surrounding ICD•10•CM will bring many benefits:

- Prevent your organization from investing in potentially obsolete equipment
- Guide you in cultivating the right skill sets required for ICD•10•CM implementation
- Allow your financial managers to prepare for the added capital and personnel investments required by the change
- Minimize the overall impact of the change for your organization

Within 12 months prior to the official date of implementation, you will want coders at your facility to undergo extensive clinical training in the use of ICD•10•CM. Until then, training should be limited to an overview of ICD•10•CM issues. Early training will result in improved planning within three business categories at your medical office:

- Training and personnel
- Information technology
- Business and finance

OBJECTIVES

- Understand the far-reaching impact of ICD•10•CM on your facility
- Prepare all departments within your facility for implementation
- Reduce last-minute crises with IS or budgeting
- Help your facility organize a task force to oversee change

TRAINING AND PERSONNEL

There is no avoiding ICD•10•CM. The new diagnostic system provides the detail lacking in the current system. Granularity, the degree to which codes are explicitly defined, is imperative to tracking disease in the United States. The statistics gathered from coding systems are used in many critical ways:

- To drive healthcare reform
- To measure both the quality and the efficacy of care
- To power payment systems
- To identify public health risks
- To detect fraud
- To monitor clinical trials and epidemics
- To track resource utilization
- To prioritize social programs

The improved data provided by ICD•10•CM codes combined with today's technology has the potential to turn medicine into a very precise science. Statistics gathered from coded claims on specific illnesses and successful patterns of care lead to medical protocols for disease management; but medical standards developed from data are only as good as the data itself. Therefore, it is important to the future of our nation's healthcare system — not just to coders or the business office — that coders are trained and committed to accuracy. Otherwise, poor decisions will result when inaccurate codes are used to track epidemics, to measure the efficacy of care, or for any of the other statistical uses mentioned above.

According to Department of Labor statistics, there are more than 600,000 coders and health information specialists in this country. Because the many uses of codes cross so many medical professions, it is no surprise that many people other than coders will be affected by ICD•10•CM. Among the people who will require training are the following:

- Clinical coders
- Physicians
- Compliance officers
- Data analysts
- Auditors
- Software vendors
- Quality assurance management
- Claims reviewers
- Human resources managers
- Accounting managers
- Information systems personnel

Clinical Personnel

The greater detail found in ICD•10•CM must be reflected in the medical records coders use for extracting information. Examples of higher clinical coding complexity include the following:

- For decubitus ulcer, one code in ICD•9•CM is replaced with a choice from among 60 codes that identify the specific site (lower back, sacral region, left buttock, etc.) and the degree of ulceration (e.g., limited to skin breakdown, fat layer exposure, necrosis of muscle or bone).
- For cardiac arrest, a single code in ICD•9•CM is replaced with choices classifying cardiac arrest due to underlying cardiac conditions, other underlying conditions; or unspecified conditions.
- For the symptom, abnormal gait, a single code has been replaced by seven codes in ICD•10•CM that identify ataxic gate, paralytic gate, difficulty in walking, falling, unsteadiness, and other abnormalities of gait.

Since coding conventions in ICD•10•CM are similar to those of ICD•9•CM, these conventions will largely be understood by experienced coders. However, be sure to provide office resources such as medical dictionaries, anatomy charts, and "self-help" instructional materials, since the level of anatomic detail is much higher in ICD•10•CM, and coders will be required to translate the language of the medical record into the language of code selection. For example, when coding a decubitus ulcer, a notation in the medical record may read, "the decubitus ulceration had invaded the subcutaneous tissue at the coccyx." The coder must determine that the correct code would be L89.051 Decubitus ulcer of sacral region limited to breakdown of the skin. To select this code, the coder must determine that subcutaneous tissue is considered part of the skin, and that the coccyx is the tail bone, a part of the sacrum. This is quite a change from the single code for decubitus ulcer in ICD•9•CM.

Specialty-specific and code-specific training should be reserved for the 12-month period preceding implementation. However, in the interim, some foundation training of clinical coders can prepare them for the change and get them oriented to using ICD•10•CM. These are some of the early training issues that can be addressed with clinical coders:

- Anatomical and physiological literacy training
- Heightened awareness of and sensitivity to documentation requirements
- Exposure to some of the new conventions of ICD•10•CM, including
  — alpha kickers for injuries that identify initial encounter, subsequent encounter, and sequelae
  — alpha kickers for coma that identify the treatment site as being in the field, at arrival to emergency department, upon hospital admission, 24 hours post admission, or an unspecified time
  — "place holding 'x' " to allow for future expansion of the code set

Communication is Key

Communication with all coders during implementation and pre-implementation is very important. When talk turns to ICD•10•CM, many experienced coders respond by outlining their retirement timetables. In many cases, people who have been coding for 20 years or more may feel threatened by the pending classification system change. They may fear they will be unseated as the resident "experts." It will be a challenge to retain experienced coders in the ICD•9•CM system, but if management presents the right attitudes regarding the change, and if all coders are encouraged to participate in the planning process for implementation, attrition can be lessened. Use the experience and knowledge of your more senior coders as you develop your implementation plans for ICD•10•CM. Your payoff will be a more comprehensive review of the impact ICD•10•CM is going to have, and a satisfied, willing staff with a vested interest in achieving a smooth implementation transition.

Whether you are a compliance officer, an auditor, a coder, or a quality assurance worker, the best early education tool for ICD•10•CM is a copy of the ICD•10•CM code book. Ingenix published a copy of the July 2002 draft of ICD•10•CM, and this version should see very little change before the final codes are published and adopted. Study the codes affecting your specialty, and familiarize yourself with the old and new conventions in ICD•10•CM. This will reduce the threat you may feel regarding the change. The added perspectives may also provide important insight into potential problem areas that need to be addressed. For example, upon learning about the alpha-numeric composition of the codes in ICD•10•CM, one clinical coder remarked to her manager that the data entry being performed by a 10-key operator would be protracted, since the 10-key operators were accustomed to numeric characters only. This observation led the facility to eliminate 10-key data entry, relying instead on full typewriter keyboards for data entry. It was expected that by the time ICD•10•CM

WORTH NOTING

A higher level of anatomical and clinical knowledge is demanded by ICD•10•CM than by ICD•9•CM. ICD•10•PCS requires even more sophistication from coders. This is because while the ICD•10•CM uses nomenclature common to the medical record, ICD•10•PCS has standardized the medical language to the point where the coder reading the medical record will be required to "translate" the language into the universal nomenclature of ICD•10•PCS. The coder will also be required to "build" the code logically by selecting the individual pieces that make up the code from the standardizes available choices.

KEY POINT

Take measures to include your more experienced coders in your facility's plans for change. Their knowledge can ease the transition to ICD•10•CM, once they are convinced the new coding system is an exciting opportunity, not a conspiracy to make their jobs more difficult.

KEY POINT

Whenever possible, coordinate work disruptions. For example, schedule an IS upgrade of coder computers for the day when your coding staff will be off-site, attending ICD•10•CM training.

was implemented, the 10-key operator would be as efficient on the keyboard as she was on the 10-key. A potential stumbling block to implementation was averted.

Understanding the new coding system, becoming familiar with the codes for their specialty, and knowing the strategic goals of their business department can help coders feel vested in the new system. When it comes to a new challenge, attitude can be the difference between success and failure.

Physicians

Physicians know the consequences of inadequate documentation as Medicare and private payers tighten their reimbursement belts. Even so, documentation continues to be the number one problem in clinical coding and reimbursement. ICD•10•CM represents the first new diagnostic coding system adopted since computers in the medical reimbursement industry raised the standards of accuracy in coding. This may provide coders and office managers with an unprecedented opportunity to train physicians who ask, "What's all this fuss about ICD•10•CM?"

The most important message that can be conveyed to physicians is that lack of compliance with the new documentation requirements of ICD•10•CM will cost them money, and cost them time. We can expect every step in the reimbursement cycle to be extended a bit during the initial stages of implementation. Nobody enjoys delayed payments, so everyone's goal will be to shrink that cycle back to its previous size. If physicians expect their staff to strive to tighten the reimbursement cycle, their best move is to lead by example.

The level of detail required in medical documentation for assignment of ICD•10•CM codes emphasizes physician participation. The patient's chart MUST specify terminology and provide complete documentation according to new standards. For example:

- For osteoporosis with pathological fracture, the origin of osteoporosis as either postmenopausal or other type, such as disuse, drug-induced, idiopathic, or, postsurgical, must be identified together with the specific site of the current fracture.
- For an injury to a nerve of the lower limb (one code in ICD•9•CM), medical documentation must show which nerve (tibial, peroneal, cutaneous sensory, or other nerve), right or left side, and whether the encounter is initial, subsequent, or to treat late effects. There are 45 choices for coding an injury to a nerve at the lower leg level in ICD•10•CM.

One "hands-on" approach to teaching physicians the issues of ICD•10•CM documentation is to perform audits on physician charts to identify documentation problems relevant to ICD•10•CM. After masking identifying information to preserve the privacy of the patient, photocopy actual medical records that are under-documented. Photocopy the page with ICD•10•CM code selections for that disorder. Highlight the documentation and the appropriate ICD•10•CM code section, and staple the two sheets together. Keep a separate file for each physician in your office, and when your file holds 10 or more examples of underdocumentation for ICD•10•CM, schedule a short meeting with the physician to go over these examples.

☑ **WORTH NOTING**

ICD•10•CM provides an unprecedented window of opportunity for physician training. It may be the only time that physicians recognize the need for change, and coders need to be armed to move when that recognition happens. A higher interest in documentation requirements can be generated if you can tie the higher level of documentation needed for ICD•10•CM to tangible reimbursement issues.

Human Resource Managers

Including human resources managers in ICD•10•CM planning may help prevent manpower shortages at implementation time. Some issues are important to HR departments as ICD•10•CM implementation nears:

- Retaining current employees
- Finding new employees

By U.S. government accounts, healthcare costs in this country topped more than one trillion dollars in 2001, and are expected to double by the end of this decade. More than half of this amount was billed through codes applied to claims at facilities and physician practices. Even without the impact of the new coding system, the Department of Labor is predicting a shortage in health information management professionals, including coders, through the rest of this decade. Qualified, experienced coders are going to be a premium commodity.

The number one goal of human resources personnel should be a successful campaign to retain current coding employees over time. A high retention rate eliminates the high costs of recruitment and training of new employees. By beginning now to measure and ensure the job satisfaction of HIM staff, human resources personnel can reduce the attrition that the new coding system threatens. The coder shortage will create competition among employers. Make sure that wages and benefits at your facility are competitive. The cost of receiving or maintaining credentialing is expensive, and coders will look elsewhere if expected to shoulder that burden at your office.

Begin networking now to develop sources for finding and recruiting new coders — through local professional organizations and placement agencies, training centers, and online employment sources.

Accounting Managers

The immediate issue affecting accounting managers regarding ICD•10•CM implementation is the capital expenditures required by the new system. Medical reimbursement offices may be required to do the following:

- Upgrade computers
- Replace software
- Hire new IS and coding personnel
- Pay for training and for coders' wages as they attend training
- Purchase reference manuals
- Manage losses in productivity

Developing a financial plan is a strategic move that is imperative to successful implementation.

A valid question is, "How will ICD•10•CM affect payment?" ICD codes are the determinants for the DRGs that are the basis for inpatient payment. Another common question is, "What is the expected impact of the change to ICD•10•CM and the potential change to ICD•10•PCS upon inpatient reimbursement?" Today reimbursement rates in the United States are based upon years of aggregate data. No one will want to give up a historically valid payment methodology when a new coding system is implemented. Instead, it is expected that for the first years,

ICD•10•CM codes and ICD•10•PCS codes will be mapped to their equivalent ICD•9•CM codes for payment determination. When sufficient data has been collected, payment schedules will be modified to reflect the more detailed information available in ICD•10•CM and ICD•10•PCS.

For those paid under CPT, the change to ICD•10•CM will only affect payment as related to medical necessity and the need to be accurate in the selection of codes. It is likely the number of rejected claims will climb during the period shortly after implementation, then settle to previous levels. If hospitals implement ICD•10•PCS, the change will be more dramatic. For the first year or so, codes in ICD•10•PCS and ICD•10•CM will be mapped to ICD•9•CM codes. Once a baseline of data has been developed, new fee schedules will be established for ICD•10•PCS and ICD•10•CM for facilities. The same issues of accuracy and claims rejection will apply at hospitals as in physician offices.

An oft-overlooked and critical factor in implementation of a new code set is its impact upon the reimbursement cycle. Each step in the reimbursement cycle has the potential to be protracted as a result of the code changes. While it is taking longer for your office to file a claim, and for the payer to reimburse you for the services, your office will be facing additional costs associated with the change: new personnel, new reference materials, new computers, training costs, productivity reductions.

No matter how well the provider does its job, it must still rely on the payer for its income. It is critical that providers contact each of their payers to be certain that procedures are coordinated and implementation is synchronized. Campaigns to work with payers can be managed by the accounting office or through the coding and billing office.

INFORMATION SYSTEMS

The move to ICD•10•CM is much bigger in the healthcare industry than Y2K ever was. Information systems (IS) personnel are major resources in the transition. As you begin budgeting and planning, remember the others who will be affected by ICD-10-CM.

Every electronic transaction requiring an ICD•9•CM code will need to be changed under ICD•10•CM or ICD•10•PCS. This includes the following:

- Medical records abstraction
- Data reporting
- Utilization
- Billing
- Fee schedules
- Payment policies
- Provider profiling
- Medical review
- Medical necessity software
- Benefits determination
- Claims submission
- Test ordering systems
- Accounting systems

KEY POINT

Don't wait until the month before implementation to discuss with your software and hardware vendors how their products will fare with ICD•10•CM, unless you want to pay a high price for substandard service. It's important to keep communication flowing in the year before implementation. From this point forward, it is also wise not to make new investments without a guarantee that the product will be "ICD•10 compatible."

CODING AXIOM

Do not assume that outside vendors will stay current with the transition.

- Case mix systems
- Groupers
- Abstracting systems
- Clinical systems

The changes will include specific functions, record format, and fields or data location sites, including the following:

- Software interfaces
- Field length formats on screens
- Report formats and layouts
- Expansions of flat files
- Coding edits and logic
- In-house custom applications

If you are using software that has ICD•9•CM codes, make sure that your software vendor and information systems personnel are preparing to accommodate ICD•10•CM codes. Systems are set up to accept code data in specific formats and the structural disparity between ICD•10•CM and ICD•9•CM requires modified software. Do not assume that outside vendors will stay current with the transition.

Planning Issues

IS will want to create a software application or an interface between the two systems. IS can work with the coding department to identify the systems and software using ICD•9•CM codes, such as computer applications in anesthesia, the emergency department, and the intensive care unit. A facility with internally developed software or interfaces needs IS to draw up long-range plans.

On the administrative side, IS can develop a system to access accurate data for longitudinal studies in finance and performance improvement. The system must be capable of creating reports during the transition. Care must be taken, however, in extracting information from longitudinal studies that may compare ICD•9•CM health patterns to ICD•10•CM health patterns. For example, the time frame for classifying myocardial infarct codes in ICD•9•CM to acute MI codes is eight weeks. In ICD•10•CM, it is four weeks. This could result in a statistical drop in the incidence of acute myocardial infarctions. Coders and code analysts would need to understand the nuances between the two coding systems to understand that the decrease was a reflection of changes in data reporting, not in the incidence of MIs.

Elements Affecting Information System (IS)

The following illustrates the differences between ICD•9•CM and ICD•10•CM and addresses issues that your IS department must consider.

Number of Characters

ICD•9•CM	*ICD•10•CM*	*Implementation Issues for ICD•10•CM*
3–5	3–7	• Any field that reads an ICD•10•CM code needs to be able to accommodate up to seven characters.

 KEY POINT

Many fonts are available that use a "European zero," a zero with a line through it: Ø. Your facility may want to consider adopting a European zero to avoid coding confusion:

000.00	Abdominal pregnancy without intrauterine pregnancy
0Ø0.ØØ	Abdominal pregnancy without intrauterine pregnancy

Some information systems drop the decimal point in ICD•9•CM to save memory space. If this practice continues, some HCPCS Level II codes may be duplicate numbers to ICD•10•CM.

Type of Character

ICD•9•CM	ICD•10•CM	Implementation Issues for ICD•10•CM
Numeric only (except V codes and E codes)	Alphanumeric	• Make sure all ICD•10-CM code fields allow for both numeric and alpha characters.
		• Reprogramming may be necessary to distinguish between numbers (0,1) and alpha characters (O,I). For example, alpha characters may need to be capitalized to distinguish between the letter I and the number one (1). A slash may need to be used with the zero to distinguish between the number and the letter O: Ø.

Decimals

ICD•9•CM	ICD•10•CM	Implementation Issues for ICD•10•CM
Decimals are used after the third character	Decimals are used after the third character	• If your system currently accommodates decimals, make sure up to four characters can be allowed after the decimal.
		• If your system does not accommodate decimals, there should be no implementation issue, other than the total number of characters required for each field.
		• Special consideration: If your system accepts both ICD and HCPCS codes, the absence of a decimal may make it difficult for your system to distinguish between HCPCS codes and 5-character ICD•10•CM codes: both have five characters with an alpha character in the first position. Examples:
		E05.00 Thyrotoxicosis with diffuse goiter without thyrotoxic crisis or storm
		E0500 IPPB machine, all types, with built-in nebulization; manual or automatic valves; internal or external power source
		L40.50 Arthropathic psoriasis, unspecified
		L4050 Replace molded calf lacer
		• Your system may need to be reprogrammed to place decimals with ICD•10•CM codes or otherwise differentiate between the ICD•10•CM and HCPCS codes.

Descriptions

ICD•9•CM	ICD•10•CM	Implementation Issues for ICD•10•CM
Tabular listing shows partial description for fourth– and fifth-digit codes	Full (stand-alone) descriptions are used for every code.	• Even though the ICD•9•CM tabular listing (book) uses partial descriptions for fourth- and fifth-digit codes, data files are available for ICD•9•CM that provide a full description for every code. If your system currently uses such a data file, then there should be no implementation issues.
		• Some ICD•9•CM data files provide the code description in multiple fields: the three-digit category description, a 4-digit subcategory description, and a five-digit subclassification description. If your system uses separate fields to accommodate category and subclassification descriptions, then reprogramming may be necessary to accept the ICD•10•CM descriptions.
		• Some ICD•9•CM data files provide abbreviated descriptions (e.g., 35-character, 48-character, 150-character). If your description field is set up to accept a specific length of description, make sure that you use a vendor who can provide ICD•10•CM abbreviated descriptions in the length you need.
		• Many of the ICD•10•CM descriptions contain several characters. Reprogramming may be necessary to expand the character limit of the description field to accept the ICD•10•CM codes and descriptions.

Hierarchy

ICD•9•CM	ICD•10•CM	Implementation Issues for ICD•10•CM
Fourth- and fifth- character codes have hierarchical relationships within a three-character category.	Fourth-, fifth-, sixth-, and seventh-character codes have hierarchical relationships within a three-character category.	• Your system may recognize the hierarchical relationship of fifth-digit codes to fourth-digit codes, and of fourth-digit codes to three-digit categories. If this is the case, then reprogramming may be necessary to accommodate an additional hierarchical relationship — sixth- and seventh-digit codes to the preceding code level.

Conventions

ICD•9•CM	ICD•10•CM	Implementation Issues for ICD•10•CM
The Tabular List may include "excludes" and "includes" notations, instructional notes, essential modifiers, nonessential modifiers, etc., in reference to any code.	The Tabular List may include excludes and includes notations, instructional notes, essential modifiers, nonessential modifiers, etc., in reference to any code.	• ICD•10•CM incorporates excludes notes, includes notes, other instructional notes, etc., in the same way as ICD•9•CM. If your program uses this information, you may need to differentiate among the three types of excludes notes.

Quantity of Codes

ICD•9•CM	ICD•10•CM	Implementation Issues for ICD•10•CM
ICD•9•CM contains more than 15,000 Vol. 1 and Vol. 3 codes. For 1999, CPT has nearly 8,000 codes.	ICD•10•CM contains more than 24,000 codes; ICD•10•PCS contains more than 20,000 codes.	• ICD•10•CM contains considerably more codes.
		• Reprogramming may be necessary to accommodate the increased number of codes and descriptions.
		• Make sure your system has sufficient memory to handle the additional data. Increasing memory may handle the increased amount of data.

Format and Availability of Data

ICD•9•CM	ICD•10•CM	Implementation Issues for ICD•10•CM
Codes and descriptions are available both in print and numerous electronic formats (e.g., tab-delimited, fixed-format, etc.)	Codes and descriptions are available in print. Access to electronic formats has not yet been determined.	• Most systems are set up to accept codes and descriptions electronically. ASCII data files are commonly used to provide codes and descriptions in specified formats: tab-delimited, fixed format, comma-delimited, etc. Because ICD•10•CM is not widely available, it may be difficult to acquire the codes and descriptions in the electronic format required by your system. Reprogramming may be required to accept a data file in a different format.

KEY POINT

Reprogramming may be necessary to accommodate the increased number of codes and descriptions in ICD•10•CM or ICD•10•PCS.

KEY POINT

Reprogramming may be necessary to accommodate the increased number of codes and descriptions in ICD•10•CM or ICD•10•PCS. Do you use shortened descriptions?

Take a look at a code like

S21.441   Puncture wound with foreign body of right back wall of thorax with penetration into thoracic cavity

A 48-character description would read:

Punc wnd w/FB; RT bk thorax, w/pen, thoracic cav

A 35-character description would read

Pun wd FB RT bk thrx, w pen thor cv

In many cases, shortened descriptions will become an impossibility due to the granularity of the descriptions.

WHAT TO DO NOW

The first step to developing a solid ICD•10•CM implementation strategy is to create a team with membership from all departments at your facility. This team will act as a task force, with the following responsibilities:

- Educate coders and physicians
- Troubleshoot implementation issues
- Track government decisions
- Communicate regularly with all employees

The task force should have membership that includes executive management, accounting, coding and billing, information services, human resources, and physicians. Divide responsibilities into major working topics, and give each member of the task force a job. Your group may need to meet monthly or quarterly, depending upon your needs and the government actions. It's important that your office be vigilant. Assign one member of your task force to read and summarize articles about implementation found in professional journals and newsletters, the Internet, and the Federal Register. E-mail these summaries to all employees, or post them in prominent areas at work. If everyone is encouraged to keep informed about ICD•10•CM, the number of surprises at implementation time will be greatly reduced.

Learning from Australia and Canada

Australia's transition to their modification, ICD•10-AM, in July 1998 and Canada's transition to ICD•10•CA in 2001 and 2002 raises several issues that the United States will be facing during the next several years. Two of these, as mentioned, are scheduling and budget. It is important to note that even though it is a good idea to learn from other countries who have already experienced implementing their own clinical modification to I-10, the U.S. may not be able to draw many direct conclusions as to how this country should proceed. Due to the circumstances of socialized medicine in other countries, the parallels may be limited. The central government does much of the coordination and decision-making in socialized medicine.

One of the greatest obstacles to implementing ICD•10•CM in the U.S. is predicted to be the lack of readiness among commercial vendors that won't be prepared for this change with appropriate functioning software and other tools needed by those in the health care industry.

Scheduling

A staggered introduction of coding classifications is an issue confronting the United States. ICD•10•CM is ready to go, possibly by 2005. A single procedural system has not been selected. In this situation, valid questions are: How will we avoid the conflicts of using two different coding systems? Will these conflicts jeopardize morbidity and mortality data collection? What about the implementation of a single system? Should it happen simultaneously, or regionally?

We can draw on the Australian experience. One-half of the country changed to ICD•10•Australian Modification (ICD•10•AM) in July 1998. The second half of the country was scheduled for July 1999.

The American Health Information Management Association surveyed Australia and other countries that have implemented ICD•10 to gather information on strategies and obstacles. Sue Prophet, director of coding policy and compliance for AHIMA, reported on this survey in testimony to the National Committee on Vital and Health Statistics on May 29, 2002. She said, in part:

Because of the many changes in the organization and structure of ICD•10, many users have found the use of computerized encoders has resulted in improvements in accuracy and efficiency. Users noted that this is largely due to the enhancements in the Alphabetic Index, which lend themselves to use in an electronic format … Canada was the first country to move to an entirely electronic product for ICD•10 codes. In other words, there are no paper ICD•10•CA code books available in Canada.

The Australian government provided two-day workshops to experienced coders as part of implementation, providing a paper copy (book) of the new ICD•10•AM code set. Canadian coders were trained first through a time-intensive correspondence course, then a two-day workshop. Only software was used for Canadian training. According to AHIMA, the average learning curve was four to six months for coding professionals to be comfortable with the new codes. The single most significant challenge reported by coders was the lack of readiness of vendors, despite ongoing communication.

WORTH NOTING

One-half of Australia changed to ICD•10•Australian Modification (ICD•10•AM) in July 1998. The second half of the country changed in July 1999. Canada changed to ICD•10•Canadian Modification (CA) in 2001 and 2002. To learn more about ICD•10•AM or -CA, search with those terms on the Internet to access many varied websites.

FOR MORE INFO

Coding Matters is the quarterly newsletter of the National Centre for the Classification of Health (NCCH). NCCH (Sydney) is funded by the Casemix Development Program, Commonwealth Department of Health and Family Services (DHFS). NCCH (Brisbane) is funded by the Casemix Development Program DHFS, the Australian Institute of Health and Welfare, the Australian Bureau of Statistics, and the Queensland University of Technology.

113

Australia's National Centre for the Classification of Health (NCCH) was advised to delay the start date until a uniform date could be set, since a staggered schedule could increase costs and affect the national data collection. Despite the advice, the NCCH went ahead with an April distribution of the ICD•10•AM and procedural classification (MSB-E) systems, as well as an errata to make the classification system as accurate as possible for users in half the country by July 1998. The Australian Bureau of Statistics (ABS) is recoding at least two years of past data into ICD•10•AM as a continuum to data collection and to assess trends using the new system.

The implementation process was a mammoth undertaking for everyone involved—coordinators and committees, health information managers, and clinical coders. However, the NCCH believed that a staggered start could actually improve coding quality. For example, the initial group of coders in the staggered schedule could identify documentation requirements and system flaws prior to national implementation.

In Australia, the NCCH had until July 1998 to produce the ICD•10•AM, according to its contractual agreement with the Division of Health and Family Services (DHFS). Government agencies such as the DHFS and the Classification and Payments Branch continue to support ICD•10•AM. Workshops, books, and training bring in additional funds. The Health Services Outcomes Branch gave funds to develop an electronic system for ICD•10•AM at NCCH Sydney, with additional funds for the project being solicited through the national press, according to the July 1998 Coding Matters. Funding levels allowed the NCCH to continue its work through June 2000, a month shy of the scheduled second edition of ICD•10•AM.

Planning for the Future

Updating ICD•10•AM is already a priority for the Australian NCCH. During the first year, NCCH stabilized the classification, although changes were anticipated due to Australian Coding Standards and typographical corrections. The NCCH maintained ICD•10 codes for mortality coding in Australia. For future editions, NCCH anticipates a 12-month lead time to publication and another five months to implementation, so that preparations would begin in the February prior to the July start date for new editions.

Procedures for updating subsequent editions in the United States probably will be similar to the process of updating ICD•9•CM. Revisions to ICD•9•CM are made once a year, effective October 1 of each year. Major changes in the time frame are published in the "Prospective Payment System, Final Rule" of the Federal Register. The ICD•9•CM Coordination and Maintenance Committee meets twice each year to discuss coding revisions proposed for the subsequent year.

Conclusion

Classification provides order and a certain control of our world. Classifying disease and death is one part of that whole system. But the real test of new coding classifications is neither the implementation process nor the technical problems related to electronic transmission. The real test, according to NCCH director Rosemary Roberts in Coding Matters, is a system that "withstands this testing crucible of real time use by real clinical coders."

 Worth Noting

"Clinical coding is a much more important function in Australia's healthcare system than it was at the time of the last change, that systems will fail if appropriate resources are not allocated," was the conclusion reached in the report, ICD•10-AM Impact Assessment on Australia by Coopers & Lybrand.

WHERE TO GO

ICD•10•CM
http://www.cdc.gov/nchs/about/otheract/icd9/icd10cm.htm - This site offers a posting of the downloadable ICD•10•CM files from the May 2002 draft of the tabular and index sections.

ICD•10•PCS
www.cms.hhs.gov/paymentsystems/icd9 - This site offers a posting of downloadable copies of ICD•10•PCS, instructions, and a PowerPoint slideshow that provides an overview of the system.

World Health Organization (WHO)
http://www.who.int/aboutwho/en/mission.html - This international agency maintains an international nomenclature of diseases, causes of death, and public health practices. WHO updated diagnostic coding with ICD•10.

National Center for Health Statistics (NCHS)
http://www.cdc.gov/nchswww/ - This U.S. government agency, together with CMS, jointly refines the diagnostic portion of ICD•9•CM and is responsible for the clinical modification of ICD•10. NCHS holds several hearings each year to consider changes or additions in diagnostic coding.

National Center for Vital and Health Statistics (NCVHS)
http://www.cdc.gov/nchswww/about/ncvhs - This is the advisory committee to the HHS for health statistics. NCVHS has become increasingly active over the past several years, addressing issues relating to uniform health data sets, medical classification systems, and the need for improved mental health statistics. The NCVHS established the objectives for the new procedural coding system, which are as follows: completeness, expandability, hierarchical structure, standardized terminology, improved accuracy, efficiency of coding, and reduced training time.

Centers for Medicare and Medicaid Services (CMS), formerly the Health Care Financing Administration (HCFA)
http://www.cms.hhs.gov/ - This organization is in charge of the federally funded healthcare programs. It is also developing a plan for proceeding with ICD•10•PCS. The steps include developing a speakers' package that would be available on the CMS homepage, testing the systems on patients who are not Medicare beneficiaries, and encouraging groups conducting ongoing research to double code with both ICD•9•CM and ICD•10•PCS. If ICD•10•PCS is selected as the national standard, CMS plans to develop a set of coding guidelines for documentation.

National Archives and Records Administration
http://www.access.gpo.gov/su_docs/aces/aces140.html#frbrowse - This is the place for the Federal Register on line, via GPO access. Users can look up specific issues of the Federal Register, which publishes notices by department. Rules and regulations for coding generally can be found under CMS.

Administrative Simplification Rules in HIPAA

http://www.hcfa.gov/medicare/edi/hipaaedi.html - This site links users to sites related to the Administrative Simplification Provision. For example: http://www.disa.org/x12 - This is the Data Interchange Standards Association web site. This site contains information on ASC X12, information on X12N subcommittees, task groups, and workgroups, including their meeting minutes. This site will contain the test conditions and results of HIPAA transactions tested at the workgroup level.

Combined Health Information DataBase (CHID)

http://chid.aerie.com/index.html - CHID is a database produced by health-related agencies of the federal government. This database provides titles, abstracts, and availability information for health information and health education resources.

American Health Information Management Association (AHIMA)

http://www.ahima.org/ - This is a professional organization for clinical data and information management. AHIMA develops industry standards advocating relevant legislation, and provides education in health information management.

DISCUSSION QUESTIONS

1. Cite the major challenges in implementing ICD•10•CM at your facility.

_____

_____

_____

2. Who at your facility will need ICD•10•CM training? ICD•10•CM certification?

_____

_____

_____

3. List the problems IS will face at implementation. How can these problems be solved or mitigated?

_____

_____

_____

4. What groups will you go to for assistance in coding or electronic transmission? Do you subscribe to the appropriate periodicals?

_____

_____

_____

5. What can we learn about implementation from Australia and Canada?

_____

_____

_____

5 Procedural Coding

Parallel procedural coding systems have been in place in U.S. medical reimbursement circles for decades. Hospitals use Volume 3 of the International Classification of Diseases, Ninth Revision, Clinical Modification (ICD•9•CM) to report inpatient care. Physicians use codes provided in the American Medical Association's (AMA) *Physicians' Current Procedural Terminology* (CPT) to report their services. CPT, first published in 1966, covers outpatient (office) services, and inpatient (hospital) procedures and other services performed and billed by the physician.

The 1990s, however, ushered in several changes in the way we deliver health care, which fueled discussions of a single system for procedural coding. For example, the advent of ambulatory surgical centers and physician office surgical suites allows once exclusively inpatient services to be performed as either outpatient or inpatient services. The administrative simplification provisions of the Health Insurance Portability and Accountability Act (HIPAA) of 1996 brought a clear demand to the issue of a single procedure coding system, which has since been the task of the Department of Health and Human Services (HHS) Coding and Classification Implementation Team.

CURRENT CODING SYSTEMS

Volume 3 of ICD•9•CM and CPT, are summarized in the following two sections.

ICD•9•CM Volume 3

In 1979, when the ninth version of ICD was published, a separate and third volume of ICD•9•CM was created to house procedure classifications. The Centers for Medicare and Medicaid Services (CMS, formerly HCFA) maintains the Volume 3 codes, which include operative, diagnostic, and therapeutic procedures. Annual code revisions are addressed at public hearings of the ICD•9•CM Coordination and Maintenance Committee, held two times a year.

Procedures in Volume 3 are catalogues in a series of two-digit category codes contained in 16 chapters. The codes are organized in a hierarchy. Codes containing the same first two digits share a common anatomical system; codes with the same first three numbers share a common anatomical system and a common type of procedure. The fourth digit further differentiates the procedures. For example, chapter 7, "Operations of the Cardiovascular System," includes the two-digit category codes 35-39. For example:

37   **Other operations on heart and pericardium**
 37.2   **Diagnostic procedures on heart and pericardium**
  37.21   **Right heart cardiac catheterization**
  37.22   **Left heart cardiac catheterization**

37.7   Insertion, revision, replacement, and removal of pacemaker leads; insertion of temporary pacemaker system; or revision of pocket

37.73   Initial insertion of transvenous lead [electrode] into atrium

37.74   Insertion or replacement of epicardial lead (electrode) into epicardium

Among the problems with ICD•9•CM Volume 3, as cited by AHIMA in testimony before the ICD•9•CM Coordination and Maintenance Committee during a 2002 hearing, are the following:

• Contains overlapping and duplicate codes
• Includes inconsistent and outdated terminology
• Lacks codes for certain types of services
• Lacks sufficient specificity and detail
• Has insufficient structure to capture new technology

CPT

The 2003 edition of CPT has been more than 30 years in the making. In 1970, the second edition marked the genesis of today's coding with the introduction of five-digit codes. The third edition, published in 1973, added new features such as modifiers. In 1977, the AMA established the annual internal review process to add, delete, and modify codes as it published its fourth edition.

The current CPT provides a listing of services and procedures and their individual codes within specific sections of CPT. There are six sections: evaluation and management, anesthesia, surgery, radiology, pathology and laboratory, and medicine. Each section is assigned a block of codes and is further broken into subsections. For example, the radiology subsections are diagnostic radiology, diagnostic ultrasound, radiation oncology, and nuclear medicine. Four appendixes follow the six sections: modifiers, summary of additions, deletions, and revisions, update to short descriptors, and clinical examples. Guidelines within each section provide definitions, explanations of terms, and factors relevant to the section. Parenthetical information found throughout the sections highlight the coding guidelines, designate coding changes such as deletions, and provide directions for finding the correct code.

Time for Change

In the late 1980s, the HHS National Committee on Vital and Health Statistics (NCVHS) characterized CPT and ICD•9•CM Volume 3 for procedures as increasingly limited in their administrative and clinical abilities. While the numeric hierarchy of Volume 3 is logical and comprehensive, it has significant drawbacks, including the inability to accommodate new medical procedures. CPT has the same shortcoming; it is running out of space to accommodate procedures under the existing subcategories.

Aside from size limitations, there has been more of a demand within the data-gathering community for a single procedural coding system that does not assign diagnoses. Procedure codes are the basis for payment, but they are also tracked to determine public and private health care policy. Many of the procedure codes in ICD•9•CM and CPT are tied to diagnoses. For example, in ICD•9•CM, code 58.5

FOR THE RECORD

According to information from the AMA, since Medicare's Prospective Payment System (PPS) began, the number of outpatient visits has climbed 137 percent, while hospital admissions have fallen by approximately 12 percent. The pace of outpatient visit growth appears to be accelerating after an annual increase of 5.4 percent in 1997.

Release of urethral stricture has little procedural detail, though it does specify a diagnosis. Similarly, CPT frequently ties procedures to diagnoses, as in codes 46937 *Cryosurgery of rectal tumor; benign* and 46938 *Cryosurgery of rectal tumor; malignant.*

In 1993, the NCVHS Subcommittee on Medical Classification Systems followed up on earlier concerns, and reported a "near consensus on the desirability of moving to a single, unified [procedure coding] system," and recommended that the HHS develop a single procedure classification system based on the following reasoning:

1. Both Volume 3 of ICD•9•CM and CPT-4 need substantial revision for precision and efficiency of coding.

2. Dual systems impede evaluation of health care based on health outcomes.

3. Changes in the organization and delivery of care require better information for monitoring and performance measurement.

4. Intensified efforts to reduce fraud and abuse require more uniformity in coding systems.

 WORTH NOTING

Two important questions should be asked as the United States considers new coding systems:

1. What are the risks, or costs, to the provider and payer community?

2. How will the change affect data collection and data integrity?

LEGISLATIVE REQUIREMENTS

HIPAA includes administrative simplification provisions that require HHS to provide technical guidance and administrative requirements for the electronic transmission of health information. In addition, the provisions warrant the application of safeguards to protect the integrity of information processed electronically, including information transmitted as code sets. HIPAA defines code sets as "any set of codes used for encoding data elements, such as tables of terms, medical concepts, medical diagnosis codes, or medical procedural codes." Since code sets are used as the standards for diagnosis, procedures, and drugs, the provision automatically affects the procedural code sets of ICD•9•CM Volume 3, CPT, and the alphanumeric HCPCS Level II (national) and III (local) codes.

The responsibility to modify the diagnostic and procedural code sets comes under the HHS secretary. Accordingly, one year after Congress passed provisions of HIPAA, the HHS National Committee for Vital Health Statistics, the federal advisory committee on health data, privacy, and health information, recommended the development of information systems to accommodate a "major change to a unified approach to coding procedures" by 2002 or 2003. Subsequently, the HHS Coding and Classification Implementation Team was charged with "moving toward a more integrated approach to procedure coding" that, since then, has been defined to include at least the following procedural categories:

- Physician services
- Physical and occupational therapy services
- Radiological procedures
- Clinical laboratory tests
- Other medical diagnostic procedures
- Hearing and vision services
- Transportation services including ambulance

NEW CODING SYSTEMS

As yet, no procedural system has been approved for national use. CPT was approved as the interim national code set when HHS published the proposed rule, "Health Insurance Reform: Standards for Electronic Transactions" in the Federal Register (1998). The rule acknowledged that "an area of weakness of CPT is that it is not always precise or unambiguous. However, there are no viable alternatives for the year 2000."

ICD•10•PCS

In 1995, the Health Care Financing Administration (HCFA, now CMS) contracted with 3-M Health Information Systems to develop a procedural coding system to replace ICD•9•CM Volume 3. The system they developed — ICD•10•PCS — is a numeric key of "smart codes" in a 7-character structure sequenced to specify the type of procedure being performed. The meaning of each character is dependent on the chapter. For example, if the procedure falls within the obstetrical section, the second character represents a body system within obstetrics. Each character has up to 34 different values. The 10 digits, 0-9, and 24 letters, A-H, J-N, and P-Z, may be assigned to each character. The letters O and I are not used in order to avoid confusion with the digits 0 and 1. In ICD•10•PCS the term "procedure" is used to refer to the complete specification of the seven characters. There is no diagnostic information, and a specific definition is applied consistently to the individual terms used in the system.

In May 1998, CMS contracted with Clinical Data Abstracting Centers (CDAC) to test the draft of ICD•10•PCS. The CDAC coders were trained on the medical surgical section of ICD•10•PCS, and testing took place in two phases: In Phase I each CDAC coded 2,500 medical records using the ICD•10•PCS system. The sample of these medical records included at least one case from each surgical diagnostic related group (DRG). Phase II consisted of a comparison between the ICD•9•CM coding system and ICD•10•PCS using sample medical records randomly selected from each monthly DRG sample. The coders' comments were evaluated and the tabular section and index were updated to address the comments. The American Health Information Management Association (AHIMA) produced a training package used at subsequent testing sites and a crosswalk was developed to bridge the transition from ICD•9•CM Volume 3 to ICD•10•PCS. Further testing was conducted on ambulatory records, records of patients who are not Medicare beneficiaries, and on the most current version of the ICD•10•PCS training manual.

CPT

The AMA is working to improve the structure and process of CPT. According to the AMA, health practitioners should anticipate changes to the editorial process of developing new and revised codes, while coders should expect structural modifications to simplify procedural coding (inpatient and outpatient) while also meeting the requirements of HIPAA. The AMA is developing a system to meet several objectives, including the following:

- Maintain CPT's position as the standard for procedural coding for the health care community, and ensure that CPT is the national and international procedural coding nomenclature that facilitates reimbursement and analysis of health care information

- Enhance the use of CPT by practicing physicians
- Improve CPT to address the needs of various non-physician health care professionals, including nurses, social workers, psychologists, optometrists, physician assistants and nurse practitioners, chiropractors, and therapists (occupational, speech, physical)
- Improve CPT to address the needs of hospitals, managed care organizations, long term care, ambulatory care professional and trade associations, clinical specialty societies, and researchers
- Develop comprehensive information regarding the correct use of CPT, including guidelines, policies, and procedures
- Develop a process to reflect changing practice patterns and new technologies
- Explore issues related to the reliability of CPT coding, i.e. that different users arrive at the same code for the same service

OBJECTIVES AND GUIDELINES

ICD•10•PCS

An early draft of the 3-M project described objectives derived from the inadequacies in the present procedural coding system. Among these objectives that were subsequently incorporated in ICD•10•PCS are the following:

- Completeness – A unique code for all substantially different procedures
- Expandability – Easy incorporation of unique codes for new procedures
- Uniformly structured – Consistent meaning of individual characters in the codes
- Standardized terminology – No multiple definitions for the same terms, and each term assigned a specific meaning (found in an accompanying glossary)

Additional attributes in the procedural coding system include the following:

- The "not elsewhere classified" option was eliminated, except for newly approved radiopharmaceuticals and new devices. The NEC option can be used prior to the addition of the radiopharmaceuticals and devices to the coding system. In every other case, ICD•10•PCS should contain all possible operations, body parts, and approaches.
- Diagnostic information is excluded from the procedure description to enhance data collection. There are no codes for specific diagnoses (e.g., aneurysm, hernia, cleft lip, enterocele).
- There are no eponyms. For example, the Bardenheuer operation is identified as ligation and suturing of an arterial fistula, rather than by the eponym.
- There is no Latin terminology. Everything is reduced to simple anatomical and procedural terms.

ICD•10•PCS Organization

The developers of ICD•10•PCS resolved problems inherent in the existing procedural coding systems by rewriting the system's salient features. Codes in ICD•10•PCS contain seven alphanumeric characters, and although there are thousands of possible codes, PCS distills all medical services into about 30 procedures. There is no numeric listing of codes. Rather, there are 16 sections filled with tables that determine code selection.

 WORTH NOTING

Nearly half of the medical specialty sections that comprise the first character of ICD•10•PCS remain undesignated. These sections cover broad medical topics, like surgery, chiropractics, mental health, and radiation oncology. In ICD•10•PCS, there is tremendous room for expansion into other medical arenas, like evaluation and management, home health services, or yet-undiscovered technologies.

ICD•10•PCS Index

The index allows codes to be located alphabetically. It is arranged by root operations with subentries by body system, body part, operation, and device. The index also may be consulted for a specific operation term such as hysterectomy, where a cross-reference advises the coder to see "Resection, Female Reproductive System, 0VT." Following is an example of entries in the index:

Fasciectomy - see Resection, Bursa, Ligaments, Fascia 0MB.
Fasciectomy - see Excision, Bursa, Ligaments, Fascia 0MT
Fascioplasty - see Repair, Bursa, Ligaments, Fascia 0MG
Fine Needle Aspiration - see Excision
Fix - see Repair
Flushing - see Irrigation
Formation - see Creation
Fragmentation
  by Body System
    Anatomical Regions 0XF
    Central Nervous System 00F
    Eye 08F
    Female Reproductive System 0VF
    Gastrointestinal System 0DF
    Heart & Great Vessels 02F
    Hepatobiliary Sytem & Pancreas 0FF
    Mouth & Throat 0CF
    Respiratory System 0BF
    Urinary Sytem 0TF
      by Body Part
        Ampulla of Vater 0FFB
        Anus 0DFQ
        Appendix 0DFJ
        Bladder 0TF8
        Bladder Neck 0TF9
        Bronchus
          Lingula 0BF9
          Lower Lobe 0BF
          Main 0BF
          Middle Lobe, Right 0BF5
          Segmental, Lingula 0BF9
          Upper Lobe 0BF

Table of Codes

Each character in each place has a specific meaning. Each code must include characters in each position. The first character identifies what type of procedure is being reported. The letter "z" is used to indicate that the character is not applicable for a specific procedure. The final draft of the ICD•10•PCS provides the following choices for first character designation:

Sections

      0   Medical and Surgical
      1   Obstetrics

 KEY POINT

The letters I and O are not used in ICD•10•PCS, so that confusion with numbers 1 and 0 can be eliminated. Therefore, each place in a seven-character ICD•10•PCS code could have any of 34 values (numbers 0-9, or any of 24 letters). This is an enormous advantage over any code systems that are strictly numeric.

2   Placement
3   Administration
4   Measurement and Monitoring
5   Imaging
6   Nuclear Medicine
7   Radiation Oncology
8   Osteopathic
9   Rehabilitation and Diagnostic Audiology
B   Extracorporeal Assistance and Performance
C   Extracorporeal Therapies
D   Laboratory
F   Mental Health
G   Chiropractic
H   Miscellaneous

Each subsequent place in the code has a specific function. The meaning of each place in a code may differ from one section to another. Thus, the fifth character in the imaging section (5) identifies the contrast material used, while the fifth character in the medical and surgical section (1) identifies the surgical approach.

For example, the seven characters for "Medical and Surgical" codes are organized as follows:

1	2	3	4	5	6	7
Section	Body System	Root Operation	Body Part	Approach	Device	Qualifier

The seven characters for "Imaging" codes are organized as follows:

1	2	3	4	5	6	7
Section	Body System	Root Types	Body Part	Contrast Qualifier	Contrast/	Qualifier/

The characters for "Extracorporeal Assistance and Performance" codes are organized as follows:

1	2	3	4	5	6	7
Section	Physiological System	Root Operation	Body System	Duration	Function	Qualifier

Medical and Surgical Section

The key to the second characters of the section, "Medical and Surgical" is as follows:

0   Central Nervous System
1   Peripheral Nervous System
2   Heart and Great Vessels
3   Upper Arteries
4   Lower Arteries
5   Upper Veins
6   Lower Veins
7   Lymphatic and Hemic System
8   Eye

KEY POINT

The second character identifies the body system in all sections except "Rehabilitation" and "Mental Health." In those sections, the second character identifies the type of procedure performed.

The third character identifies the root operation, except in "Radiation Oncology," "Rehabilitation," and "Mental Health." In many sections, only a few root operations are performed and these operations are defined for use in that section (i.e., irrigation in the section, "Administration"). The section, "Medical and Surgical," however, uses an extensive list of root operations. The sections, "Obstetrics" and "Placement" also use some of these root operations in addition to section-specific root operations.

9	Ear, Nose, Sinus
B	Respiratory System
C	Mouth and Throat
D	Gastrointestinal System
F	Hepatobiliary System and Pancreas
G	Endocrine System
H	Skin and Breast
J	Subcutaneous Tissue
K	Muscles
L	Tendons
M	Bursa, Ligaments, Fascia
N	Head and Facial Bones
P	Upper Bones
Q	Lower Bones
R	Upper Joints
S	Lower Joints
T	Urinary System
V	Female Reproductive System
W	Male Reproductive System
X	Anatomical Regions
Y	Upper Extremities
Z	Lower Extremities

The third character in the section, "Medical Surgical" represents the root operation, which specifies the underlying objective of the procedure (e.g., bypass). There are 30 root operations in the medical and surgical section. Each root operation is given a precise definition. The root operation characters are consistent through all body systems.

The fourth character indicates the specific part of the body system on which the procedure was performed (e.g., appendix). Body parts are not to be equated with organs. For example, the upper, middle, and lower esophagus are three body parts, and each can be excised or resected. The body part includes lesions, polyps, etc. found in/on the body part.

The fifth character indicates the approach used to perform the procedure (e.g., open). The approach characters are consistent through all body systems. There are 13 different approaches.

The sixth character indicates whether any device was used in the procedure (e.g., synthetic substitute). This character is used to specify only devices that remain after the procedure is completed.

The seventh character is a qualifier that has a unique meaning for individual procedures. Examples of qualifiers include:

- Type of transplant
- Second site for a transplant
- Second site for a bypass
- Original procedure in a revision
- Type of fluid taken out during a drainage

Imaging Section

The root procedure and definitions for imaging are represented by the third character. Some examples are:

- Plain radiography planar display of an image developed from the capture of external ionizing radiation on photographic or photoconductive plate
- Fluoroscopy single plane or bi-plane real time display of an image developed from the capture of external ionizing radiation on fluorescent screen. The image may also be stored by either digital or analog means
- Computerized Tomography (CT Scan)
- Computer reformatted digital display of multiplanar images developed from the capture of multiple exposures of external ionizing radiation
- Magnetic Resonance Imaging (MRI)
- Computer reformatted digital display of multiplanar images developed from the capture of radio frequency signals emitted by nuclei in a body site excited within a magnetic field
- Ultrasonography
- Real time display of images of anatomy or flow information developed from the capture of reflected and attenuated high frequency sound waves

Body parts are further specified in the fourth character.

The fifth character specifies the type of contrast material used in the imaging procedures. Contrast is differentiated by the concentration of the contrast material (high or low osmolar). The specific contrast is specified when the concentration of the contrast is not relevant.

The sixth character provides either further detail about the contrast material, such as the route of administration (e.g., IV, direct, via colostomy), or contains a qualifier specific to the root type of imaging procedure, such as portable for plain radiography procedures.

The seventh character is a qualifier that has a unique meaning for individual imaging procedures. Qualifiers include:

- Cine evaluation
- Plain film subtraction
- Guidance for invasive procedures
- 3D reconstruction
- Type of views (AP/PA, decubitus, limited)
- Foreign body localization
- Tomography, one or multiple planes

Medical and Surgical Root Procedures

The following is the key to procedures reported as the third character in the medical and surgical section of ICD•10•PCS. The official description for ICD•10•PCS follows, along with some examples in parentheses of appropriate services reported under each defined procedure.

1. Alteration: Modifying the natural anatomical structure of a body part without affecting the function of the body part (facelift or breast augmentation)

2. Bypass: Altering the route of passage of the contents of a tubular body part (gastrojejunal bypass or coronary artery bypass)

3. Change: Taking out or off a device from a body part and putting back an identical or similar device in or on the same body part without cutting or puncturing the skin or a mucous membrane (recasting a fracture or replacing an ostomy tube)

4. Control: Stopping, or attempting to stop, postprocedural bleeding (control of bleeding following tonsillectomy)

5. Creation: Making a new structure that does not physically take the place of a body part (sex change operation)

6. Destruction: Eradicating all or a portion of a body part (crush fallopian tube or fulgurate rectal polyps)

7. Detachment: Cutting off all or a portion of an extremity (amputation of foot or partial penectomy)

8. Dilation: Expanding the orifice or the lumen of a tubular body part (tracheal or urethral dilation)

9. Division: Separating, without taking out, all or a portion of a body part (nerve division)

10. Drainage: Taking or letting out fluids and/or gases from a body part (I&D of abscess, arthrocentesis, or\ thoracentesis)

11. Excision: Cutting out or off, without replacement, a portion of a body part (wedge ostectomy, partial nephrectomy, pulmonary segmentectomy)

12. Extirpation: Taking or cutting out solid matter from a body part (sequestrectomy or cholelithotomy)

13. Extraction: Taking out or off all or a portion of a body part (vein stripping, tooth extraction, phrenic nerve avulsion, or dermabrasion)

14. Fragmentation: Breaking down solid matter in a body part (lithotripsy)

15. Fusion: Joining together portions of an articular body part rendering the articular body part immobile (spinal fusion, ankle arthrodesis)

16. Insertion: Putting in a nonbiological appliance that monitors, assists, performs, or prevents a physiological function, but does not physically take the place of a body part (pacemaker insertion)

17. Inspection: Visually and/or manually exploring a body part (diagnostic arthroscopy or exploratory laparotomy)

18. Map: Locating the route of passage of electrical impulses and/or locating functional areas in a body part (mapping cardiac conduction pathways, local cortical areas)

19. Occlusion: Completely closing the orifice or lumen of a tubular body part (ligation of vas deferens or ligation of fallopian tube)

20. Reattachment: Putting back in or on all or a portion of a body part (replant parathyroid, reattach amputated finger, or reattach severed kidney)

21. Release: Freeing a body part (lysis of peritoneal adhesions or freeing the median nerve)

22. Removal: Taking out or off a device from a body part (pacemaker removal or stent removal)

23. Repair: Restoring to the extent possible, a body part to its natural anatomic structure (tracheoplasty, suture laceration, herniorrhaphy or repair of episiotomy)

24. Replacement: Putting in or on a biological or synthetic material that physically takes the place of all or a portion of a body part (total knee replacement, intraocular lens insertion)

25. Reposition: Moving to its normal location or other suitable location all or a portion of a body part (position undescended testicle or reposition aberrant kidney)

26. Resection: Cutting out or off, without replacement, all of a body part (cholecystectomy or total gastrectomy)

27. Restriction: Partially closing the orifice or lumen of a tubular body part (fundoplication or cervical cerclage)

28. Revision: Correcting a portion of a previously performed procedure (revision of hip replacement, strabismus surgery, or gastroenterostomy)

29. Transfer: Moving, without taking out, all or a portion of a body part to another location to take over the function of all or a portion of a body part (nerve transfer or tendon transfer)

30. Transplantation: Putting in or on all or a portion of a living body part taken from another individual or animal to physically take the place and/or function of all or a portion of a similar body part (lung, kidney, or heart transplant)

It's important to note that the definitions in ICD•10•PCS do not always mirror the language of the medical record. There is no use of Latin terminology or eponyms. This poses some challenges for coders, and will demand a much higher level of anatomic literacy and understanding of procedural terminology from coders, along with a resolve to be more concise and detailed in documentation by physicians.

ICD•10•PCS Tabular List

In ICD•10•PCS, a separate table is created for each possible combination of the first three characters of a code. For each body system, the Tabular List begins with a listing of the operations performed (i.e., the root operations). When a procedure involves distinct parts, multiple codes are provided. Following is a listing from the section of the operations performed for the central nervous system:

- Bypass
- Change
- Destruction
- Division
- Drainage
- Excision

The Tabular List for each body system also includes a listing of the body parts, approaches, devices, and qualifiers for that system. Each root operation in the body system follows these listings. At the top of each of the tables is the name of the section, body system, and root operation, as well as the definition of the root operation. The list is formatted as a grid with rows and columns. The four columns in

WORTH NOTING

An example of the complex language issues of ICD•10•PCS is the use of the terms, "excision" and "resection." In CPT and in common medical documentation, "excision" can report the removal of a part, or all, of an organ. The term is sometimes used interchangeably with "resection." Coders may find themselves in a quandary when using ICD•10•PCS, because ICD•10•PCS defines an "excision" as removal of "a part" of an organ, and "resection" as removal of the whole organ. While the medical record may report the "excision" of a hot appendix, the appropriate code would report the "resection" of a hot appendix. Physicians will need to familiarize themselves with the procedural definitions of ICD•10•PCS to reduce confusion.

the grid represent the last four characters of the code (which are labeled, "Body Part," "Approach," "Device," and "Qualifier" for the obstetrics and medical surgical sections). Each row in the grid specifies the allowable combinations of the last four characters. For example, following is the table that would be referenced to determine the correct code for the fragmentation of calculus in the left renal pelvis.

0: Medical and surgical	T: Urinary system	F: Fragmentation	
Body Part Character 4	Approach Character 5	Device Character 6	Qualifier Character 7
3 Kidney pelvis, right	0 open	Z none	Z none
4 Kidney pelvis, left	1 open intraluminal		

OTF Rubic

0: Medical and surgical	T: Urinary system	F: Fragmentation	
Body Part Character 4	Approach Character 5	Device Character 6	Qualifier Character 7
3 Kidney pelvis, right	0 open	Z none	Z none
4 Kidney pelvis, left	1 open intraluminal		
5 Ureter, right	2 open intraluminal endoscopic		
6 Ureter, left	3 percutaneous		
8 Bladder	4 percutaneous endoscopic		
9 Bladder neck	5 percutaneous intraluminal		
B Urethra	6 percutaneous intraluminal endoscopic		
	7 transorifice intraluminal		
	8 transorifice intraluminal endoscopic		
	Z none		

ICD•10•PCS was endorsed in September by the subcommittee on coding standards of the National Committee on Vital and Health Statistics. It is up to the full committee to endorse the system, which could then be adopted by the Secretary of Health and Human Services and as a HIPAA standard. It is unlikely that ICD•10•PCS could be implemented before October 2005, and unknown whether it would be implemented concurrent to ICD•10•CM implementation. In the initial years of ICD•10•PCS implementation, facility payment would by facilitated by mapping ICD•10•PCS and ICD•10•CM diagnostic codes to ICD•9•CM diagnostic and procedural codes, for the selection of the diagnosis related group (DRG) that determines payment. It is expected that once ICD•10•PCS and ICD•10•CM have been producing sufficient data for comprehensive analysis of fees, a new payment methodology using ICD•10•CM and ICD•10•PCS to determine DRGs would be established.

CPT

ICD•10•PCS was developed to complement ICD•10•CM in the inpatient arena, but is vastly different from CPT in terms of its design, intent, structure, and maintenance. The five-digit coding system has been undergoing some minor revisions in past years as the AMA works to maintain CPT's relevance in an increasingly demanding world. Michael Beebe, project director over CPT at the AMA, wrote in the Journal of AHIMA:

In the past, CPT has been used primarily as a billing and administrative code set. This is both a strength and a weakness as it moves forward as a national standard code set for physician services. With its foundation in billing and administration, CPT has developed into a working terminology that describes services as they are performed by the clinician. Also, the code set has a broad user base with well-understood and generally accepted coding conventions. However, other code sets claim greater clinical relevance, specificity, and methodological rigor.

With the elimination of local codes under HIPAA and the increased integration of CPT with clinical and administrative computer systems, greater demands will be placed on CPT beyond billing and administration. CPT must evolve to meet the challenges presented by changes in medical practice and its status as a standard national code set.

SUMMARY

Advances in medicine, technology, and electronic transmission of information prompted the National Committee of Vital Health Statistics to admit that the health care industry was operating with "structurally flawed and wastefully redundant procedural codes sets." Public criticism from the health care industry echoed the concern, which was ultimately resolved with a legislative prerogative for a singular procedural coding system to replace ICD•9•CM Volume 3 and CPT-4.

Two organizations, which had anticipated the ultimatum, moved ahead in earnest to develop the preeminent system. CMS, the federal agency that administers the public health programs, contracted with an organization to develop a system, as required by the protocol of the Department of Health and Human Services. The AMA ran headlong into a process to develop a system that would maintain the organization's hold on procedural coding. While the former, ICD•10•PCS, has been tested and revised according to coders' concerns, the other, CPT-5, is being implemented through the existing CPT process. However, neither system has been approved as the definitive procedural coding system, as mandated by the Health Insurance Portability and Accountability Act of 1996.

In the interim, CPT has been selected as the national standard for reporting medical services and procedures. As a result, the AMA is moving forward to improve the electronic capabilities of CPT and modifying the current system to meet the pressing demands of the health care industry. While we can say change is coming, no one, as yet, can say which system will become the industry standard, or how soon the conversion will take place.

DISCUSSION QUESTIONS

1. Describe the legislation affecting procedural coding.

   _____

   _____

   _____

2. What is a "smart code" system and what are its benefits?

   _____

   _____

   _____

3. Describe the AMA's proposed changes to CPT-5, as compared to CPT-4.

   _____

   _____

   _____

4. How do ICD•10•PCS and CPT-5 accommodate new technologies?

   _____

   _____

   _____

6 National Standards

HEALTH INSURANCE PORTABILITY AND ACCOUNTABILITY ACT OF 1996

Provisions to set standards for patient privacy, data security, electronic transactions, and other administrative simplification issues were adopted by Congress as part of the Health Insurance Portability and Accountability Act of 1996 (HIPAA), Public Law 104-191, which was enacted on August 21, 1996. The original intent of the administrative simplification provisions of HIPAA was to develop a single set of standards for the transmission of electronic data to effectively promote widespread reliance on these electronic transactions. From that original intent, HIPAA and its administrative simplification have grown to become much more than that, and will have a significant effect on the way the health care industry uses and transmits data.

Standards of Administrative Simplification

Two years after HIPAA won congressional approval, the secretary of the Department of Health and Human Services began releasing Notices of Proposed Rulemaking (NPRM) regarding various standards pertaining to administrative simplification provisions. Many of these NPRMs have now become final rules, and include the following:

- Standards for Electronic Transactions and Code Sets (issued August 17, 2000)
- Standards for Privacy of Individually Identifiable Health Information (issued December 28, 2000, modified August 14, 2002)
- National Standard Unique Employer Identifier (issued May 31, 2002)

In addition, the administrative simplification provisions include several other standards that have not been finalized to date, including:

- Standards for security and electronic signatures (proposed rule published August 12, 1998)
- Unique identifiers for individuals (which has been since postponed indefinitely due to privacy concerns)
- National Standard Health Care Provider Identifier (proposed rule published May 7, 1998)

FINAL RULE – STANDARDS FOR ELECTRONIC TRANSACTIONS AND CODE SETS

A final rule published in the August 17, 2000 Federal Register acted on the standards of electronic health care transactions, as well as established the medical data sets (code sets) that are suitable for use in electronic transactions. Compliance with this rule is required by October 16, 2002. Small health plans were given until October 16, 2003. In May 2002, Congress adopted a law known as the Administrative Simplification Compliance Act, Public Law 107-105, which allows for a one-year extension in the

KEY POINT

National standards for electronic health care transactions are meant to encourage electronic commerce in the health care industry and simplify the processes involved. The anticipated results of a standardized system include savings from the reduction in the administrative burdens of Medicare, Medicaid, and the State Children's Health Insurance Plan on health care providers and health plans. All private sector health plans and government health plans, all health care clearinghouses, and all health care providers must use the standards for electronic transactions when conducting any of the defined transactions covered under the HIPAA. A health care clearinghouse may accept nonstandard transactions from health care providers for translating and sending. The Department of Health and Human Services (HHS) can impose penalties of not more than $100 for each violation of the standard, except that the total amount imposed on any one person in each calendar year may not exceed $25,000 for violations of one requirement. Enforcement procedures will be published in a future regulation. Public Law 107-105, the Administrative Simplification Compliance Act, requires all affected entities to either be in compliance with the rules, or file a timely compliance plan. Failure to comply with this law can result in exclusion from federal health care programs.

DEFINITION

Code set. Any set of codes used for encoding data elements, such as tables of terms, medical concepts, medical diagnosis codes, or medical procedure codes. A code set includes both the codes and the descriptors that accompany the codes.

Covered entity. Any health plan, health care clearinghouse, or health care provider who transmits any health information in electronic form in connection with a HIPAA transaction.

Electronic Data Interchange (EDI). The electronic transfer of information, such as electronic media health claims, in a standard format that is fast and cost effective. Currently there are about 400 formats for electronic health claims being used in the United States. The lack of standardization makes it difficult and expensive to develop and maintain software.

Health Insurance Portability and Accountability Act of 1996 (HIPAA). Amends the Internal Revenue Code of 1986 to improve portability and continuity of health insurance coverage in the group and individual markets. Among its many provisions, HIPAA addresses improved access to long-term care services and coverage, and simplifies the administration of health insurance.

KEY POINT

Cost estimates for long-term expenses due to electronic transmission are expected to be negligible since the majority of costs are one-time costs related to implementation. There are on-going costs associated with administrative simplification, such as subscribing to or purchasing documentation and implementation specifications related to code sets and standard formats, and obtaining current health plan and health care provider identifier directories or data files.

HIPAA required standards to be developed, when possible, by private sector organizations accredited by the American National Standards Institute (ANSI). These are not government agencies and all standards are from the Accredited Standards Committee (ASC) X12N except the standards for retail pharmacy transactions, which are from the National Council for Prescription Drug Programs (NCPDP).

compliance date for covered entities filing a timely compliance plan with the Centers for Medicare and Medicaid Services (CMS, formerly HCFA). Small health plans are not eligible for the extension.

Standards for Electronic Transactions

The final rule lists the following summary of formats acceptable for electronic transactions, selected on the basis of 10 guiding principles that were used to designate a standard as a HIPAA standard. Some of these standards may be altered based on two National Proposed Rule Makings (NPRMs) that were issued on May 31, 2002. These NPRMs are still awaiting finalization.

Retail Pharmacy Specifications

Health care providers that submit retail pharmacy claims, and health care plans that process retail pharmacy claims, currently use the National Council for Prescription Drug Programs (NCPDP) format. The NCPDP claim and equivalent encounter is used either in online interactive or batch mode. Since all pharmacy health care providers and health plans use the NCPDP claim format, there are no specific impacts to health care providers.

ASC X12N 837 for Submission of Institutional Health Care Claims, Professional Health Care Claims, Dental Claims, and Coordination of Benefits

All health care providers and health plans are required to use the ASC X12N 837 for submitting electronic health care claims (hospital, physician/supplier, and dental), and have the option of using a health care clearinghouse to satisfy the HIPAA standard requirements. The ASC X12N 837 was selected as the standard for the institutional (hospital, nursing facilities, and similar inpatient institutions) claim and will replace the UB-92 Format developed by CMS for Medicare claims.

ASC X12N 835 for Receipt of Health Care Remittance

Health care providers that conduct EDI with health plans and that do not change their internal systems will have to convert the ASC X12N 835 transactions received from health plans into a format compatible with their internal systems, either by using a translator or a health care clearinghouse. Health plans that want to transmit remittance advice directly to health care providers and that do not use the ASC X12N 835 will also incur costs to convert to the standard.

ASC X12N 276/277 for Health Care Claim Status/Response

Most health care providers that are currently using an electronic format for claim status inquiries may request claim status electronically using the ASC X12N 276/277. After implementation, health care providers will be able to request and receive the status of claims in one standard format from all health care plans. Health plans that do not currently directly accept electronic claim status requests and do not directly send electronic claims status responses will have to modify their systems to accept the ASC X12N 276 and to send the ASC X12N 277. No disruptions in claims processing or payment should occur.

ASC X12N 834 for Benefit Enrollment and Maintenance in a Health Plan

Employers may use the ASC X12N 834 to electronically enroll or disenroll its subscribers into or out of a health plan. Currently, most small and medium size employers and other sponsors conduct subscriber enrollments using paper forms. In addition, the ASC X12N 834 supports detailed enrollment information on the subscriber's dependents, which is often lacking in current practice.

ASC X12N 270/271 for Eligibility for a Health Plan

The ASC X12N 270/271 transaction may be used by a health care provider to electronically request and receive eligibility information from a health care plan prior to providing or billing for a dental, professional, or institutional health care service.

ASC X12N 820 for Payroll Deducted and Other Group Premium Payment for Insurance Product

An employer can respond to a bill by using the ASC X12N 820 to electronically transmit a remittance notice and payment for health insurance premiums. Payment may be by paper check or an electronic funds transfer transaction. The ASC X12N 820 can be sent with electronic funds transfer instructions that are routed directly to the Federal Reserve System's automated health care clearinghouses or with payments generated directly by the employer's or other sponsor's bank.

ASC X12N 278 for Referral Certification and Authorization

A health care provider may use the ASC X12N 278 to electronically request and receive authorization for a health care service from a health plan prior to providing a health care service.

Code Sets

In order to be designated as a HIPAA code set, the criteria must be met. According to the Federal Register 63, no. 88, May 7, 1998, a code set must do the following:

- Improve the efficiency and effectiveness of the health care system by leading to cost reductions for or improvements in benefits from electronic health care transactions
- Meet the needs of the user community, especially providers, health plans, and clearinghouses
- Be consistent and uniform with other HIPAA standards in data element definitions and privacy requirement
- Have low additional development and implementation costs relative to benefits of using the standard
- Be supported by an ANSI-accredited standards organization or other organization
- Be timely in development, testing, implementation, and updating
- Be technologically independent of computer platforms and transmission protocols
- Be precise, simple, and unambiguous
- Be efficient in terms of paper work burdens on users
- Incorporate flexibility to adapt to change in health care industry infrastructure and information technology

When conducting standard transactions as discussed above, the code sets that have been adopted as the standard medical data code sets are to be used. As new code sets become available, such as ICD•10•CM, and are adequately tested and revised, they may be considered for inclusion in the list of standard medical code sets. This is a decision that would be weighed by the Designated Standard Maintenance

Organization and the National Committee on Vital and Health Statistics, and presented to the secretary for the Department of Health and Human Services. It would then be submitted through the NPRM process for public comment, and all affected entities would have a minimum of 24 months to become compliant with the new code set once a change becomes final. Following are the code sets as adopted in the August 17, 2000 Federal Register:

- International Classification of Diseases, 9th Edition, Clinical Modification, (ICD•9•CM), Volumes 1 and 2 (including The Official ICD•9•CM Guidelines for Coding and Reporting), as updated and distributed by HHS, for the following conditions:

    1. Diseases

    2. Injuries

    3. Impairments

    4. Other health related problems and their manifestations

    5. Causes of injury, disease, impairment, or other health-related problems

- International Classification of Diseases, 9th Edition, Clinical Modification, (ICD•9•CM), Volume 3 Procedures (including The Official ICD•9•CM Guidelines for Coding and Reporting), as updated and distributed by HHS, for the following procedures or other actions taken for diseases, injuries, and impairments on hospital inpatients reported by hospitals:

    1. Prevention

    2. Diagnosis

    3. Treatment

    4. Management

- National Drug Codes (NDC), as updated and distributed by HHS, in collaboration with drug manufacturers, for the following:

    1. Drugs

    2. Biologics

        Note: It has been proposed in an NPRM dated May 31, 2002 that the use of National Drug Codes as the standard medical code set for reporting drugs and biologics in all standard transactions be repealed. NDC codes will continue to be used in retail pharmacy transactions, per the NCPDP claim format. This change is still in proposed form, but would eliminate the required use of NDC codes by health plans, care providers, and clearinghouses not involved in retail pharmacy transactions. These covered entities could use HCPCS codes in place of the NDC code. See below for further information on HCPCS codes.

- Code on Dental Procedures and Nomenclature, as updated and distributed by the American Dental Association, for dental services.

- The combination of Healthcare Common Procedure Coding System (HCPCS), as updated and distributed by HHS, and *Physician's Current Procedural Terminology*, Fourth Edition (CPT), as updated and distributed by the American Medical Association, for physician services and other health related services. These services include, but are not limited to, the following:

 FOR MORE INFO

The implementation guides for the ASC X12N standards are available from the Washington Publishing Company, PMB 161, 5284 Randolph Road, Rockville, MD, 20852-2116; telephone: 301-949-9740; FAX: 301-949-9742. These guides are also available at no cost through the Washington Publishing Company on the Internet at http://www.wpc-edi.com/hipaa/. The implementation guide for retail pharmacy standards is available from the National Council for Prescription Drug Programs, 9240 East Raintree Drive, Scottsdale, AZ, 85260-7518; telephone: 480-477-1000; FAX: 480-767-1042. It is also available from the NCPDP's website at http://www.ncpdp.org.

1. Physician services

2. Physical and occupational therapy services

3. Radiological procedures

4. Clinical laboratory tests

5. Other medical diagnostic procedures

6. Hearing and vision services

7. Transportation services including ambulance

- The Healthcare Common Procedure Coding System (HCPCS), as updated and distributed by CMSHHS, for all other substances, equipment, supplies, or other items used in health care services. These items include, but are not limited to, the following:

   1. Medical supplies

   2. Orthotic and prosthetic devices

   3. Durable medical equipment

      Note: A proposed rule published May 31, 2002, would make HCPCS codes available for use with drugs and biologics to health plans, care providers, and clearinghouses not involved in retail pharmacy transactions. Under this proposal, there would be no standard medical data code set for drugs and biologics, except in retail pharmacy transactions. It is expected that most health care providers will continue to make use of the above-mentioned HCPCS codes.

All local codes will be eliminated. Users that need additional codes must apply to the appropriate organizations (e.g., CMS for HCPCS codes, the AMA for CPT codes) for national codes.

STANDARDS FOR PRIVACY OF INDIVIDUALLY IDENTIFIABLE HEALTH INFORMATION

HIPAA gave Congress until August 21, 1999, to pass health privacy legislation. However, after three years went by without an act of Congress, HHS used the authority granted by HIPAA regulations to develop privacy protections. The final rule published in December 2000 (Federal Register) covers health plans, health care clearinghouses, and those health care providers who conduct certain financial and administrative transactions. The regulations protect all medical records and other identifiable health information held by a covered entity, whether communicated electronically, on paper, or orally. The privacy regulations were effective on April 14, 2001, but most covered entities have until April 14, 2003, to become fully compliant. Several modifications to the final privacy rule were made final on August 14, 2002.

The fundamental purpose of the privacy rule is to set a federal "floor" of basic protections to prevent those who do not need identifiable health information from accessing or using it for purposes never intended or known by the individual who is the subject of that information. It affords certain rights to patients regarding the use of their information, and gives patients the right to file a complaint about any perceived violation of the privacy rule. It also provides covered entities with the ability to use protected health information for treatment, payment, and health care operations, provided that entity has made a good faith effort to notify the patient about these uses.

STANDARD UNIQUE EMPLOYER IDENTIFIER

This rule adopts the use of the employer identification number (EIN) as assigned by the Internal Revenue Service as a standard identifier for employers in standard transactions. The use of this identifier mainly applies to employers as sponsors of health insurance for employees, and would be used in electronic transactions to enroll employees in a health plan (or remove employees) or make premium payments to health plans on behalf of their employees. Health care providers would only be required to use it on a situational basis, such as with X12N 270/271 eligibility transactions when the employer is the holder of that information.

STANDARDS AWAITING FINAL RULES

Several provisions still remain waiting to be resolved by final rule at the time of this publication, most notably provisions for data security.

Standards for Security and Electronic Signatures

An NPRM regarding data security and electronic signatures was published on August 12, 1998. The purpose of the security standards is to address the steps that must be taken by a covered entity to prevent the unintentional disclosure, destruction, or corruption of personal health information maintained or transmitted by health plans, health care providers, and health care clearinghouses. It includes administrative procedures, physical safeguards, technical security services, and technical security mechanisms. A final rule on the security portion is expected in the fourth quarter of 2002. Due to a lack of consensus regarding the standardization of electronic signatures, it is expected that this section will be dropped from the final security rule, and a separate new NPRM will be filed.

National Standard Health Care Provider Identifier (NPI)

The NPI is a proposed 10-position numeric identifier for health care providers submitting claims or conducting other transactions specified by HIPAA. A health care provider is an individual, group, or organization that provides medical or other health services or supplies. This includes physicians and other practitioners, physician/practitioner groups, institutions such as hospitals, laboratories, and nursing homes, organizations such as health maintenance organizations, and suppliers such as pharmacies and medical supply companies. This rule is expected to simplify the cumbersome process of receiving and administering multiple provider identification numbers.

The proposed rule was published in the Federal Register on May 7, 1998. Public comment ended July 6, 1998. No final rule has been published, though it is expected sometime in the near future.

SUMMARY

The Health Insurance Portability and Accountability Act of 1996 (HIPAA) was established to improve health care coverage in individual and group markets. The

KEY POINT

The privacy regulations provide for a federal minimum standard to be met regarding the protection of individually identifiable health information, which can be preempted by a more stringent state law. Be sure to check the patient privacy laws in your state to determine whether they are more or less stringent than the privacy rule. If they are more stringent than HIPAA, they will be the standard in your state.

administrative simplification provisions of HIPAA apply directly to health providers because of the requirements for electronic transmission of health care information and the related issues, such as the privacy of patient and medical information. In the past five years, final rules in accordance to HIPAA regulations include those establishing formats for electronic transmission, the code sets (diagnostic and procedural) acceptable for electronic transmission, and privacy rules to protect the patient and medical record. Still awaiting final rule are the requirements for security and provider identifiers.

DISCUSSION QUESTIONS

1. List the administrative simplification provisions in HIPAA as they apply to the health care provider.

    _____

    _____

    _____

2. Briefly describe the administrative simplification regulations so far approved by final rule.

    _____

    _____

    _____

3. Who must use the electronic transmission requirements, and when do the requirements go into effect?

    _____

    _____

    _____

4. List the code sets adopted as the standard under administrative simplification provisions.

    _____

    _____

    _____

5. If state and federal patient privacy provisions conflict, which set of regulations will prevail?

    _____

    _____

    _____

7 Documentation

ICD•10•CM is largely a coding system built for the future. Its architecture is of a scale that offers incredible potential for growth to meet the future reporting demands of medical science worldwide.

In creating the clinical modification for ICD•10 in this country, the National Center for Health Statistics (NCHS) has clearly decided the future is already here. The number of diagnostic codes available for use in the ICD•10•CM coding system is larger than the number available in ICD•9•CM by thousands.

This greater level of detail, called "granularity," is good news for the nosologists and government researchers tracking disease in the United States. Don't underestimate the importance of this work; their statistics help drive healthcare reform, research, payment systems, and social programs. The granularity of ICD•10•CM does indeed provide benefits for everyone in our society.

DOCUMENTATION NEEDS

For the coders in the trenches, the drawbacks to the new coding system are obvious: if more detail is to be reported with ICD•10•CM, more detail will be required in the medical records from which the data for coding is extracted. For coders who are already wrangling with daily insufficiencies in documentation, the increased details needed to report ICD•10•CM may seem foreboding.

Let's look at some specific examples of conditions that require more information to code in ICD•10•CM than they did in ICD•9•CM, and the relevant issues that must be specified in documentation.

OBJECTIVES

- Preview examples of documentation requirements for ICD•10•CM
- Learn how increased granularity affects documentation, coding, and the reimbursement cycle.
- Examine how data collection affects outcomes.
- Discuss society's advantage in using a coding system with greater granularity.

DEFINITION

Nosologist. A scientist who studies the classification of diseases.

Example 1

Term	Coding Component	Codes	
Hypertrophy (benign) of Prostate	Specify: without complication with obstruction with hematuria with obstruction and hematuria with other complication	N40.00	Hypertrophy (benign) of prostate without complication
		N40.01	Hypertrophy (benign) of prostate with obstruction
		N40.02	Hypertrophy (benign) of prostate with hematuria
		N40.03	Hypertrophy (benign) of prostate with obstruction and hematuria
		N40.09	Hypertrophy (benign) of prostate with other complication

This information on the prostate is pertinent because under ICD•9•CM, one code, 600.0 Hypertrophy (benign) of prostate, is used to report all of these prostatic hypertrophy conditions, regardless of the presence of blood in urine or an obstruction. Medical staff members must know about the changes in the requirements for choosing a code for benign hypertrophy of the prostate so they can start to make gradual adjustments now in how they document.

In this example, the information listed in the coding component column is information that has not been required under ICD•9•CM, but will be required with ICD•10•CM. You may find that information not essential to choosing the code in ICD•9•CM, but necessary for selecting the code in ICD•10•CM, may already be present in the medical record, such as when the doctor notes that the patient with benign hypertrophy of the prostate also has hematuria.

Example 2

Term	Coding Component	Codes
Pregnancy	With bladder infection, specify trimester: first second third	O23.10 Infections of bladder in pregnancy, unspecified trimester O23.11 Infections of bladder in pregnancy, first trimester O23.12 Infections of bladder in pregnancy, second trimester O23.13 Infections of bladder in pregnancy, third trimester

In this case, the new documentation component required for ICD•10•CM code selection is one that you would already expect to find in the medical record. In ICD•10•CM, code selection in pregnancy includes a trimester component. One would normally expect medical charts to include this data, or it could be derived from the patient's due date.

Also, in ICD•10•CM, laterality must be reported for injuries when laterality applies. For instance, one code reports a subluxation of the right scapula, another reports a subluxation of the left scapula. Typically, a coder should expect to find laterality information in the medical record.

Keep in mind, though, that issues like laterality are not documentation issues for ICD•10•CM alone. Physicians must meet the legal and professional standards for documentation that demand a level of granularity in the medical record.

Example 3

Term	Coding Component	Codes

Decubitus ulcer	Specify site:
	    unspecified part of back
	    left upper back
	    right upper back
	    left lower back
	    right lower back
	    sacral region
	    right buttock
	    left buttock
	    contiguous site of back and buttock
	    other site
	Identify extent of ulcer:
	    limited to skin breakdown
	    exposure of fat layer
	    muscle necrosis
	    bone necrosis
		L89.051 Decubitus ulcer of sacral region limited to breakdown of the skin
		
		L89.052 Decubitus ulcer of sacral region with fat layer exposed
		
		L89.053 Decubitus ulcer of sacral region with necrosis of muscle
		
		L89.054 Decubitus ulcer of sacral region with necrosis of bone
		
		L89.059 Decubitus ulcer of sacral region with unspecified severity

This example shows a case in which information specifying the extent to which the condition has progressed, as well as the site where it is occurring, is necessary for choosing the most appropriate code. This is a big departure from the single code used in ICD•9•CM for decubitus ulcer.

Sometimes the necessary components are not other conditions, complications, or manifestations that the physician may also have documented somewhere in the medical record. In these cases, it becomes especially important to educate medical staff members about the changes in the necessary code components and the documentation requirements for choosing a code. This is also true for conditions that may be classified as different types, or with different nomenclature, such as early or late onset Alzheimer's disease and follicular non-Hodgkin's lymphoma small cleaved cell, mixed small cleaved and large cell, or large cell, as opposed to nodular lymphoma used in ICD•9•CM.

While information about the upcoming changes, given to all medical staff members, is pertinent and important, individual studies that focus on providers' documentation habits and the particular conditions they are likely to report may also be useful in determining areas for improvement.

Holding smaller, focused inservices that cover changes in coding components and documentation requirements for conditions often encountered within certain specialties may be another way to improve documentation.

DOCUMENTATION AND THE REIMBURSEMENT PROCESS

No one will deny that documentation plays an important role in the reimbursement process. The lack of it can create bottlenecks at certain points along the way that delay billing and hence payment. While it may seem that the implementation of ICD•10•CM holds only the disadvantages of slowing down your cycle of payment, there are going to be definite advantages that ICD•10•CM will also bring. Before we look at what those advantages are, let's examine some of the potential scenarios that

 WORTH NOTING

One physician, upon hearing a coder from another clinic complain about her doctor's documentation, offered this anecdote:

"My daughter came home from school yesterday with a report card and all subjects were marked with the grade, 'incomplete.' I scheduled an appointment with the teacher, since my daughter said she had turned in all of her homework and felt the tests were very easy. At the meeting with the teacher, I asked how a student who does such sterling work could be awarded 'incomplete' in every class. The teacher looked me straight in the eye and said, with a bit of a chip on his shoulder, 'You know, I didn't get into teaching to do paper work...'

"Doctors," this physician continued, "could learn a lot from that story. Your job isn't done until your paper work is done."

 CODING AXIOM

Build documentation compliance for physicians into your compliance plan, with provisions for fines or other punitive actions for chronic noncompliance. One New York clinic noted a significant reduction in underdocumentation after a provision for a $100 fine was written into the clinic's compliance plan. The fine was levied at the third documented instance for a documentation mistake (for example, not noting the type of diabetes) found by the same coder. Who were the checks made out to? The coders whose work was hampered by the documentation problems.

may happen while your facility captures the learning curve on documenting with ICD•10•CM requirements.

The reimbursement process functions something like this in its basic format, although your facility or practice may have other steps along the way:

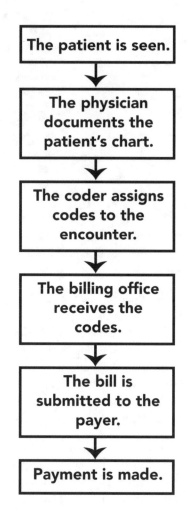

The bottlenecking that can occur because of the increased granularity and documentation requirements of ICD•10•CM is most likely to happen in the early steps. The coder will be the first to recognize that important information is missing. The coder must then query the doctor for more information and the doctor has to ensure that it gets into the medical record before the coding part of the process can proceed.

If the doctor wasn't aware of the components required to assign a code, he or she may not have that information and will have to go back to the patient. Avoiding this last possibility is one of the reasons why disseminating information about ICD•10•CM granularity and the accompanying documentation necessities is so important. By studying the differences in coding components and adjusting documentation habits now, future paperwork bottlenecks can be minimized.

These areas of bottlenecking along the reimbursement process are already very familiar to us now with ICD•9•CM. A certain amount of "documentation chasing" is always going to be in the picture, so it is safe to say that the increase in time until billing that you will experience with the implementation of ICD•10•CM will not remain a constant. As the learning curve is conquered, the time spent on these steps will return to a usual operating level.

Advantages of ICD•10•CM Within the Reimbursement Process

There are also some definite advantages to using ICD•10•CM within the reimbursement cycle that occur at the coding stage and beyond. Since the codes are so much more defined in their subclassification, the coder experiences a reduction in the manual processing time of choosing the codes. Coders are also much more likely to choose the correct code the first time. There is much less ambiguity left open for discussion in ICD•10•CM.

The whole billing process is made much more complicated when "extra documentation" has to be mailed in to clarify the situation. This is hard to do electronically and these extra documents have to be read and manually processed in order for the payer to make a decision. ICD•10•CM generates much less of a problem when it comes to submitting paper because the codes intrinsically paint a clearer and more complete picture of the patient's condition.

This leads us into another advantage of ICD•10•CM that happens at the payer's end. There is much less room for denial based on the diagnosis not matching the procedure for medical necessity. With ICD•10•CM, the diagnosis comes much closer to being "married" to the procedure, and since it gives a more complete description of the condition intrinsically, it leaves a smaller gap for denial.

INCREASED GRANULARITY

When we think about the purposes that a coding system fulfills, it seems that we focus only on the billing and reimbursement function for using codes. The primary reason for creating a coding system that assigns a number to the diagnosis or condition is simply to record and retrieve information in an efficient way. One of the main purposes we use this for is — and always has been — to gather data for research and statistics. The awareness of this purpose seems to have fallen into the background against the daily rush to assign codes for billing third party payers.

Nosologists, medical researchers, and epidemiologists are constantly tracking disease in the United States. Where do they get their data? What are their findings doing for the country? Our coding system with its assigned codes for morbidity cases is how they are able to pull their data, whether they are looking at a certain subpopulation, a specific disease or condition, or procedures performed.

A coding system for documenting and reporting cases allows the researchers, the statisticians, and the epidemiologists to gather the information with which they work. Their statistics and their research findings are very important. They help drive healthcare reform, make decisions about the most effective and appropriate treatments, determine what research to be pursuing, and aid in structuring our social programs concerned with health and well-being. For answering these purposes, increased granularity is a mighty tool.

Understanding these crucial functions of a coding system can assuage some of the apprehension surrounding the implementation of ICD•10•CM and our need for it. How can you know where you are going and make informed, educated decisions for the future if you don't know what's happening? To track what is happening, you need data. Data affects your outcomes. Good data can help change our world. Coders are literally building the database that drives our future every time they choose the codes that are used in painting our statistical pictures and conducting research.

The increased granularity, or in other words, the greater level of detail that ICD•10•CM brings with it gives us the better data that we need and it will lead to better clinical outcomes and more cost-effective disease management, which benefits everyone. ICD•10•CM has the power to begin turning medicine from an art into a science.

Improving Treatment Management

Let's look at how ICD•10•CM can improve the management and treatment of disease for the individual. With ICD•10•CM, the codes provided for diabetic conditions include the manifestation with the type in the code itself. There are separate categories for diabetes due to underlying condition (E08), drug or chemical induced diabetes (E09), gestational diabetes (O24.4-), type I diabetes (E10), and type II diabetes (E11). A code for the current use of insulin is also provided, Z79.7.

A diabetic patient has an accident while traveling and must go to another hospital. The patient's records are faxed for the emergency and the physician treating this new patient can see, according to ICD•10•CM classification, that the patient is a type II diabetic who also has a foot ulcer and does currently use insulin. The doctor is now aware of this before he or she even talks to the patient, and it didn't require reading through hand-written notations to discover if the patient is on insulin or not.

Under ICD•9•CM, another code is needed to identify which manifestation is occurring, and the fifth digit that specifies type II, NIDDM, or noninsulin dependent diabetes mellitus is also used for type II patients who do require insulin. This has always been confusing and doesn't tell the provider looking at the diagnosis whether or not the patient is on insulin.

Establishing Better Clinical Outcomes and Treatment Protocols

ICD•10•CM will not only aid in improving disease management and treatment for all individuals within a certain diagnostic group, but it will help us achieve better treatment protocols that yield better clinical outcomes for future cases. In the race against cancer, for instance, there is an advantage waiting to be exploited for research purposes and better treatment outcomes within the ICD•10•CM system for reporting morbidity. This is especially true when combined with the ICD•10•PCS system for documenting procedures.

With the greater granularity that the detail of ICD•10•CM provides, researchers will be able to study diseases, together with the current treatments being used, on a much finer level. They will begin to see patterns emerging and can track those patterns and outcomes to find the critical connections needed to develop new treatments and speed research.

For example, carcinoma in situ of the breast can be tracked by only one code in ICD•9•CM, 233.0. There are 24 separate codes in the rubric for carcinoma in situ of

WORTH NOTING

The Joint Commission on Accreditation of Healthcare Organizations (JCAHO) has set standards for record-keeping that, if rigorously followed by physicians, would eliminate many of the documentation problems present in the medical record today. Among the elements it requires are the following:

- Progress notes made by medical staff and other authorized staff
- Reports on any diagnostic or therapeutic procedures, such as pathology and clinical laboratory examinations, and radiology and nuclear medicine examinations or treatments
- Medical history
- Impressions and conclusions drawn from history and examination
- Plan for patient care
- Consultation reports
- Final diagnoses
- Discharge instructions

the breast in ICD•10•CM, with axes for lobular, intraductal, other, and unspecified carcinoma, the right or the left breast, and male or female gender. Together with the ICD•10•PCS system for reporting the procedures with greater detail, researchers can track the specific outcomes of the different types of radioactive materials versus surgical procedures used in treating those cases. They may start discovering certain trends that would have been very difficult, if not impossible, to see with less specific data.

Researchers may discover, for instance, that one particular isotope used for treating lobular cancer results in a better response than other isotopes, or the same treatment doesn't yield the same outcome on intraductal carcinoma, or surgical intervention proves more effective than radiation in females; these are only examples of the kinds of trends and patterns that could be discovered when research is done with better data. Data always affects the outcome. When you can marry the procedure to the diagnosis, you get definitive trackable outcomes. This is also why there will be less room for denial on the reimbursement side of using ICD•10•CM to document medical necessity.

Other Advantages of Increased Granularity

We may see other advantages happen from the sidelines with the implementation of ICD•10•CM. For instance, under ICD•9•CM, there is only one code available for reporting Down syndrome, 758.0. There are, in fact, three different types of Down syndrome: nonmosaicism (meiotic nondisjunction), mosaicism (mitotic nondisjunction), and translocation. With ICD•10•CM, the following are the codes to choose from:

Q90.0   **Trisomy 21, nonmosaicism (meiotic nondisjunction)**
Q90.1   **Trisomy 21, mosaicism (mitotic nondisjunction)**
Q90.2   **Trisomy 21, translocation**
Q90.9   **Down syndrome, unspecified**

Once the distinction is made in the clinical coding system, it allows for gathering documented data on a much higher level of detail, and researchers will be using that data; ultimately it may prove to be a catalyst in making genetic testing a standard practice rather than leaving such testing undone, as it currently is in so many cases. This could have far-reaching effects for making all kinds of discoveries. The increased granularity of the ICD•10•CM coding system has many deep and extensive advantages that are worth celebrating.

DISCUSSION QUESTIONS

1. What are some action plans that your facility can use to educate physicians about documentation requirements?

    _____

    _____

    _____

2. How will better documentation habits help the reimbursement process?

    _____

    _____

    _____

3. Explain how the data we use affects the outcome when establishing protocols for treating disease.

    _____

    _____

    _____

4. Evaluate the importance of increased granularity in the data used and the role that granularity plays in shaping the future.

    _____

    _____

    _____

8 ICD•10•CM Three-Digit Categories

CHAPTER 1

Certain Infectious and Parasitic Diseases (A00-B99)

Intestinal Infectious Diseases (A00-A09)

A00	Cholera
A01	Typhoid and paratyphoid fevers
A02	Other salmonella infections
A03	Shigellosis
A04	Other bacterial intestinal infections
A05	Other bacterial foodborne intoxications
A06	Amebiasis
A07	Other protozoal intestinal diseases
A08	Viral and other specified intestinal infections
A09	Infectious gastroenteritis and colitis, unspecified

Tuberculosis (A15-A19)

A15	Respiratory tuberculosis
A17	Tuberculosis of nervous system
A18	Tuberculosis of other organs
A19	Miliary tuberculosis

Certain Zoonotic Bacterial Diseases (A20-A28)

A20	Plague
A21	Tularemia
A22	Anthrax
A23	Brucellosis
A24	Glanders and melioidosis
A25	Rat-bite fevers
A26	Erysipeloid
A27	Leptospirosis
A28	Other zoonotic bacterial diseases, not elsewhere classified

Other Bacterial Diseases (A30-A49)

A30	Leprosy [Hansen's disease]
A31	Infection due to other mycobacteria
A32	Listeriosis
A33	Tetanus neonatorum
A34	Obstetrical tetanus

A35   Other tetanus
A36   Diphtheria
A37   Whooping cough
A38   Scarlet fever
A39   Meningococcal infection
A40   Streptococcal septicemia
A41   Other septicemia
A42   Actinomycosis
A43   Nocardiosis
A44   Bartonellosis
A46   Erysipelas
A48   Other bacterial diseases, not elsewhere classified
A49   Bacterial infection of unspecified site

Infections With A Predominantly Sexual Mode of Transmission (A50-A64)

A50   Congenital syphilis
A51   Early syphilis
A52   Late syphilis
A53   Other and unspecified syphilis
A54   Gonococcal infection
A55   Chlamydial lymphogranuloma (venereum)
A56   Other sexually transmitted chlamydial diseases
A57   Chancroid
A58   Granuloma inguinale
A59   Trichomoniasis
A60   Anogenital herpesviral [herpes simplex] infections
A63   Other predominantly sexually transmitted diseases, not elsewhere classified
A64   Unspecified sexually transmitted disease

Other Spirochetal Diseases (A65-A69)

A65   Nonvenereal syphilis
A66   Yaws
A67   Pinta [carate]
A68   Relapsing fevers
A69   Other spirochetal infections

Other Diseases Caused by Chlamydiae (A70-A74)

A70   Chlamydia psittaci infections
A71   Trachoma
A74   Other diseases caused by chlamydiae

Rickettsioses (A75-A79)

A75   Typhus fever
A77   Spotted fever [tick-borne rickettsioses]
A78   Q fever
A79   Other rickettsioses

Viral Infections of the Central Nervous System (A80-A89)

A80   Acute poliomyelitis

A81   Atypical virus infections of central nervous system
A82   Rabies
A83   Mosquito-borne viral encephalitis
A84   Tick-borne viral encephalitis
A85   Other viral encephalitis, not elsewhere classified
A86   Unspecified viral encephalitis
A87   Viral meningitis
A88   Other viral infections of central nervous system, not elsewhere classified
A89   Unspecified viral infection of central nervous system

Arthropod-borne Viral Fevers and Viral Hemorrhagic Fevers (A90-A99)

A90   Dengue fever [classical dengue]
A91   Dengue hemorrhagic fever
A92   Other mosquito-borne viral fevers
A93   Other arthropod-borne viral fevers, not elsewhere classified
A94   Unspecified arthropod-borne viral fever
A95   Yellow fever
A96   Arenaviral hemorrhagic fever
A98   Other viral hemorrhagic fevers, not elsewhere classified
A99   Unspecified viral hemorrhagic fever

Viral Infections Characterized by Skin and Mucous Membrane Lesions (B00-B09)

B00   Herpesviral [herpes simplex] infections
B01   Varicella [chickenpox]
B02   Zoster [herpes zoster]
B03   Smallpox
B04   Monkeypox
B05   Measles
B06   Rubella [German measles]
B07   Viral warts
B08   Other viral infections characterized by skin and mucous membrane lesions, not elsewhere classified
B09   Unspecified viral infection characterized by skin and mucous membrane lesions

Viral Hepatitis (B15-B19)

B15   Acute hepatitis A
B16   Acute hepatitis B
B17   Other acute viral hepatitis
B18   Chronic viral hepatitis
B19   Unspecified viral hepatitis

Human Immunodeficiency Virus [HIV] Disease (B20)

B20   Human immunodeficiency virus [HIV] disease

Other Viral Diseases (B25-B34)

B25   Cytomegaloviral disease
B26   Mumps

B27   Infectious mononucleosis
B30   Viral conjunctivitis
B33   Other viral diseases, not elsewhere classified
B34   Viral infection of unspecified site

Mycoses (B35-B49)

B35   Dermatophytosis
B36   Other superficial mycoses
B37   Candidiasis
B38   Coccidioidomycosis
B39   Histoplasmosis
B40   Blastomycosis
B41   Paracoccidioidomycosis
B42   Sporotrichosis
B43   Chromomycosis and pheomycotic abscess
B44   Aspergillosis
B45   Cryptococcosis
B46   Zygomycosis
B47   Mycetoma
B48   Other mycoses, not elsewhere classified
B49   Unspecified mycosis

Protozoal Diseases (B50-B64)

B50   Plasmodium falciparum malaria
B51   Plasmodium vivax malaria
B52   Plasmodium malariae malaria
B53   Other specified malaria
B54   Unspecified malaria
B55   Leishmaniasis
B56   African trypanosomiasis
B57   Chagas' disease
B58   Toxoplasmosis
B59   Pneumocystosis
B60   Other protozoal diseases, not elsewhere classified
B64   Unspecified protozoal disease

Helminthiases (B65-B83)

B65   Schistosomiasis [bilharziasis]
B66   Other fluke infections
B67   Echinococcosis
B68   Taeniasis
B69   Cysticercosis
B70   Diphyllobothriasis and sparganosis
B71   Other cestode infections
B72   Dracunculiasis
B73   Onchocerciasis
B74   Filariasis
B75   Trichinellosis
B76   Hookworm diseases
B77   Ascariasis

B78   Strongyloidiasis
B79   Trichuriasis
B80   Enterobiasis
B81   Other intestinal helminthiases, not elsewhere classified
B82   Unspecified intestinal parasitism
B83   Other helminthiases

Pediculosis, Acariasis and Other Infestations (B85-B89)

B85   Pediculosis and phthiriasis
B86   Scabies
B87   Myiasis
B88   Other infestations
B89   Unspecified parasitic disease

Sequelae of Infectious and Parasitic Diseases (B90-B94)

B90   Sequelae of tuberculosis
B91   Sequelae of poliomyelitis
B92   Sequelae of leprosy
B94   Sequelae of other and unspecified infectious and parasitic diseases

Bacterial, Viral and Other Infectious Agents (B95-B97)

B95   Streptococcus, Staphylococcus, and Enterococcus as the cause of diseases classified to other chapters
B96   Other bacterial agents as the cause of diseases classified to other chapters
B97   Viral agents as the cause of diseases classified to other chapters

Other Infectious Diseases (B99)

B99   Other and unspecified infectious diseases

Chapter 2

Neoplasms (C00-D49)

Malignant Neoplasms (C00-C96)

Malignant Neoplasm of Lip, Oral Cavity and Pharynx (C00-C14)

C00   Malignant neoplasm of lip
C01   Malignant neoplasm of base of tongue
C02   Malignant neoplasm of other and unspecified parts of tongue
C03   Malignant neoplasm of gum
C04   Malignant neoplasm of floor of mouth
C05   Malignant neoplasm of palate
C06   Malignant neoplasm of other and unspecified parts of mouth
C07   Malignant neoplasm of parotid gland
C08   Malignant neoplasm of other and unspecified major salivary glands
C09   Malignant neoplasm of tonsil
C10   Malignant neoplasm of oropharynx
C11   Malignant neoplasm of nasopharynx
C12   Malignant neoplasm of pyriform sinus

C13   Malignant neoplasm of hypopharynx

C14   Malignant neoplasm of other and ill-defined sites in the lip, oral cavity and pharynx

Malignant Neoplasm of Digestive Organs (C15-C26)

C15   Malignant neoplasm of esophagus

C16   Malignant neoplasm of stomach

C17   Malignant neoplasm of small intestine

C18   Malignant neoplasm of colon

C19   Malignant neoplasm of rectosigmoid junction

C20   Malignant neoplasm of rectum

C21   Malignant neoplasm of anus and anal canal

C22   Malignant neoplasm of liver and intrahepatic bile ducts

C23   Malignant neoplasm of gallbladder

C24   Malignant neoplasm of other and unspecified parts of biliary tract

C25   Malignant neoplasm of pancreas

C26   Malignant neoplasm of other and ill-defined digestive organs

Malignant Neoplasm of Respiratory and Intrathoracic Organs (C30-C39)

C30   Malignant neoplasm of nasal cavity and middle ear

C31   Malignant neoplasm of accessory sinuses

C32   Malignant neoplasm of larynx

C33   Malignant neoplasm of trachea

C34   Malignant neoplasm of bronchus and lung

C37   Malignant neoplasm of thymus

C38   Malignant neoplasm of heart, mediastinum and pleura

C39   Malignant neoplasm of other and ill-defined sites in the respiratory system and intrathoracic organs

Malignant Neoplasm of Bone and Articular Cartilage (C40-C41)

C40   Malignant neoplasm of bone and articular cartilage of limbs

C41   Malignant neoplasm of bone and articular cartilage of other and unspecified sites

Melanoma and Other Malignant Neoplasms of Skin (C43-C44)

C43   Malignant melanoma of skin

C44   Other malignant neoplasm of skin

Malignant Neoplasms of Mesothelial and Soft Tissue (C45-C49)

C45   Mesothelioma

C46   Kaposi's sarcoma

C47   Malignant neoplasm of peripheral nerves and autonomic nervous system

C48   Malignant neoplasm of retroperitoneum and peritoneum

C49   Malignant neoplasm of other connective and soft tissue

Malignant Neoplasm of Breast (C50)

C50   Malignant neoplasm of breast

Malignant Neoplasm of Female Genital Organs (C51-C58)

C51   Malignant neoplasm of vulva

C52   Malignant neoplasm of vagina
C53   Malignant neoplasm of cervix uteri
C54   Malignant neoplasm of corpus uteri
C55   Malignant neoplasm of uterus, part unspecified
C56   Malignant neoplasm of ovary
C57   Malignant neoplasm of other and unspecified female genital organs
C58   Malignant neoplasm of placenta

Malignant Neoplasms of Male Genital Organs (C60-C63)

C60   Malignant neoplasm of penis
C61   Malignant neoplasm of prostate
C62   Malignant neoplasm of testis
C63   Malignant neoplasm of other and unspecified male genital organs

Malignant Neoplasm of Urinary Tract (C64-C68)

C64   Malignant neoplasm of kidney, except renal pelvis
C65   Malignant neoplasm of renal pelvis
C66   Malignant neoplasm of ureter
C67   Malignant neoplasm of bladder
C68   Malignant neoplasm of other and unspecified urinary organs

Malignant Neoplasms of Eye, Brain and Other Parts of Central Nervous System (C69-C72)

C69   Malignant neoplasm of eye and adnexa
C70   Malignant neoplasm of meninges
C71   Malignant neoplasm of brain
C72   Malignant neoplasm of spinal cord, cranial nerves and other parts of central nervous system

Malignant Neoplasm of Thyroid and Other Endocrine Glands (C73-C75)

C73   Malignant neoplasm of thyroid gland
C74   Malignant neoplasm of adrenal gland
C75   Malignant neoplasm of other endocrine glands and related structures

Malignant Neoplasms of Ill-defined, Secondary and Unspecified Sites (C76-C80)

C76   Malignant neoplasm of other and ill-defined sites
C77   Secondary and unspecified malignant neoplasm of lymph nodes
C78   Secondary malignant neoplasm of respiratory and digestive organs
C79   Secondary malignant neoplasm of other sites
C80   Malignant neoplasm without specification of site

Malignant Neoplasms of Lymphoid, Hematopoietic and Related Tissue (C81-C96)

C81   Hodgkin's disease
C82   Follicular [nodular] non-Hodgkin's lymphoma
C83   Diffuse non-Hodgkin's lymphoma
C84   Peripheral and cutaneous T-cell lymphomas
C85   Other and unspecified types of non-Hodgkin's lymphoma
C88   Malignant immunoproliferative diseases
C90   Multiple myeloma and malignant plasma cell neoplasms
C91   Lymphoid leukemia
C92   Myeloid leukemia

C93 Monocytic leukemia
C94 Other leukemias of specified cell type
C95 Leukemia of unspecified cell type
C96 Other and unspecified malignant neoplasms of lymphoid, hematopoietic and related tissue

In Situ Neoplasms (D00-D09)

D00 Carcinoma in situ of oral cavity, esophagus and stomach
D01 Carcinoma in situ of other and unspecified digestive organs
D02 Carcinoma in situ of middle ear and respiratory system
D03 Melanoma in situ
D04 Carcinoma in situ of skin
D05 Carcinoma in situ of breast
D06 Carcinoma in situ of cervix uteri
D07 Carcinoma in situ of other and unspecified genital organs
D09 Carcinoma in situ of other and unspecified sites

Benign Neoplasms (D10-D36)

D10 Benign neoplasm of mouth and pharynx
D11 Benign neoplasm of major salivary glands
D12 Benign neoplasm of colon, rectum, anus and anal canal
D13 Benign neoplasm of other and ill-defined parts of digestive system
D14 Benign neoplasm of middle ear and respiratory system
D15 Benign neoplasm of other and unspecified intrathoracic organs
D16 Benign neoplasm of bone and articular cartilage
D17 Benign lipomatous neoplasm
D18 Hemangioma and lymphangioma, any site
D19 Benign neoplasm of mesothelial tissue
D20 Benign neoplasm of soft tissue of retroperitoneum and peritoneum
D21 Other benign neoplasms of connective and other soft tissue
D22 Melanocytic nevi
D23 Other benign neoplasms of skin
D24 Benign neoplasm of breast
D25 Leiomyoma of uterus
D26 Other benign neoplasms of uterus
D27 Benign neoplasm of ovary
D28 Benign neoplasm of other and unspecified female genital organs
D29 Benign neoplasm of male genital organs
D30 Benign neoplasm of urinary organs
D31 Benign neoplasm of eye and adnexa
D32 Benign neoplasm of meninges
D33 Benign neoplasm of brain and other parts of central nervous system
D34 Benign neoplasm of thyroid gland
D35 Benign neoplasm of other and unspecified endocrine glands
D36 Benign neoplasm of other and unspecified sites

Neoplasms of Uncertain Behavior (D37-D48)

D37 Neoplasm of uncertain behavior of oral cavity and digestive organs
D38 Neoplasm of uncertain behavior of middle ear and respiratory and intrathoracic organs

D39 Neoplasm of uncertain behavior of female genital organs

D40 Neoplasm of uncertain behavior of male genital organs

D41 Neoplasm of uncertain behavior of urinary organs

D42 Neoplasm of uncertain behavior of meninges

D43 Neoplasm of uncertain behavior of brain and central nervous system

D44 Neoplasm of uncertain behavior of endocrine glands

D45 Polycythemia vera

D46 Myelodysplastic syndromes

D47 Other neoplasms of uncertain behavior of lymphoid, hematopoietic and related tissue

D48 Neoplasm of uncertain behavior of other and unspecified sites

D49 Neoplasms of unspecified behavior

CHAPTER 3

Diseases of the blood and blood-forming organs and certain disorders involving the immune mechanism (D50-D89)

Nutritional Anemias (D50-D53)

D50 Iron deficiency anemia

D51 Vitamin B12 deficiency anemia

D52 Folate deficiency anemia

D53 Other nutritional anemias

Hemolytic Anemias (D55-D59)

D55 Anemia due to enzyme disorders

D56 Thalassemia

D57 Sickle-cell disorders

D58 Other hereditary hemolytic anemias

D59 Acquired hemolytic anemia

Aplastic and Other Anemias (D60-D64)

D60 Acquired pure red cell aplasia [erythroblastopenia]

D61 Other aplastic anemias

D62 Acute posthemorrhagic anemia

D63 Anemia in chronic diseases classified elsewhere

D64 Other anemias

Coagulation Defects, Purpura and Other Hemorrhagic Conditions (D65-D69)

D65 Disseminated intravascular coagulation [defibrination syndrome]

D66 Hereditary factor VIII deficiency

D67 Hereditary factor IX deficiency

D68 Other coagulation defects

D69 Purpura and other hemorrhagic conditions

Other Diseases of Blood and Blood-forming Organs (D70-D78)

D70 Neutropenia

D71 Functional disorders of polymorphonuclear neutrophils

D72 Other disorders of white blood cells

D73 Diseases of spleen

D74 Methemoglobinemia

D75 Other diseases of blood and blood-forming organs

D76 Certain diseases involving lymphoreticular tissue and reticulohistiocytic system

D77 Other disorders of blood and blood-forming organs in diseases classified elsewhere

D78 Intraoperative and postprocedural complications of procedures on the spleen

Certain Disorders Involving the Immune Mechanism (D80-D89)

D80 Immunodeficiency with predominantly antibody defects

D81 Combined immunodeficiencies

D82 Immunodeficiency associated with other major defects

D83 Common variable immunodeficiency

D84 Other immunodeficiencies

D86 Sarcoidosis

D89 Other disorders involving the immune mechanism, not elsewhere classified

CHAPTER 4

Endocrine, nutritional and metabolic diseases (E00-E90)

Disorders of Thyroid Gland (E00-E07)

E00 Congenital iodine-deficiency syndrome

E01 Iodine-deficiency related thyroid disorders and allied conditions

E02 Subclinical iodine-deficiency hypothyroidism

E03 Other hypothyroidism

E04 Other nontoxic goiter

E05 Thyrotoxicosis [hyperthyroidism]

E06 Thyroiditis

E07 Other disorders of thyroid

Diabetes Mellitus (E08-E14)

E08 Diabetes mellitus due to underlying condition

E09 Drug or chemical induced diabetes mellitus

E10 Type I diabetes mellitus

E11 Type II diabetes mellitus

E13 Other specified diabetes mellitus

E14 Unspecified diabetes mellitus

Other Disorders of Glucose Regulation and Pancreatic Internal Secretion (E15-E16)

E15 Nondiabetic hypoglycemic coma

E16 Other disorders of pancreatic internal secretion

Disorders of Other Endocrine Glands (E20-E36)

E20 Hypoparathyroidism

E21 Hyperparathyroidism and other disorders of parathyroid gland

E22   Hyperfunction of pituitary gland
E23   Hypofunction and other disorders of the pituitary gland
E24   Cushing's syndrome
E25   Adrenogenital disorders
E26   Hyperaldosteronism
E27   Other disorders of adrenal gland
E28   Ovarian dysfunction
E29   Testicular dysfunction
E30   Disorders of puberty, not elsewhere classified
E31   Polyglandular dysfunction
E32   Diseases of thymus
E34   Other endocrine disorders
E35   Disorders of endocrine glands in diseases classified elsewhere
E36   Intraoperative and postprocedural complications of endocrine procedures

Malnutrition (E40-E46)

E40   Kwashiorkor
E41   Nutritional marasmus
E42   Marasmic kwashiorkor
E43   Unspecified severe protein-calorie malnutrition
E44   Protein-calorie malnutrition of moderate and mild degree
E45   Retarded development following protein-calorie malnutrition
E46   Unspecified protein-calorie malnutrition

Other Nutritional Deficiencies (E50-E64)

E50   Vitamin A deficiency
E51   Thiamine deficiency
E52   Niacin deficiency [pellagra]
E53   Deficiency of other B group vitamins
E54   Ascorbic acid deficiency
E55   Vitamin D deficiency
E56   Other vitamin deficiencies
E58   Dietary calcium deficiency
E59   Dietary selenium deficiency
E60   Dietary zinc deficiency
E61   Deficiency of other nutrient elements
E63   Other nutritional deficiencies
E64   Sequelae of malnutrition and other nutritional deficiencies

Obesity and Other Hyperalimentation (E65-E68)

E65   Localized adiposity
E66   Obesity
E67   Other hyperalimentation
E68   Sequelae of hyperalimentation

Metabolic Disorders (E70-E90)

E70   Disorders of aromatic amino-acid metabolism
E71   Disorders of branched-chain amino-acid metabolism and fatty-acid metabolism

E72 Other disorders of amino-acid metabolism

E73 Lactose intolerance

E74 Other disorders of carbohydrate metabolism

E75 Disorders of sphingolipid metabolism and other lipid storage disorders

E76 Disorders of glycosaminoglycan metabolism

E77 Disorders of glycoprotein metabolism

E78 Disorders of lipoprotein metabolism and other lipidemias

E79 Disorders of purine and pyrimidine metabolism

E80 Disorders of porphyrin and bilirubin metabolism

E83 Disorders of mineral metabolism

E84 Cystic fibrosis

E85 Amyloidosis

E86 Volume depletion

E87 Other disorders of fluid, electrolyte and acid-base balance

E88 Other and unspecified metabolic disorders

E89 Postprocedural endocrine and metabolic disorders, not elsewhere classified

E90 Nutritional and metabolic disorders in diseases classified elsewhere

Chapter 5

Mental and behavioral disorders (F01-F99)

Mental Disorders Due to Known Physiological Conditions (F01-F09)

F01 Vascular dementia

F02 Dementia in other diseases classified elsewhere

F03 Unspecified dementia

F04 Amnestic disorder due to known physiological condition

F05 Delirium due to known physiological condition

F06 Other mental disorders due to known physiological condition

F07 Personality and behavioral disorders due to known physiological condition

F09 Unspecified mental disorder due to known physiological condition

Mental and Behavioral Disorders Due to Psychoactive Substance Use (F10-F19)

F10 Alcohol-related disorders

F11 Opioid-related disorders

F12 Cannabis-related disorders

F13 Sedative, hypnotic, or anxiolytic-related disorders

F14 Cocaine-related disorders

F15 Other stimulant-related disorders

F16 Hallucinogen-related disorders

F17 Nicotine dependence

F18 Inhalant-related disorders

F19 Other psychoactive substance-related disorders

Schizophrenia, Schizotypal, Delusional, and Other Non-mood Psychotic Disorders (F20-F29)

F20   Schizophrenia
F21   Schizotypal disorder
F22   Delusional disorders
F23   Brief psychotic disorder
F24   Shared psychotic disorder
F25   Schizoaffective disorders
F28   Other psychotic disorder not due to a substance or known physiological condition
F29   Unspecified psychosis not due to a substance or known physiological condition

Mood [Affective] Disorders (F30-F39)

F30   Manic episode
F31   Bipolar disorder
F32   Major depressive disorder, single episode
F33   Major depressive disorder, recurrent
F34   Persistent mood [affective] disorders
F39   Unspecified mood [affective] disorder

Anxiety, Dissociative, Stress-related, Somatoform and Other Nonpsychotic Mental Disorders (F40-F48)

F40   Phobic anxiety disorders
F41   Other anxiety disorders
F42   Obsessive-compulsive disorder
F43   Reaction to severe stress, and adjustment disorders
F44   Dissociative and conversion disorders
F45   Somatoform disorders
F48   Other nonpsychotic mental disorders

Behavioral Syndromes Associated With Physiological Disturbances and Physical Factors (F50-F59)

F50   Eating disorders
F51   Sleep disorders not due to a substance or known physiological condition
F52   Sexual dysfunction not due to a substance or known physiological condition
F53   Puerperal psychosis
F54   Psychological and behavioral factors associated with disorders or diseases classified elsewhere
F55   Abuse of non-psychoactive substances
F59   Unspecified behavioral syndromes associated with physiological disturbances and physical factors

Disorders of Adult Personality and Behavior (F60-F69)

F60   Specific personality disorders
F63   Impulse disorders
F64   Gender identity disorders
F65   Paraphilias

F66   Other sexual disorders

F68   Other disorders of adult personality and behavior

F69   Unspecified disorder of adult personality and behavior

Mental Retardation (F70-F79)

F70   Mild mental retardation

F71   Moderate mental retardation

F72   Severe mental retardation

F73   Profound mental retardation

F78   Other mental retardation

F79   Unspecified mental retardation

Pervasive and Specific Developmental Disorders (F80-F89)

F80   Specific developmental disorders of speech and language

F81   Specific developmental disorders of scholastic skills

F82   Specific developmental disorder of motor function

F84   Pervasive developmental disorders

F88   Other disorders of psychological development

F89   Unspecified disorder of psychological development

Behavioral and Emotional Disorders With Onset Usually Occurring In Childhood and Adolescence (F90-F98)

F90   Attention-deficit hyperactivity disorders

F91   Conduct disorders

F93   Emotional disorders with onset specific to childhood

F94   Disorders of social functioning with onset specific to childhood and adolescence

F95   Tic disorder

F98   Other behavioral and emotional disorders with onset usually occurring in childhood and adolescence

Unspecified Mental Disorder (F99)

F99   Mental disorder, not otherwise specified

CHAPTER 6

Diseases of the nervous system (G00-G99)

Inflammatory Diseases of the Central Nervous System (G00-G09)

G00   Bacterial meningitis, not elsewhere classified

G01   Meningitis in bacterial diseases classified elsewhere

G02   Meningitis in other infectious and parasitic diseases classified elsewhere

G03   Meningitis due to other and unspecified causes

G04   Encephalitis, myelitis and encephalomyelitis

G05   Encephalitis, myelitis and encephalomyelitis in diseases classified elsewhere

G06   Intracranial and intraspinal abscess and granuloma

G07   Intracranial and intraspinal abscess and granuloma in diseases classified elsewhere

G08   Intracranial and intraspinal phlebitis and thrombophlebitis
G09   Sequelae of inflammatory diseases of central nervous system

Systemic Atrophies Primarily Affecting the Central Nervous System (G10-G13)

G10   Huntington's disease
G11   Hereditary ataxia
G12   Spinal muscular atrophy and related syndromes
G13   Systemic atrophies primarily affecting central nervous system in diseases classified elsewhere

Extrapyramidal and Movement Disorders (G20-G26)

G20   Parkinson's disease
G21   Secondary parkinsonism
G22   Parkinsonism in diseases classified elsewhere
G23   Other degenerative diseases of basal ganglia
G24   Dystonia
G25   Other extrapyramidal and movement disorders
G26   Extrapyramidal and movement disorders in diseases classified elsewhere

Other Degenerative Diseases of the Nervous System (G30-G32)

G30   Alzheimer's disease
G31   Other degenerative diseases of nervous system, not elsewhere classified
G32   Other degenerative disorders of nervous system in diseases classified elsewhere

Demyelinating Diseases of the Central Nervous System (G35-G37)

G35   Multiple sclerosis
G36   Other acute disseminated demyelination
G37   Other demyelinating diseases of central nervous system

Episodic and Paroxysmal Disorders (G40-G47)

G40   Epilepsy
G43   Migraine
G44   Other headache syndromes
G45   Transient cerebral ischemic attacks and related syndromes
G46   Vascular syndromes of brain in cerebrovascular diseases
G47   Organic sleep disorders

Nerve, Nerve Root and Plexus Disorders (G50-G59)

G50   Disorders of trigeminal nerve
G51   Facial nerve disorders
G52   Disorders of other cranial nerves
G53   Cranial nerve disorders in diseases classified elsewhere
G54   Nerve root and plexus disorders
G55   Nerve root and plexus compressions in diseases classified elsewhere
G56   Mononeuropathies of upper limb
G57   Mononeuropathies of lower limb

G58   Other mononeuropathies

G59   Mononeuropathy in diseases classified elsewhere

Polyneuropathies and Other Disorders of the Peripheral Nervous System (G60-G65)

G60   Hereditary and idiopathic neuropathy

G61   Inflammatory polyneuropathy

G62   Other and unspecified polyneuropathies

G63   Polyneuropathy in diseases classified elsewhere

G64   Other disorders of peripheral nervous system

G65   Sequelae of inflammatory and toxic polyneuropathies

Diseases of Myoneural Junction and Muscle (G70-G73)

G70   Myasthenia gravis and other myoneural disorders

G71   Primary disorders of muscles

G72   Other and unspecified myopathies

G73   Disorders of myoneural junction and muscle in diseases classified elsewhere

Cerebral Palsy and Other Paralytic Syndromes (G80-G83)

G80   Infantile cerebral palsy

G81   Hemiplegia and hemiparesis

G82   Paraplegia (paraparesis) and Quadriplegia (quadriparesis)

G83   Other paralytic syndromes

Other Disorders of the Nervous System (G90-G99)

G90   Disorders of autonomic nervous system

G91   Hydrocephalus

G92   Toxic encephalopathy

G93   Other disorders of brain

G94   Other disorders of brain in diseases classified elsewhere

G95   Other diseases of spinal cord

G96   Other disorders of central nervous system

G97   Intraoperative and postprocedural complications and disorders of nervous system, not elsewhere classified

G98   Other disorders of nervous system not elsewhere classified

G99   Other disorders of nervous system in diseases classified elsewhere

CHAPTER 7

Diseases of the eye and adnexa (H00-H59)

Disorders of Eyelid, Lacrimal System and Orbit (H00-H05)

H00   Hordeolum and chalazion

H01   Other inflammation of eyelid

H02   Other disorders of eyelid

H04   Disorders of lacrimal system

H05   Disorders of orbit

Disorders of Conjunctiva (H10-H11)

H10   Conjunctivitis
H11   Other disorders of conjunctiva

Disorders of Sclera, Cornea, Iris and Ciliary Body (H15-H21)

H15   Disorders of sclera
H16   Keratitis
H17   Corneal scars and opacities
H18   Other disorders of cornea
H20   Iridocyclitis
H21   Other disorders of iris and ciliary body

Disorders of Lens (H25-H28)

H25   Age-related cataract
H26   Other cataract
H27   Other disorders of lens
H28   Cataract in diseases classified elsewhere

Disorders of Choroid and Retina (H30-H36)

H30   Chorioretinal inflammation
H31   Other disorders of choroid
H32   Chorioretinal disorders in diseases classified elsewhere
H33   Retinal detachments and breaks
H34   Retinal vascular occlusions
H35   Other retinal disorders
H36   Retinal disorders in diseases classified elsewhere

Glaucoma (H40-H42)

H40   Glaucoma
H42   Glaucoma in diseases classified elsewhere

Disorders of Vitreous Body and Globe (H43-H44)

H43   Disorders of vitreous body
H44   Disorders of globe

Disorders of Optic Nerve and Visual Pathways (H46-H47)

H46   Optic neuritis
H47   Other disorders of optic [2nd] nerve and visual pathways

Disorders of Ocular Muscles, Binocular Movement, Accommodation and Refraction (H49-H52)

H49   Paralytic strabismus
H50   Other strabismus
H51   Other disorders of binocular movement
H52   Disorders of refraction and accommodation

Visual Disturbances and Blindness (H53-H54)

H53   Visual distubances
H54   Blindness and low vision

Other Disorders of Eye and Adnexa (H55-H59)

H55   Nystagmus and other irregular eye movements

H57   Other disorders of eye and adnexa

H59   Intraoperative and postprocedural complications and disorders of eye and adnexa, not elsewhere classified

CHAPTER 8

Diseases of the ear and mastoid process (H60-H95)

Diseases of External Ear (H60-H62)

H60   Otitis externa

H61   Other disorders of external ear

H62   Disorders of external ear in diseases classified elsewhere

Diseases of Middle Ear and Mastoid (H65-H75)

H65   Nonsuppurative otitis media

H66   Suppurative and unspecified otitis media

H67   Otitis media in diseases classified elsewhere

H68   Eustachian salpingitis and obstruction

H69   Other and unspecified disorders of Eustachian tube

H70   Mastoiditis and related conditions

H71   Cholesteatoma of middle ear

H72   Perforation of tympanic membrane

H73   Other disorders of tympanic membrane

H74   Other disorders of middle ear mastoid

H75   Other disorders of middle ear and mastoid in diseases classified elsewhere

Diseases of Inner Ear (H80-H83)

H80   Otosclerosis

H81   Disorders of vestibular function

H82   Vertiginous syndromes in diseases classified elsewhere

H83   Other diseases of inner ear

Other Disorders of Ear (H90-H95)

H90   Conductive and sensorineural hearing loss

H91   Other and unspecified hearing loss

H92   Otalgia and effusion of ear

H93   Other disorders of ear, not elsewhere classified

H94   Other disorders of ear in diseases classified elsewhere

H95   Intraoperative and postprocedural complications and disorders of ear and mastoid process, not elsewhere classified

CHAPTER 9

Diseases of the circulatory system (I00-I99)

Acute Rheumatic Fever (I00-I02)

I00   Rheumatic fever without heart involvement
I01   Rheumatic fever with heart involvement
I02   Rheumatic chorea

Chronic Rheumatic Heart Diseases (I05-I09)

I05   Rheumatic mitral valve diseases
I06   Rheumatic aortic valve diseases
I07   Rheumatic tricuspid valve diseases
I08   Multiple valve diseases
I09   Other rheumatic heart diseases

Hypertensive Diseases (I10-I15)

I10   Essential (primary) hypertension
I11   Hypertensive heart disease
I12   Hypertensive renal disease
I13   Hypertensive heart and renal disease
I15   Secondary hypertension

Ischemic Heart Diseases (I20-I25)

I20   Angina pectoris
I21   Acute myocardial infarction
I22   Subsequent acute myocardial infarction
I23   Certain current complications following acute myocardial infarction (within the 28 day period)
I24   Other acute ischemic heart diseases
I25   Chronic ischemic heart disease

Pulmonary Heart Disease and Diseases of Pulmonary Circulation (I26-I28)

I26   Pulmonary embolism
I27   Other pulmonary heart diseases
I28   Other diseases of pulmonary vessels

Other Forms of Heart Disease (I30-I52)

I30   Acute pericarditis
I31   Other diseases of pericardium
I32   Pericarditis in diseases classified elsewhere
I33   Acute and subacute endocarditis
I34   Nonrheumatic mitral valve disorders
I35   Nonrheumatic aortic valve disorders
I36   Nonrheumatic tricuspid valve disorders
I37   Nonrheumatic pulmonary valve disorders
I38   Endocarditis, valve unspecified
I39   Endocarditis and heart valve disorders in diseases classified elsewhere
I40   Acute myocarditis
I41   Myocarditis in diseases classified elsewhere

I42   Cardiomyopathy
I43   Cardiomyopathy in diseases classified elsewhere
I44   Atrioventricular and left bundle-branch block
I45   Other conduction disorders
I46   Cardiac arrest
I47   Paroxysmal tachycardia
I48   Atrial fibrillation and flutter
I49   Other cardiac arrhythmias
I50   Heart failure
I51   Complications and ill-defined descriptions of heart disease
I52   Other heart disorders in diseases classified elsewhere

Cerebrovascular Diseases (I60-I69)

I60   Subarachnoid hemorrhage
I61   Nontraumatic intracerebral hemorrhage
I62   Other and unspecified nontraumatic intracranial hemorrhage
I63   Cerebral infarction
I64   Stroke, not specified as hemorrhage or infarction
I65   Occlusion and stenosis of precerebral arteries, not resulting in cerebral infarction
I66   Occlusion and stenosis of cerebral arteries, not resulting in cerebral infarction
I67   Other cerebrovascular diseases
I68   Cerebrovascular disorders in diseases classified elsewhere
I69   Sequelae of cerebrovascular disease

Diseases of Arteries, Arterioles and Capillaries (I70-I79)

I70   Atherosclerosis
I71   Aortic aneurysm and dissection
I72   Other aneurysm
I73   Other peripheral vascular diseases
I74   Arterial embolism and thrombosis
I77   Other disorders of arteries and arterioles
I78   Diseases of capillaries
I79   Disorders of arteries, arterioles and capillaries in diseases classified elsewhere

Diseases of Veins, Lymphatic Vessels and Lymph Nodes, Not Elsewhere Classified (I80-I89)

I80   Phlebitis and thrombophlebitis
I81   Portal vein thrombosis
I82   Other venous embolism and thrombosis
I83   Varicose veins of lower extremities
I84   Hemorrhoids
I85   Esophageal varices
I86   Varicose veins of other sites
I87   Other disorders of veins
I88   Nonspecific lymphadenitis
I89   Other noninfective disorders of lymphatic vessels and lymph nodes

Other and Unspecified Disorders of the Circulatory System (I95-I99)

I95	Hypotension
I96	Gangrene, not elsewhere classified
I97	Intraoperative and postprocedural complications and disorders of the circulatory system, not elsewhere classified
I99	Other and unspecified disorders of circulatory system

CHAPTER 10

Diseases of the respiratory system (J00-J99)

Acute Upper Respiratory Infections (J00-J06)

J00	Acute nasopharyngitis [common cold]
J01	Acute sinusitis
J02	Acute pharyngitis
J03	Acute tonsillitis
J04	Acute laryngitis and tracheitis
J05	Acute obstructive laryngitis [croup] and epiglottitis
J06	Acute upper respiratory infections of multiple and unspecified sites

Influenza and Pneumonia (J10-J18)

J10	Influenza
J12	Viral pneumonia, not elsewhere classified
J13	Pneumonia due to Streptococcus pneumoniae
J14	Pneumonia due to Hemophilus influenza
J15	Bacterial pneumonia, not elsewhere classified
J16	Pneumonia due to other infectious organisms, not elsewhere classified
J17	Pneumonia in diseases classified elsewhere
J18	Pneumonia, unspecified organism

Other Acute Lower Respiratory Infections (J20-J22)

J20	Acute bronchitis
J21	Acute bronchiolitis
J22	Unspecified acute lower respiratory infection

Other Diseases of Upper Respiratory Tract (J30-J39)

J30	Vasomotor and allergic rhinitis
J31	Chronic rhinitis, nasopharyngitis and pharyngitis
J32	Chronic sinusitis
J33	Nasal polyp
J34	Other and unspecified disorders of nose and nasal sinuses
J35	Chronic diseases of tonsils and adenoids
J36	Peritonsillar abscess
J37	Chronic laryngitis and laryngotracheitis
J38	Diseases of vocal cords and larynx, not elsewhere classified
J39	Other diseases of upper respiratory tract

Chronic Lower Respiratory Diseases (J40-J47)

J40	Bronchitis, not specified as acute or chronic

J41	Simple and mucopurulent chronic bronchitis
J42	Unspecified chronic bronchitis
J43	Emphysema
J44	Other chronic obstructive pulmonary disease
J45	Asthma
J47	Bronchiectasis

Lung Diseases Due To External Agents (J60-J70)

J60	Coalworker's pneumoconiosis
J61	Pneumoconiosis due to asbestos and other mineral fibers
J62	Pneumoconiosis due to dust containing silica
J63	Pneumoconiosis due to other inorganic dusts
J64	Unspecified pneumoconiosis
J65	Pneumoconiosis associated with tuberculosis
J66	Airway disease due to specific organic dust
J67	Hypersensitivity pneumonitis due to organic dust
J68	Respiratory conditions due to inhalation of chemicals, gases, fumes and vapors
J69	Pneumonitis due to solids and liquids
J70	Respiratory conditions due to other external agents

Other Respiratory Diseases Principally Affecting the Interstitium (J80-J84)

J80	Adult respiratory distress syndrome
J81	Pulmonary edema
J82	Pulmonary eosinophilia, not elsewhere classified
J84	Other interstitial pulmonary diseases

Suppurative and Necrotic Conditions of the Lower Respiratory Tract (J85-J86)

J85	Abscess of lung and mediastinum
J86	Pyothorax

Other Diseases of the Pleura (J90-J94)

J90	Pleural effusion, not elsewhere classified
J91	Pleural effusion in conditions classified elsewhere
J92	Pleural plaque
J93	Pneumothorax
J94	Other pleural conditions

Other Diseases of the Respiratory System (J95-J99)

J95	Intraoperative and postprocedural complications and disorders of the respiratory system, not elsewhere classified
J96	Respiratory failure, not elsewhere classified
J98	Other respiratory disorders
J99	Respiratory disorders in diseases classified elsewhere

CHAPTER 11

Diseases of the digestive system (K00-K94)

Diseases of Oral Cavity and Salivary Glands (K00-K14)

K00   Disorders of tooth development and eruption
K01   Embedded and impacted teeth
K02   Dental caries
K03   Other diseases of hard tissues of teeth
K04   Diseases of pulp and periapical tissues
K05   Gingivitis and periodontal diseases
K06   Other disorders of gingiva and edentulous alveolar ridge
K08   Other disorders of teeth and supporting structures
K09   Cysts of oral region, not elsewhere classified
K11   Diseases of salivary glands
K12   Stomatitis and related lesions
K13   Other diseases of lip and oral mucosa
K14   Diseases of tongue

Diseases of Esophagus, Stomach and Duodenum (K20-K31)

K20   Esophagitis
K21   Gastro-esophageal reflux disease
K22   Other diseases of esophagus
K23   Disorders of esophagus in diseases classified elsewhere
K25   Gastric ulcer
K26   Duodenal ulcer
K27   Peptic ulcer, site unspecified
K28   Gastrojejunal ulcer
K29   Gastritis and duodenitis
K30   Dyspepsia
K31   Other diseases of stomach and duodenum

Diseases of Appendix (K35-K38)

K35   Acute appendicitis
K36   Other appendicitis
K37   Unspecified appendicitis
K38   Other diseases of appendix

Hernia (K40-K46)

K40   Inguinal hernia
K41   Femoral hernia
K42   Umbilical hernia
K43   Ventral hernia
K44   Diaphragmatic hernia
K45   Other abdominal hernia
K46   Unspecified abdominal hernia

Noninfective Enteritis and Colitis (K50-K52)

K50   Crohn's disease [regional enteritis]
K51   Ulcerative colitis

K52   Other and unspecified noninfective gastroenteritis and colitis

Other Diseases of Intestines (K55-K63)

K55   Vascular disorders of intestine
K56   Paralytic ileus and intestinal obstruction without hernia
K57   Diverticular disease of intestine
K58   Irritable bowel syndrome
K59   Other functional intestinal disorders
K60   Fissure and fistula of anal and rectal regions
K61   Abscess of anal and rectal regions
K62   Other diseases of anus and rectum
K63   Other diseases of intestine

Diseases of Peritoneum and Retroperitoneum (K65-K68)

K65   Peritonitis
K66   Other disorders of peritoneum
K67   Disorders of peritoneum in infectious diseases classified elsewhere
K68   Disorders of retroperitoneum

Diseases of Liver (K70-K77)

K70   Alcoholic liver disease
K71   Toxic liver disease
K72   Hepatic failure, not elsewhere classified
K73   Chronic hepatitis, not elsewhere classified
K74   Fibrosis and cirrhosis of liver
K75   Other inflammatory liver diseases
K76   Other diseases of liver
K77   Liver disorders in diseases classified elsewhere

Disorders of Gallbladder, Biliary Tract and Pancreas (K80-K87)

K80   Cholelithiasis
K81   Cholecystitis
K82   Other diseases of gallbladder
K83   Other diseases of biliary tract
K85   Acute pancreatitis
K86   Other diseases of pancreas
K87   Disorders of gallbladder, biliary tract and pancreas in diseases classified elsewhere

Other Diseases of the Digestive System (K90-K94)

K90   Intestinal malabsorption
K91   Intraoperative and postprocedural complications and disorders of digestive system, not elsewhere classified
K92   Other diseases of digestive system
K93   Disorders of other digestive organs in diseases classified elsewhere
K94   Complications of artificial openings of the digestive system

CHAPTER 12

Diseases of the skin and subcutaneous tissue (L00-L99)

Infections of the Skin and Subcutaneous Tissue (L00-L08)

L00   Staphylococcal scalded skin syndrome
L01   Impetigo
L02   Cutaneous abscess, furuncle and carbuncle
L03   Cellulitis and acute lymphangitis
L04   Acute lymphadenitis
L05   Pilonidal cyst
L08   Other local infections of skin and subcutaneous tissue

Bullous Disorders (L10-14)

L10   Pemphigus
L11   Other acantholytic disorders
L12   Pemphigoid
L13   Other bullous disorders
L14   Bullous disorders in diseases classified elsewhere

Dermatitis and Eczema (L20-L30)

L20   Atopic dermatitis
L21   Seborrheic dermatitis
L22   Diaper dermatitis
L23   Allergic contact dermatitis
L24   Irritant contact dermatitis
L25   Unspecified contact dermatitis
L26   Exfoliative dermatitis
L27   Dermatitis due to substances taken internally
L28   Lichen simplex chronicus and prurigo
L29   Pruritus
L30   Other and unspecified dermatitis

Papulosquamous Disorders (L40-L45)

L40   Psoriasis
L41   Parapsoriasis
L42   Pityriasis rosea
L43   Lichen planus
L44   Other papulosquamous disorders
L45   Papulosqamous disorders in diseases classified elsewhere

Urticaria and Erythema (L50-L54)

L50   Urticaria
L51   Erythema multiforme
L52   Erythema nodosum
L53   Other erythematous conditions
L54   Erythema in diseases classified elsewhere

Radiation-related Disorders of the Skin and Subcutaneous Tissue (L55-L59)

L55 Sunburn
L56 Other acute skin changes due to ultraviolet radiation
L57 Skin changes due to chronic exposure to nonionizing radiation
L58 Radiodermatitis
L59 Other disorders of skin and subcutaneous tissue related to radiation

Disorders of Skin Appendages (L60-L75)

L60 Nail disorders
L62 Nail disorders in diseases classified elsewhere
L63 Alopecia areata
L64 Androgenic alopecia
L65 Other nonscarring hair loss
L66 Cicatricial alopecia [scarring hair loss]
L67 Hair color and hair shaft abnormalities
L68 Hypertrichosis
L70 Acne
L71 Rosacea
L72 Follicular cysts of skin and subcutaneous tissue
L73 Other follicular disorders
L74 Eccrine sweat disorders
L75 Apocrine sweat disorders

Intraoperative and Postprocedural Complications of Dermatologic Procedures (L76)

L76 Intraoperative and postprocedural complications of dermatologic procedures

Other Disorders of the Skin and Subcutaneous Tissue (L80-L99)

L80 Vitiligo
L81 Other disorders of pigmentation
L82 Seborrheic keratosis
L83 Acanthosis nigricans
L84 Corns and callosities
L85 Other epidermal thickening
L86 Keratoderma in diseases classified elsewhere
L87 Transepidermal elimination disorders
L88 Pyoderma gangrenosum
L89 Decubitus ulcer
L90 Atrophic disorders of skin
L91 Hypertrophic disorders of skin
L92 Granulomatous disorders of skin and subcutaneous tissue
L93 Lupus erythematosus
L94 Other localized connective tissue disorders
L95 Vasculitis limited to skin, not elsewhere classified
L97 Non-decubitus chronic ulcer of lower limb, not elsewhere classified
L98 Other disorders of skin and subcutaneous tissue, not elsewhere classified

    L99   Other disorders of skin and subcutaneous tissue in diseases classified elsewhere

CHAPTER 13

Diseases of the musculoskeletal system and connective tissue (M00-M99)

Arthropathies (M00-M25)

Infectious Arthropathies (M00-M02)
    M00   Pyogenic arthritis
    M01   Direct infections of joint in infectious and parasitic diseases classified elsewhere
    M02   Postinfective and reactive arthropathies

Inflammatory Polyarthropathies (M05-M14)
    M05   Rheumatoid arthritis with rheumatoid factor
    M06   Other rheumatoid arthritis
    M07   Enteropathic arthropathies
    M08   Juvenile arthritis
    M10   Gout
    M11   Other crystal arthropathies
    M12   Other specific arthropathies
    M13   Other arthritis
    M14   Arthropathies in other diseases classified elsewhere

Osteoarthritis (M15-M19)
    M15   Polyosteoarthritis
    M16   Osteoarthritis of hip
    M17   Osteoarthritis of knee
    M18   Osteoarthritis of first carpometacarpal joint
    M19   Other and unspecified osteoarthritis

Other Joint Disorders (M20-M25)
    M20   Acquired deformities of fingers and toes
    M21   Other acquired deformities of limbs
    M22   Disorder of patella
    M23   Internal derangement of knee
    M24   Other specific joint derangements
    M25   Other joint disorder, not elsewhere classified

Dentofacial Anomalies [Including Malocclusion] and Other Disorders of Jaw (M26-M27)
    M26   Dentofacial anomalies [including malocclusion]
    M27   Other diseases of jaws

Systemic Connective Tissue Disorders (M30-M36)
    M30   Polyarteritis nodosa and related conditions
    M31   Other necrotizing vasculopathies

M32 Systemic lupus erythematosus
M33 Dermatopolymyositis
M34 Systemic sclerosis [scleroderma]
M35 Other systemic involvement of connective tissue
M36 Systemic disorders of connective tissue in diseases classified elsewhere

Dorsopathies (M40-M54)

Deforming Dorsopathies (M40-M43)

M40 Kyphosis and lordosis
M41 Scoliosis
M42 Spinal osteochondrosis
M43 Other deforming dorsopathies

Spondylopathies (M45-M49)

M45 Ankylosing spondylitis
M46 Other inflammatory spondylopathies
M47 Spondylosis
M48 Other spondylopathies
M49 Spondylopathies in diseases classified elsewhere

Other Dorsopathies (M50-M54)

M50 Cervical disc disorders
M51 Thoracic, thoracolumbar, and lumbosacral intervertebral disc disorders
M53 Other and unspecified dorsopathies, not elsewhere classified
M54 Dorsalgia

Soft tissue disorders (M60-M79)

Disorders of Muscles (M60-M63)

M60 Myositis
M61 Calcification and ossification of muscle
M62 Other disorders of muscle
M63 Disorders of muscle in diseases classified elsewhere

Disorders of Synovium and Tendon (M65-M67)

M65 Synovitis and tenosynovitis
M66 Spontaneous rupture of synovium and tendon
M67 Other disorders of synovium and tendon

Other Soft Tissue Disorders (M70-M79)

M70 Soft tissue disorders related to use, overuse and pressure
M71 Other bursopathies
M72 Fibroblastic disorders
M75 Shoulder lesions
M76 Enthesopathies of lower limb, excluding foot
M77 Other enthesopathies
M79 Other soft tissue disorders, not elsewhere classified

Disorders of Bone Density and Structure (M80-M85)

M80 Osteoporosis with current pathological fracture
M81 Osteoporosis without current pathological fracture
M83 Adult osteomalacia
M84 Disorder of continuity of bone
M85 Other disorders of bone density and structure

Other Osteopathies (M86-M90)

M86 Osteomyelitis
M87 Osteonecrosis
M88 Osteitis deformans [Paget's disease of bone]
M89 Other disorders of bone
M90 Osteopathies in diseases classified elsewhere

Chondropathies (M91-M94)

M91 Juvenile osteochondrosis of hip and pelvis
M92 Other juvenile osteochondrosis
M93 Other osteochondropathies
M94 Other disorders of cartilage

Other Disorders of the Musculoskeletal System and Connective Tissue (M95-M99)

M95 Other acquired deformities of musculoskeletal system and connective tissue
M96 Intraoperative and postprocedural complications and disorders of the musculoskeletal system, not elsewhere classified
M99 Biomechanical lesions, not elsewhere classified

CHAPTER 14

Diseases of the genitourinary system (N00-N99)

Glomerular Diseases (N00-N08)

N00 Acute nephritic syndrome
N01 Rapidly progressive nephritic syndrome
N02 Recurrent and persistent hematuria
N03 Chronic nephritic syndrome
N04 Nephrotic syndrome
N05 Unspecified nephritic syndrome
N06 Isolated proteinuria with specified morphological lesion
N07 Hereditary nephropathy, not elsewhere classified
N08 Glomerular disorders in diseases classified elsewhere

Renal Tubulo-interstitial Diseases (N10-N16)

N10 Acute tubulo-interstitial nephritis
N11 Chronic tubulo-interstitial nephritis
N12 Tubulo-interstitial nephritis, not specified as acute or chronic
N13 Obstructive and reflux uropathy
N14 Drug- and heavy-metal-induced tubulo-interstitial and tubular conditions

N15 Other renal tubulo-interstitial diseases
N16 Renal tubulo-interstitial disorders in diseases classified elsewhere

Renal Failure (N17-N19)

N17 Acute renal failure
N18 Chronic renal failure
N19 Unspecified renal failure

Urolithiasis (N20-N23)

N20 Calculus of kidney and ureter
N21 Calculus of lower urinary tract
N22 Calculus of urinary tract in diseases classified elsewhere
N23 Unspecified renal colic

Other Disorders of Kidney and Ureter (N25-N29)

N25 Disorders resulting from impaired renal tubular function
N26 Unspecified contracted kidney
N27 Small kidney of unknown cause
N28 Other disorders of kidney and ureter, not elsewhere classified
N29 Other disorders of kidney and ureter in diseases classified elsewhere

Other Diseases of the Urinary System (N30-N39)

N30 Cystitis
N31 Neuromuscular dysfunction of bladder, not elsewhere classified
N32 Other disorders of bladder
N33 Bladder disorders in diseases classified elsewhere
N34 Urethritis and urethral syndrome
N35 Urethral stricture
N36 Other disorders of urethra
N37 Urethral disorders in diseases classified elsewhere
N39 Other disorders of urinary system

Diseases of Male Genital Organs (N40-N53)

N40 Hyperplasia of prostate
N41 Inflammatory diseases of prostate
N42 Other disorders of prostate
N43 Hydrocele and spermatocele
N44 Noninflammatory disorders of testis
N45 Orchitis and epididymitis
N46 Male infertility
N47 Disorders of prepuce
N48 Other disorders of penis
N49 Inflammatory disorders of male genital organs, not elsewhere classified
N50 Other and unspecified disorders of male genital organs
N51 Disorders of male genital organs in diseases classified elsewhere
N52 Male erectile dysfunction
N53 Male sexual dysfunction

Disorders of Breast (N60-N64)

N60　Benign mammary dysplasia
N61　Inflammatory disorders of breast
N62　Hypertrophy of breast
N63　Unspecified lump in breast
N64　Other disorders of breast

Inflammatory Diseases of Female Pelvic Organs (N70-N77)

N70　Salpingitis and oophoritis
N71　Inflammatory disease of uterus, except cervix
N72　Inflammatory disease of cervix uteri
N73　Other female pelvic inflammatory diseases
N74　Female pelvic inflammatory disorders in diseases classified elsewhere
N75　Diseases of Bartholin's gland
N76　Other inflammation of vagina and vulva
N77　Vulvovaginal ulceration and inflammation in diseases classified elsewhere

Noninflammatory Disorders of Female Genital Tract (N80-N98)

N80　Endometriosis
N81　Female genital prolapse
N82　Fistulae involving female genital tract
N83　Noninflammatory disorders of ovary, fallopian tube and broad ligament
N84　Polyp of female genital tract
N85　Other noninflammatory disorders of uterus, except cervix
N86　Erosion and ectropion of cervix uteri
N87　Dysplasia of cervix uteri
N88　Other noninflammatory disorders of cervix uteri
N89　Other noninflammatory disorders of vagina
N90　Other noninflammatory disorders of vulva and perineum
N91　Absent, scanty and rare menstruation
N92　Excessive, frequent and irregular menstruation
N93　Other abnormal uterine and vaginal bleeding
N94　Pain and other conditions associated with female genital organs and menstrual cycle
N95　Menopausal and other perimenopausal disorders
N96　Habitual aborter
N97　Female infertility
N98　Complications associated with artificial fertilization

Other Disorders of the Genitourinary System (N99)

N99　Intraoperative complications and postprocedural disorders of genitourinary system, not elsewhere classified

CHAPTER 15

Pregnancy, childbirth and the puerperium (O00-O99)

Pregnancy With Abortive Outcome (O00-O09)

O00 Ectopic pregnancy
O01 Hydatidiform mole
O02 Other abnormal products of conception
O03 Spontaneous abortion
O04 Complications following (induced) termination of pregnancy
O07 Failed attempted termination of pregnancy
O08 Complications following ectopic and molar pregnancy
O09 Supervision of high-risk pregnancy

Edema, Proteinuria and Hypertensive Disorders In Pregnancy, Childbirth and the Puerperium (O10-O16)

O10 Pre-existing hypertension complicating pregnancy, childbirth and the puerperium
O11 Pre-existing hypertensive disorder with superimposed proteinuria
O12 Gestational [pregnancy-induced] edema and proteinuria without hypertension
O13 Gestational [pregnancy-induced] hypertension without significant proteinuria
O14 Gestational [pregnancy-induced] hypertension with significant proteinuria
O15 Eclampsia
O16 Unspecified maternal hypertension

Other Maternal Disorders Predominantly Related to Pregnancy (O20-O29)

O20 Hemorrhage in early pregnancy
O21 Excessive vomiting in pregnancy
O22 Venous complications in pregnancy
O23 Infections of genitourinary tract in pregnancy
O24 Diabetes mellitus in pregnancy, childbirth, and the puerperium
O25 Malnutrition in pregnancy, childbirth and the puerperium
O26 Maternal care for other conditions predominantly related to pregnancy
O28 Abnormal findings on antenatal screening of mother
O29 Complications of anesthesia during pregnancy

Maternal Care Related to the Fetus and Amniotic Cavity and Possible Delivery Problems (O30-O48)

O30 Multiple gestation
O31 Complications specific to multiple gestation
O32 Maternal care for malpresentation of fetus
O33 Maternal care for disproportion
O34 Maternal care for abnormality of pelvic organs
O35 Maternal care for known or suspected fetal abnormality and damage
O36 Maternal care for other fetal problems

O37   Fetal care for fetal abnormality and damage
O40   Polyhydramnios
O41   Other disorders of amniotic fluid and membranes
O42   Premature rupture of membranes
O43   Placental disorders
O44   Placenta previa
O45   Premature separation of placenta [abruptio placentae]
O46   Antepartum hemorrhage, not elsewhere classified
O47   False labor
O48   Late pregnancy

Complications of Labor and Delivery (O60-O77)

O60   Preterm labor
O61   Failed induction of labor
O62   Abnormalities of forces of labor
O63   Long labor
O64   Obstructed labor due to malposition and malpresentation of fetus
O65   Obstructed labor due to maternal pelvic abnormality
O66   Other obstructed labor
O67   Labor and delivery complicated by intrapartum hemorrhage, not
       elsewhere classified
O68   Labor and delivery complicated by abnormality of fetal acid-base
       balance
O69   Labor and delivery complicated by umbilical cord complications
O70   Perineal laceration during delivery
O71   Other obstetric trauma
O72   Postpartum hemorrhage
O73   Retained placenta and membranes, without hemorrhage
O74   Complications of anesthesia during labor and delivery
O75   Other complications of labor and delivery, not elsewhere classified
O76   Abnormality in fetal heart rate and rhythm complicating labor and
       delivery
O77   Other fetal stress complicating labor and delivery

Delivery (O80)

O80   Encounter for full-term uncomplicated delivery

Complications Predominantly Related to the Puerperium (O85-O92)

O85   Puerperal sepsis
O86   Other puerperal infections
O87   Venous complications in the puerperium
O88   Obstetric embolism
O89   Complications of anesthesia during the puerperium
O90   Complications of the puerperium, not elsewhere classified
O91   Infections of breast associated with pregnancy, the puerperium and
       lactation
O92   Other disorders of breast associated with pregnancy, the puerperium,
       and lactation

Sequelae of Complication of Pregnancy, Childbirth, and the Puerperium (O93)

O93 Sequelae of complication of pregnancy, childbirth, and the puerperium

Other Obstetric Conditions, Not Elsewhere Classified (O94-O99)

O94 Maternal malignant neoplasma, traumatic injuries and abuse classifiable elsewhere but complicating prenancy, childbirth and the puerperium

O98 Maternal infectious and parasitic diseases classifiable elsewhere but complicating pregnancy, childbirth and the puerperium

O99 Other maternal diseases classifiable elsewhere but complicating pregnancy, childbirth and the puerperium

CHAPTER 16

Certain conditions originating in the perinatal period (P00-P96)

Newborn Affected by Maternal Factors and by Complications of Pregnancy, Labor, and Delivery (P00-P04)

P00 Newborn (suspected) affected by maternal conditions that may be unrelated to present pregnancy

P01 Newborn (suspected) affected by maternal complications of pregnancy

P02 Newborn (suspected) affected by maternal complications of placenta, cord and membranes

P03 Newborn (suspected) affected by other complications of labor and delivery

P04 Newborn (suspected) affected by noxious influences transmitted via placenta or breast milk

Disorders of Newborn Related To Length of Gestation and Fetal Growth (P05-P08)

P05 Disorders of newborn related to slow fetal growth and fetal malnutrition

P07 Disorders of newborn related to short gestation and low birth weight, not elsewhere classified

P08 Disorders of newborn related to long gestation and high birth weight

Birth Trauma (P10-P15)

P10 Intracranial laceration and hemorrhage due to birth injury
P11 Other birth injuries to central nervous sytem
P12 Birth injury to scalp
P13 Birth injury to skeleton
P14 Birth injury to peripheral nervous system
P15 Other birth injuries

Respiratory and Cardiovascular Disorders Specific to the Perinatal Period (P19-P29)

P19   Metabolic acidemia in newborn
P22   Respiratory distress of newborn
P23   Congenital pneumonia
P24   Neonatal aspiration syndromes
P25   Interstitial emphysema and related conditions originating in the perinatal period
P26   Pulmonary hemorrhage originating in the perinatal period
P27   Chronic respiratory disease originating in the perinatal period
P28   Other respiratory conditions originating in the perinatal period
P29   Cardiovascular disorders originating in the perinatal period

Infections Specific To the Perinatal Period (P35-P39)

P35   Congenital viral diseases
P36   Bacterial sepsis of newborn
P37   Other congenital infectious and parasitic diseases
P38   Omphalitis of newborn
P39   Other infections specific to the perinatal period

Hemorrhagic and Hematological Disorders of Newborn (P50-P61)

P50   Newborn affected by (intrauterine) blood loss
P51   Umbilical hemorrhage of newborn
P52   Intracranial nontraumatic hemorrhage of newborn
P53   Hemorrhagic disease of newborn
P54   Other neonatal hemorrhages
P55   Hemolytic disease of newborn
P56   Hydrops fetalis due to hemolytic disease
P57   Kernicterus
P58   Neonatal jaundice due to other excessive hemolysis
P59   Neonatal jaundice from other and unspecified causes
P60   Disseminated intravascular coagulation of newborn
P61   Other perinatal hematological disorders

Transitory Endocrine and Metabolic Disorders Specific To Newborn (P70-P74)

P70   Transitory disorders of carbohydrate metabolism specific to newborn
P71   Transitory neonatal disorders of calcium and magnesium metabolism
P72   Other transitory neonatal endocrine disorders
P74   Other transitory neonatal electrolyte and metabolic disturbances

Digestive System Disorders of Newborn (P75-P78)

P75   Meconium ileus
P76   Other intestinal obstruction of newborn
P77   Necrotizing enterocolitis of newborn
P78   Other perinatal digestive system disorders

Conditions Involving the Integument and Temperature Regulation Of Newborn (P80-P83)

P80   Hypothermia of newborn
P81   Other disturbances of temperature regulation of newborn
P83   Other conditions of integument specific to newborn

Other Problems with Newborn (P84)

P84   Other problems with newborn

Other Disorders Originating In the Perinatal Period (P90-P96)

P90   Convulsions of newborn
P91   Other disturbances of cerebral status of newborn
P92   Feeding problems of newborn
P93   Reactions and intoxications due to drugs administered to newborn
P94   Disorders of muscle tone of newborn
P95   Stillbirth
P96   Other conditions originating in the perinatal period

CHAPTER 17

Congenital malformations, deformations and chromosomal abnormalities (Q00-Q99)

Congenital Malformations Of the Nervous System (Q00-Q07)

Q00   Anencephaly and similar malformations
Q01   Encephalocele
Q02   Microcephaly
Q03   Congenital hydrocephalus
Q04   Other congenital malformations of brain
Q05   Spina bifida
Q06   Other congenital malformations of spinal cord
Q07   Other congenital malformations of nervous system

Congenital Malformations Of Eye, Ear, Face and Neck (Q10-Q18)

Q10   Congenital malformations of eyelid, lacrimal apparatus and orbit
Q11   Anophthalmos, microphthalmos and macrophthalmos
Q12   Congenital lens malformations
Q13   Congenital malformations of anterior segment of eye
Q14   Congenital malformations of posterior segment of eye
Q15   Other congenital malformations of eye
Q16   Congenital malformations of ear causing impairment of hearing
Q17   Other congenital malformations of ear
Q18   Other congenital malformations of face and neck

Congenital Malformations of the Circulatory System (Q20-Q28)

Q20   Congenital malformations of cardiac chambers and connections
Q21   Congenital malformations of cardiac septa
Q22   Congenital malformations of pulmonary and tricuspid valves
Q23   Congenital malformations of aortic and mitral valves
Q24   Other congenital malformations of heart

Q25   Congenital malformations of great arteries
Q26   Congenital malformations of great veins
Q27   Other congenital malformations of peripheral vascular system
Q28   Other congenital malformations of circulatory system

Congenital Malformations of the Respiratory System (Q30-Q34)

Q30   Congenital malformations of nose
Q31   Congenital malformations of larynx
Q32   Congenital malformations of trachea and bronchus
Q33   Congenital malformations of lung
Q34   Other congenital malformations of respiratory system

Cleft Lip and Cleft Palate (Q35-Q37)

Q35   Cleft palate
Q36   Cleft lip
Q37   Cleft palate with cleft lip

Other Congenital Malformations of the Digestive System (Q38-Q45)

Q38   Other congenital malformations of tongue, mouth and pharynx
Q39   Congenital malformations of esophagus
Q40   Other congenital malformations of upper alimentary tract
Q41   Congenital absence, atresia and stenosis of small intestine
Q42   Congenital absence, atresia and stenosis of large intestine
Q43   Other congenital malformations of intestine
Q44   Congenital malformations of gallbladder, bile ducts and liver
Q45   Other congenital malformations of digestive system

Congenital Malformations Of Genital Organs (Q50-Q56)

Q50   Congenital malformations of ovaries, fallopian tubes and broad ligaments
Q51   Congenital malformations of uterus and cervix
Q52   Other congenital malformations of female genitalia
Q53   Undescended and ectopic testicle
Q54   Hypospadias
Q55   Other congenital malformations of male genital organs
Q56   Indeterminate sex and pseudohermaphroditism

Congenital Malformations Of the Urinary System (Q60-Q64)

Q60   Renal agenesis and other reduction defects of kidney
Q61   Cystic kidney disease
Q62   Congenital obstructive defects of renal pelvis and congenital malformations of ureter
Q63   Other congenital malformations of kidney
Q64   Other congenital malformations of urinary system

Congenital Malformations and Deformations Of the Musculoskeletal System (Q65-Q79)

Q65   Congenital deformities of hip
Q66   Congenital deformities of feet

Q67   Congenital musculoskeletal deformities of head, face, spine and chest
Q68   Other congenital musculoskeletal deformities
Q69   Polydactyly
Q70   Syndactyly
Q71   Reduction defects of upper limb
Q72   Reduction defects of lower limb
Q73   Reduction defects of unspecified limb
Q74   Other congenital malformations of limb(s)
Q75   Other congenital malformations of skull and face bones
Q76   Congenital malformations of spine and bony thorax
Q77   Osteochondrodysplasia with defects of growth of tubular bones and spine
Q78   Other osteochondrodysplasias
Q79   Congenital malformations of musculoskeletal system, not elsewhere classified

Other Congenital Malformations (Q80-Q89)

Q80   Congenital ichthyosis
Q81   Epidermolysis bullosa
Q82   Other congenital malformations of skin
Q83   Congenital malformations of breast
Q84   Other congenital malformations of integument
Q85   Phakomatoses, not elsewhere classified
Q86   Congenital malformation syndromes due to known exogenous causes, not elsewhere classified
Q87   Other specified congenital malformation syndromes affecting multiple systems
Q89   Other congenital malformations, not elsewhere classified

Chromosomal Abnormalities, Not Elsewhere Classified (Q90-Q99)

Q90   Down syndrome
Q91   Trisomy 18 and Trisomy 13
Q92   Other trisomies and partial trisomies of the autosomes, not elsewhere classified
Q93   Monosomies and deletions from the autosomes, not elsewhere classified
Q95   Balanced rearrangements and structural markers, not elsewhere classified
Q96   Turner syndrome
Q97   Other sex chromosome abnormalities, female phenotype, not elsewhere classified
Q98   Other sex chromosome abnormalities, male phenotype, not elsewhere classified
Q99   Other chromosome abnormalities, not elsewhere classified

CHAPTER 18

Symptoms, signs and abnormal clinical and laboratory findings, not elsewhere classified (R00-R99)

Symptoms and Signs Involving the Circulatory and Respiratory Systems (R00-R09)

R00   Abnormalities of heart beat
R01   Cardiac murmurs and other cardiac sounds
R03   Abnormal blood-pressure reading, without diagnosis
R04   Hemorrhage from respiratory passages
R05   Cough
R06   Abnormalities of breathing
R07   Pain in throat and chest
R09   Other symptoms and signs involving the circulatory and respiratory system

Symptoms and Signs Involving the Digestive System and Abdomen (R10-R19)

R10   Abdominal and pelvic pain
R11   Nausea and vomiting
R12   Heartburn
R13   Aphagia and dysphagia
R14   Flatulence and related conditions
R15   Fecal incontinence
R16   Hepatomegaly and splenomegaly, not elsewhere classified
R17   Unspecified jaundice
R18   Ascites
R19   Other symptoms and signs involving the digestive system and abdomen

Symptoms and Signs Involving the Skin and Subcutaneous Tissue (R20-R23)

R20   Disturbances of skin sensation
R21   Rash and other nonspecific skin eruption
R22   Localized swelling, mass and lump of skin and subcutaneous tissue
R23   Other skin changes

Symptoms and Signs Involving the Nervous and Musculoskeletal Systems (R25-R29)

R25   Abnormal involuntary movements
R26   Abnormalities of gait and mobility
R27   Other lack of coordination
R29   Other symptoms and signs involving the nervous and musculoskeletal systems

Symptoms and Signs Involving the Genitourinary System (R30-R39)

R30   Pain associated with micturition
R31   Hematuria

R32	Unspecified urinary incontinence
R33	Retention of urine
R34	Anuria and oliguria
R35	Polyuria
R36	Urethral discharge
R37	Sexual sysfunction, unspecified
R39	Other and unspecified symptoms and signs involving the urinary system

Symptoms and Signs Involving Cognition, Perception, Emotional State and Behavior (R40-R46)

R40	Somnolence, stupor and coma
R41	Other symptoms and signs involving cognitive functions and awareness
R42	Dizziness and giddiness
R43	Disturbances of smell and taste
R44	Other symptoms and signs involving general sensations and perceptions
R45	Symptoms and signs involving emotional state
R46	Symptoms and signs involving appearance and behavior

Symptoms and Signs Involving Speech and Voice (R47-R49)

R47	Speech disturbances, not elsewhere classified
R48	Dyslexia and other symbolic dysfunctions, not elsewhere classified
R49	Voice disturbances

General Symptoms and Signs (R50-R69)

R50	Fever
R51	Headache
R52	Pain, not elsewhere classified
R53	Malaise and fatigue
R54	Age-related physical debility
R55	Syncope and collapse
R56	Convulsions, not elsewhere classified
R57	Shock, not elsewhere classified
R58	Hemorrhage, not elsewhere classified
R59	Enlarged lymph nodes
R60	Edema, not elsewhere classified
R61	Hyperhidrosis
R62	Lack of expected normal physiological development in childhood and adults
R63	Symptoms and signs concerning food and fluid intake
R64	Cachexia
R68	Other general symptoms and signs
R69	Illness NOS

Abnormal Findings on Examination of Blood, Without Diagnosis (R70-R79)

R70	Elevated erythrocyte sedimentation rate and abnormality of plasma viscosity

R71   Abnormality of red blood cells

R72   Abnormality of white blood cells, not elsewhere classified

R73   Elevated blood glucose level

R74   Abnormal serum enzyme levels

R75   Inconclusive laboratory evidence of human immunodeficiency virus [HIV]

R76   Other abnormal immunological findings in serum

R77   Other abnormalities of plasma proteins

R78   Findings of drugs and other substances, not normally found in blood

R79   Other abnormal findings of blood chemistry

Abnormal Findings on Examination of Urine, Without Diagnosis (R80-R82)

R80   Proteinuria

R81   Glycosuria

R82   Other and unspecified abnormal findings in urine

Abnormal Findings on Examination of Other Body Fluids, Substances and Tissues, Without Diagnosis (R83-R89)

R83   Abnormal findings in cerebrospinal fluid

R84   Abnormal findings in specimens from respiratory organs and thorax

R85   Abnormal findings in specimens from digestive organs and abdominal cavity

R86   Abnormal findings in specimens from male genital organs

R87   Abnormal findings in specimens from female genital organs

R88   Abnormal findings in other body fluids and substances

R89   Abnormal findings in specimens from other organs, systems and tissues

Abnormal Findings on Diagnostic Imaging and in Function Studies, Without Diagnosis (R90-R94)

R90   Abnormal findings on diagnostic imaging of central nervous system

R91   Abnormal findings on diagnostic imaging of lung

R92   Abnormal findings on diagnostic imaging of breast

R93   Abnormal findings on diagnostic imaging of other body structures

R94   Abnormal results of function studies

Ill-defined and Unknown Cause of Mortality (R99)

R99   Ill-defined and unknown cause of mortality

CHAPTER 19

Injury, poisoning and certain other consequences of external causes (S00-T88)

Injuries To the Head (S00-S09)

S00   Superficial injury of head

S01   Open wound of head

S02   Fracture of skull and facial bones

S03   Dislocation and sprain of joints and ligaments of head

S04   Injury of cranial nerve
S05   Injury of eye and orbit
S06   Intracranial injury
S07   Crushing injury of head
S08   Avulsion and traumatic amputation of part of head
S09   Other and unspecified injuries of head

Injuries To the Neck (S10-S19)

S10   Superficial injury of neck
S11   Open wound of neck
S12   Fracture of cervical vertebra and other parts of neck
S13   Dislocation and sprain of joints and ligaments at neck level
S14   Injury of nerves and spinal cord at neck level
S15   Injury of blood vessels at neck level
S16   Injury of muscle and tendon at neck level
S17   Crushing injury of neck
S19   Other and unspecified injuries of neck

Injuries To the Thorax (S20-S29)

S20   Superficial injury of thorax
S21   Open wound of thorax
S22   Fracture of rib(s), sternum and thoracic spine
S23   Dislocation and sprain of joints and ligaments of thorax
S24   Injury of nerves and spinal cord at thorax level
S25   Injury of blood vessels of thorax
S26   Injury of heart
S27   Injury of other and unspecified intrathoracic organs
S28   Crushing injury of thorax, and traumatic amputation of part of thorax
S29   Other and unspecified injuries of thorax

Injuries to the Abdomen, Lower Back, Lumbar Spine and Pelvis (S30-S39)

S30   Superficial injury of abdomen, lower back and pelvis
S31   Open wound of abdomen, lower back and pelvis
S32   Fracture of lumbar spine and pelvis
S33   Dislocation and sprain of joints and ligaments of lumbar spine and pelvis
S34   Injury of lumbar and sacral spinal cord and nerves at abdomen, lower back and pelvis level
S35   Injury of blood vessels at abdomen, lower back and pelvis level
S36   Injury of intra-abdominal organs
S37   Injury of pelvic organs
S38   Crushing injury, and traumatic amputation of part of abdomen, lower back and pelvis
S39   Other and unspecified injuries of abdomen, lower back and pelvis

Injuries to the Shoulder and Upper Arm (S40-S49)

S40   Superficial injury of shoulder and upper arm
S41   Open wound of shoulder and upper arm
S42   Fracture of shoulder and upper arm

S43   Dislocation and sprain of joints and ligaments of shoulder girdle
S44   Injury of nerves at shoulder and upper arm level
S45   Injury of blood vessels at shoulder and upper arm level
S46   Injury of muscle and tendon at shoulder and upper arm level
S47   Crushing injury of shoulder and upper arm
S48   Traumatic amputation of shoulder and upper arm
S49   Other and unspecified injuries of shoulder and upper arm

Injuries to the Elbow and Forearm (S50-S59)

S50   Superficial injury of elbow and forearm
S51   Open wound of elbow and forearm
S52   Fracture of forearm
S53   Dislocation and sprain of joints and ligaments of elbow
S54   Injury of nerves at forearm level
S55   Injury of blood vessels at forearm level
S56   Injury of muscle and tendon at forearm level
S57   Crushing injury of elbow and forearm
S58   Traumatic amputation of elbow and forearm
S59   Other and unspecified injuries of elbow and forearm

Injuries to the Wrist, Hand, and Fingers (S60-S69)

S60   Superficial injury of wrist, hand and fingers
S61   Open wound of wrist, hand and fingers
S62   Fracture at wrist and hand level
S63   Dislocation and sprain of joints and ligaments at wrist and hand level
S64   Injury of nerves at wrist and hand level
S65   Injury of blood vessels at wrist and hand level
S66   Injury of muscle and tendon at wrist and hand level
S67   Crushing injury of wrist, hand, and fingers
S68   Traumatic amputation of wrist, hand, and fingers
S69   Other and unspecified injuries of wrist, hand, and finger(s)

Injuries to the Hip and Thigh (S70-S79)

S70   Superficial injury of hip and thigh
S71   Open wound of hip and thigh
S72   Fracture of femur
S73   Dislocation and sprain of joint and ligaments of hip
S74   Injury of nerves at hip and thigh level
S75   Injury of blood vessels at hip and thigh level
S76   Injury of muscle and tendon at hip and thigh level
S77   Crushing injury of hip and thigh
S78   Traumatic amputation of hip and thigh
S79   Other and unspecified injuries of hip and thigh

Injuries to the Knee and Lower Leg (S80-S89)

S80   Superficial injury of knee and lower leg
S81   Open wound of knee and lower leg
S82   Fracture of lower leg, including ankle
S83   Dislocation and sprain of joints and ligaments of knee

S84 Injury of nerves at lower leg level
S85 Injury of blood vessels at lower leg level
S86 Injury of muscle and tendon at lower leg level
S87 Crushing injury of lower leg
S88 Traumatic amputation of lower leg
S89 Other and unspecified injuries of lower leg

Injuries to the Ankle and Foot (S90-S99)

S90 Superficial injury of ankle, foot and toes
S91 Open wound of ankle, foot and toes
S92 Fracture of foot and toe, except ankle
S93 Dislocation and sprain of joints and ligaments at ankle, foot and toe level
S94 Injury of nerves at ankle and foot level
S95 Injury of blood vessels at ankle and foot level
S96 Injury of muscle and tendon at ankle and foot level
S97 Crushing injury of ankle and foot
S98 Traumatic amputation of ankle and foot
S99 Other and unspecified injuries of ankle and foot

Injury, poisoning and certain other consequences of external causes (T07-T88)

Injuries Involving Multiple Body Regions (T07)

T07 Unspecified multiple injuries

Injuries of Unspecified Body Region (T14)

T14 Injury of unspecified body region

Effects of Foreign Body Entering Through Natural Orifice (T15-T19)

T15 Foreign body on external eye
T16 Foreign body in ear
T17 Foreign body in respiratory tract
T18 Foreign body in alimentary tract
T19 Foreign body in genitourinary tract

Burns and Corrosions (T20-T32)

Burns and Corrosions of External Body Surface, Specified by Site (T20-T25)

T20 Burns and corrosion of head, face, and neck
T21 Burn and corrosion of trunk
T22 Burn and corrosion of shoulder and upper limb, except wrist and hand
T23 Burn and corrosion of wrist and hand
T24 Burn and corrosion of lower limb, except ankle and foot
T25 Burn and corrosion of ankle and foot

Burns and Corrosions Confined to Eye and Internal Organs (T26-T28)

T26 Burn and corrosion confined to eye and adnexa
T27 Burn and corrosion of respiratory tract
T28 Burn and corrosion of other internal organs

Burns and Corrosions Of Multiple and Unspecified Body Regions (T30-T32)

T30   Burns and corrosion, body region unspecified
T31   Burns classified according to extent of body surface involved
T32   Corrosions classified according to extent of body surface involved

Frostbite (T33-T34)

T33   Superficial frostbite
T34   Frostbite with tissue necrosis

Poisoning By and Adverse Effects of Drugs, Medicaments and Biological Substances (T36-T50)

T36   Poisoning by and adverse effect of systemic antibiotics
T37   Poisoning by and adverse effect of other systemic anti-infectives and antiparasitics
T38   Poisoning by and adverse effect of hormones and their synthetic substitutes and antagonists, not elsewhere classified
T39   Poisoning by and adverse effect of nonopioid analgesics, antipyretics and antirheumatics
T40   Poisoning by and adverse effect of narcotics and psychodysleptics [hallucinogens]
T41   Poisoning by and adverse effect of anesthetics and therapeutic gases
T42   Poisoning by and adverse effect of antiepileptic, sedative-hypnotic and antiparkinsonism drugs
T43   Poisoning by and adverse effect of psychotropic drugs, not elsewhere classified
T44   Poisoning by and adverse effect of drugs primarily affecting the autonomic nervous system
T45   Poisoning by and adverse effect of primarily systemic and hematological agents, not elsewhere classified
T46   Poisoning by and adverse effect of agents primarily affecting the cardiovascular system
T47   Poisoning by and adverse effect of agents primarily affecting the gastrointestinal system
T48   Poisoning by and adverse effect of agents primarily acting on smooth and skeletal muscles and the respiratory system
T49   Poisoning by and adverse effect of topical agents primarily affecting skin and mucous membrane and by ophthalmological, otorhinorlaryngological and dental drugs
T50   Poisoning by and adverse effect of diuretics and other and unspecified drugs, medicaments and biological substances

Toxic Effects of Substances Chiefly Nonmedicinal as to Source (T51-T65)

T51   Toxic effect of alcohol
T52   Toxic effect of organic solvents
T53   Toxic effect of halogen derivatives of aliphatic and aromatic hydrocarbons
T54   Toxic effect of corrosive substances
T55   Toxic effect of soaps and detergents
T56   Toxic effect of metals
T57   Toxic effect of other inorganic substances

T58   Toxic effect of carbon monoxide

T59   Toxic effect of other gases, fumes and vapors

T60   Toxic effect of pesticides

T61   Toxic effect of noxious substances eaten as seafood

T62   Toxic effect of other noxious substances eaten as food

T63   Toxic effect of contact with venomous animals and plants

T64   Toxic effect of aflatoxin and other mycotoxin food contaminants

T65   Toxic effect of other and unspecified substances

Other and Unspecified Effects of External Causes (T66-T78)

T66   Unspecified effects of radiation

T67   Effects of heat and light

T68   Hypothermia

T69   Other effects of reduced temperature

T70   Effects of air pressure and water pressure

T71   Asphyxiation

T73   Effects of other deprivation

T74   Adult and child abuse, neglect and other maltreatment, confirmed

T75   Other and unspecified effects of other external causes

T76   Adult and child abuse, neglect and other maltreatment, suspected

T78   Adverse effects, not elsewhere classified

Certain Early Complications of Trauma (T79)

T79   Certain early complications of trauma, not elsewhere classified

Complications of Surgical and Medical Care, Not Elsewhere Classified (T80-T88)

T80   Complications following infusion, transfusion and therapeutic injection

T81   Complication of procedures, not elsewhere classified

T82   Complications of cardiac and vascular prosthetic devices, implants and grafts

T83   Complications of genitourinary prosthetic devices, implants and grafts

T84   Complications of internal orthopedic prosthetic devices, implants and grafts

T85   Complications of other internal prosthetic devices, implants and grafts

T86   Complications of transplanted organs and tissue

T87   Complications peculiar to reattachment and amputation

T88   Other complications of surgical and medical care, not elsewhere classified

CHAPTER 20

External causes of morbidity (V00-Y97)

Transport accidents (V00-V99)

Pedestrian Injured In Transport Accident (V00-V09)

V00   Pedestrian conveyance accident
V01   Pedestrian injured in collision with pedal cycle
V02   Pedestrian injured in collision with two- or three-wheeled motor vehicle
V03   Pedestrian injured in collision with car, pick-up truck or van
V04   Pedestrian injured in collision with heavy transport vehicle or bus
V05   Pedestrian injured in collision with railway train or railway vehicle
V06   Pedestrian injured in collision with other nonmotor vehicle
V09   Pedestrian injured in other and unspecified transport accidents

Pedal Cycle Rider Injured In Transport Accident (V10-V19)

V10   Pedal cycle rider injured in collision with pedestrian or animal
V11   Pedal cycle rider injured in collision with other pedal cycle
V12   Pedal cycle rider injured in collision with two- or three-wheeled motor vehicle
V13   Pedal cycle rider injured in collision with car, pick-up truck or van
V14   Pedal cycle rider injured in collision with heavy transport vehicle or bus
V15   Pedal cycle rider injured in collision with railway train or railway vehicle
V16   Pedal cycle rider injured in collision with other nonmotor vehicle
V17   Pedal cycle rider injured in collision with fixed or stationary object
V18   Pedal cycle rider injured in noncollision transport accident
V19   Pedal cycle rider injured in other and unspecified transport accidents

Motorcycle Rider Injured In Transport Accident (V20-V29)

V20   Motorcycle rider injured in collision with pedestrian or animal
V21   Motorcycle rider injured in collision with pedal cycle
V22   Motorcycle rider injured in collision with two- or three-wheeled motor vehicle
V23   Motorcycle rider injured in collision with car, pick-up truck or van
V24   Motorcycle rider injured in collision with heavy transport vehicle or bus
V25   Motorcycle rider injured in collision with railway train or railway vehicle
V26   Motorcycle rider injured in collision with other nonmotor vehicle
V27   Motorcycle rider injured in collision with fixed or stationary object
V28   Motorcycle rider injured in noncollision transport accident
V29   Motorcycle rider injured in other and unspecified transport accidents

Occupant Of Three-wheeled Motor Vehicle Injured In Transport Accident (V30-V39)

V30 Occupant of three-wheeled motor vehicle injured in collision with pedestrian or animal

V31 Occupant of three-wheeled motor vehicle injured in collision with pedal cycle

V32 Occupant of three-wheeled motor vehicle injured in collision with two- or three-wheeled motor vehicle

V33 Occupant of three-wheeled motor vehicle injured in collision with car, pick-up truck or van

V34 Occupant of three-wheeled motor vehicle injured in collision with heavy transport vehicle or bus

V35 Occupant of three-wheeled motor vehicle injured in collision with railway train or railway vehicle

V36 Occupant of three-wheeled motor vehicle injured in collision with other nonmotor vehicle

V37 Occupant of three-wheeled motor vehicle injured in collision with fixed or stationary object

V38 Occupant of three-wheeled motor vehicle injured in noncollision transport accident

V39 Occupant of three-wheeled motor vehicle injured in other and unspecified transport accidents

Car Occupant Injured In Transport Accident (V40-V49)

V40 Car occupant injured in collision with pedestrian or animal

V41 Car occupant injured in collision with pedal cycle

V42 Car occupant injured in collision with two- or three-wheeled motor vehicle

V43 Car occupant injured in collision with car, pick-up truck or van

V44 Car occupant injured in collision with heavy transport vehicle or bus

V45 Car occupant injured in collision with railway train or railway vehicle

V46 Car occupant injured in collision with other nonmotor vehicle

V47 Car occupant injured in collision with fixed or stationary object

V48 Car occupant injured in noncollision transport accident

V49 Car occupant injured in other and unspecified transport accidents

Occupant Of Pick-up Truck Or Van Injured In Transport Accident (V50-V59)

V50 Occupant of pick-up truck or van injured in collision with pedestrian or animal

V51 Occupant of pick-up truck or van injured in collision with pedal cycle

V52 Occupant of pick-up truck or van injured in collision with two- or three-wheeled motor vehicle

V53 Occupant of pick-up truck or van injured in collision with car, pick-up truck or van

V54 Occupant of pick-up truck or van injured in collision with heavy transport vehicle or bus

V55 Occupant of pick-up truck or van injured in collision with railway train or railway vehicle

V56   Occupant of pick-up truck or van injured in collision with other nonmotor vehicle

V57   Occupant of pick-up truck or van injured in collision with fixed or stationary object

V58   Occupant of pick-up truck or van injured in noncollision transport accident

V59   Occupant of pick-up truck or van injured in other and unspecified transport accidents

Occupant Of Heavy Transport Vehicle Injured In Transport Accident (V60-V69)

V60   Occupant of heavy transport vehicle injured in collision with pedestrian or animal

V61   Occupant of heavy transport vehicle injured in collision with pedal cycle

V62   Occupant of heavy transport vehicle injured in collision with two- or three-wheeled motor vehicle

V63   Occupant of heavy transport vehicle injured in collision with car, pick-up truck or van

V64   Occupant of heavy transport vehicle injured in collision with heavy transport vehicle or bus

V65   Occupant of heavy transport vehicle injured in collision with railway train or railway vehicle

V66   Occupant of heavy transport vehicle injured in collision with other nonmotor vehicle

V67   Occupant of heavy transport vehicle injured in collision with fixed or stationary object

V68   Occupant of heavy transport vehicle injured in noncollision transport accident

V69   Occupant of heavy transport vehicle injured in other and unspecified transport accidents

Bus Occupant Injured In Transport Accident (V70-V79)

V70   Bus occupant injured in collision with pedestrian or animal

V71   Bus occupant injured in collision with pedal cycle

V72   Bus occupant injured in collision with two- or three-wheeled motor vehicle

V73   Bus occupant injured in collision with car, pick-up truck or van

V74   Bus occupant injured in collision with heavy transport vehicle or bus

V75   Bus occupant injured in collision with railway train or railway vehicle

V76   Bus occupant injured in collision with other nonmotor vehicle

V77   Bus occupant injured in collision with fixed or stationary object

V78   Bus occupant injured in noncollision transport accident

V79   Bus occupant injured in other and unspecified transport accidents

Other Land Transport Accidents (V80-V89)

V80   Animal-rider or occupant of animal-drawn vehicle injured in transport accident

V81   Occupant of railway train or railway vehicle injured in transport accident

V82   Occupant of powered streetcar injured in transport accident

V83   Occupant of special vehicle mainly used on industrial premises injured in transport accident

V84   Occupant of special vehicle mainly used in agriculture injured in transport accident

V85   Occupant of special construction vehicle injured in transport accident

V86   Occupant of special all-terrain or other motor vehicle, injured in transport accident

V87   Traffic accident of specified type but victim's mode of transport unknown

V88   Nontraffic accident of specified type but victim's mode of transport unknown

V89   Motor- or nonmotor-vehicle accident, type of vehicle unspecified

Water Transport Accidents (V90-V94)

V90   Drowning and submersion due to accident to watercraft

V91   Other injury due to accident to watercraft

V92   Drowning and submersion due to accident on board watercraft, without accident to watercraft

V93   Other injury due to accident on board watercraft, without accident to watercraft

V94   Other and unspecified water transport accidents

Air and Space Transport Accidents (V95-V97)

V95   Accident to powered aircraft causing injury to occupant

V96   Accident to nonpowered aircraft causing injury to occupant

V97   Other specified air transport accidents

Other and Unspecified Transport Accidents (V98-V99)

V98   Other specified transport accidents

V99   Unspecified transport accident

Other External Causes of Accidental Injury (W00-X58)

Falls (W00-W19)

W00   Fall due to ice and snow

W01   Fall on same level from slipping, tripping and stumbling

W03   Other fall on same level due to collision with another person

W04   Fall while being carried or supported by other persons

W05   Fall from non-moving wheelchair

W06   Fall from bed

W07   Fall from chair

W08   Fall from other furniture

W09   Fall on and from playground equipment

W10   Fall on and from stairs and steps

W11   Fall on and from ladder

W12   Fall on and from scaffolding

W13   Fall from, out of or through building or structure

W14   Fall from tree

W15   Fall from cliff

W16 Fall, jump or diving into water
W17 Other fall from one level to another
W18 Other fall on same level
W19 Unspecified fall

Exposure To Inanimate Mechanical Forces (W20-W49)

W20 Struck by thrown, projected or falling object
W21 Striking against or struck by sports equipment
W22 Striking against or struck by other objects
W23 Caught, crushed, jammed or pinched in or between objects
W24 Contact with lifting and transmission devices, not elsewhere classified
W25 Contact with sharp glass
W26 Contact with knife, sword or dagger
W27 Contact with nonpowered hand tool
W28 Contact with powered lawnmower
W29 Contact with other powered hand tools and household machinery
W30 Contact with agricultural machinery
W31 Contact with other and unspecified machinery
W32 Accidental handgun discharge
W33 Accidental rifle, shotgun and larger firearm discharge
W34 Accidental discharge from other and unspecified firearms and guns
W35 Explosion and rupture of boiler
W36 Explosion and rupture of gas cylinder
W37 Explosion and rupture of pressurized tire, pipe or hose
W38 Explosion and rupture of other specified pressurized devices
W39 Discharge of firework
W40 Explosion of other materials
W42 Exposure to noise
W45 Foreign body or object entering through skin
W49 Exposure to other inanimate mechanical forces

Exposure To Animate Mechanical Forces (W50-W64)

W50 Accidental hit, strick, kick, twist, bite or scratch by another person
W51 Accidental striking against or bumped into by another person
W52 Crushed, pushed or stepped on by crowd or human stampede
W53 Contact with rodent
W54 Contact with dog
W55 Contact with other mammals
W56 Contact with nonvenomous marine animal
W57 Bitten or stung by nonvenomous insect and other nonvenomous arthropods
W58 Bitten or struck by crocodile or alligator
W59 Contact with other nonvenomous reptiles
W60 Contact with nonvenomous plant thorns and spines and sharp leaves
W61 Contact with birds
W62 Contact with nonvenomous amphibians
W64 Exposure to other animate mechanical forces

Accidental Non-transport Drowning and Submersion (W65-W74)

W65   Accidental drowning and submersion while in bath-tub
W67   Accidental drowning and submersion while in swimming-pool
W69   Accidental drowning and submersion while in natural water
W73   Other specified cause of accidental non-transport drowning and submersion
W74   Unspecified cause of accidental drowning and submersion

Exposure To Electric Current, Radiation and Extreme Ambient Air Temperature and Pressure (W85-W99)

W85   Exposure to electric transmission lines
W86   Exposure to other specified electric current
W88   Exposure to ionizing radiation
W89   Exposure to man-made visible and ultraviolet light
W90   Exposure to other nonionizing radiation
W92   Exposure to excessive heat of man-made origin
W93   Exposure to excessive cold of man-made origin
W94   Exposure to high and low air pressure and changes in air pressure
W99   Exposure to other man-made environmental factors

Exposure To Smoke, Fire and Flames (X00-X08)

X00   Exposure to uncontrolled fire in building or structure
X01   Exposure to uncontrolled fire, not in building or structure
X02   Exposure to controlled fire in building or structure
X03   Exposure to controlled fire, not in building or structure
X04   Exposure to ignition of highly flammable material
X05   Exposure to ignition or melting of nightwear
X06   Exposure to ignition or melting of other clothing and apparel
X08   Exposure to other specified smoke, fire and flames

Contact With Heat and Hot Substances (X10-X19)

X10   Contact with hot drinks, food, fats and cooking oils
X11   Contact with hot tap-water
X12   Contact with other hot fluids
X13   Contact with steam and other hot vapors
X14   Contact with hot air and other hot gases
X15   Contact with hot household appliances
X16   Contact with hot heating appliances, radiators and pipes
X17   Contact with hot engines, machinery and tools
X18   Contact with other hot metals
X19   Contact with other heat and hot substances

Exposure To Forces Of Nature (X30-X39)

X30   Exposure to excessive natural heat
X31   Exposure to excessive natural cold
X32   Exposure to sunlight
X34   Earthquake
X35   Volcanic eruption
X36   Avalanche, landslide and other earth movements
X37   Cataclysmic storm

X38   Flood
X39   Exposure to other forces of nature

Overexertion, Travel and Privation (X50-X52)

X50   Overexertion and strenuous or repetitive movements
X51   Travel and motion
X52   Prolonged stay in weightless environment

Accidental Exposure To Other and Unspecified Factors (X58)

X58   Exposure to other specified factors

Intentional Self-harm (X71-X83)

X71   Intentional self-harm by drowning and submersion
X72   Intentional self-harm by handgun discharge
X73   Intentional self-harm by rifle, shotgun and larger firearm discharge
X74   Intentional self-harm by other and unspecified firearm and gun discharge
X75   Intentional self-harm by explosive material
X76   Intentional self-harm by smoke, fire and flames
X77   Intentional self-harm by steam, hot vapors and hot objects
X78   Intentional self-harm by sharp object
X79   Intentional self-harm by blunt object
X80   Intentional self-harm by jumping from a high place
X81   Intentional self-harm by jumping or lying before moving object
X82   Intentional self-harm by crashing of motor vehicle
X83   Intentional self-harm by other specified means

Assault (X92-Y08)

X92   Assault by drowning and submersion
X93   Assault by handgun discharge
X94   Assault by rifle, shotgun and larger firearm discharge
X95   Assault by other and unspecified firearm and gun discharge
X96   Assault by explosive material
X97   Assault by smoke, fire and flames
X98   Assault by steam, hot vapors and hot objects
X99   Assault by sharp object
Y00   Assault by blunt object
Y01   Assault by pushing from high place
Y02   Assault by pushing or placing victim before moving object
Y03   Assault by crashing of motor vehicle
Y04   Assault by bodily force
Y05   Sexual assault
Y07   Perpetrator of maltreatment and neglect
Y08   Assault by other specified means

Event Of Undetermined Intent (Y21-Y33)

Y21   Drowning and submersion, undetermined intent
Y22   Handgun discharge, undetermined intent
Y23   Rifle, shotgun and larger firearm discharge, undetermined intent
Y24   Other and unspecified firearm discharge, undetermined intent

Y25   Contact with explosive material, undetermined intent

Y26   Exposure to smoke, fire and flames, undetermined intent

Y27   Contact with steam, hot vapors and hot objects, undetermined intent

Y28   Contact with sharp object, undetermined intent

Y29   Contact with blunt object, undetermined intent

Y30   Falling, jumping or pushed from a high place, undetermined intent

Y31   Falling, lying or running before or into moving object, undetermined intent

Y32   Crashing of motor vehicle, undetermined intent

Y33   Other specified events, undetermined intent

Legal Intervention, Operations Of War, Military Operations, and Terrorism (Y35-Y38)

Y35   Legal intervention

Y36   Operations of war

Y37   Military operations

Y38   Terrorism

Complications of medical and surgical care (Y62-Y84)

Misadventures to Patients During Surgical and Medical Care (Y62-Y69)

Y62   Failure of sterile precautions during surgical and medical care

Y63   Failure in dosage during surgical and medical care

Y64   Contaminated medical or biological substances

Y65   Other misadventures during surgical and medical care

Y66   Nonadministration of surgical and medical care

Y69   Unspecified misadventure during surgical and medical care

Medical Devices Associated With Adverse Incidents In Diagnostic and Therapeutic Use (Y70-Y82)

Y70   Anesthesiology devices associated with adverse incidents

Y71   Cardiovascular devices associated with adverse incidents

Y72   Otorhinolaryngological devices associated with adverse incidents

Y73   Gastroenterology and urology devices associated with adverse incidents

Y74   General hospital and personal-use devices associated with adverse incidents

Y75   Neurological devices associated with adverse incidents

Y76   Obstetric and gynecological devices associated with adverse incidents

Y77   Ophthalmic devices associated with adverse incidents

Y78   Radiological devices associated with adverse incidents

Y79   Orthopedic devices associated with adverse incidents

Y80   Physical medicine devices assiociated with adverse incidents

Y81   General- and plastic-surgery devices associated with adverse incidents

Y82   Other and unspecified medical devices associated with adverse incidents

Surgical and Other Medical Procedures As the Cause Of Abnormal Reaction Of the Patient, Or Of Later Complication, Without Mention Of Misadventure At the Time Of the Procedure (Y83-Y84)

- Y83 Surgical operation and other surgical procedures as the cause of abnormal reaction of the patient, or of later complication, without mention of misadventure at the time of the procedure
- Y84 Other medical procedures as the cause of abnormal reaction of the patient, or of later complication, without mention of misadventure at the time of the procedure

Supplementary Factors Related To Causes Of Morbidity Classified Elsewhere (Y90-Y97)

- Y90 Evidence of alcohol involvement determined by blood alcohol level
- Y92 Place of occurrence of the external cause
- Y93 Activity Code
- Y95 Nosocomial condition
- Y96 Work-related condition
- Y97 Environmental-pollution-related condition

CHAPTER 21

Factors influencing health status and contact with health services (Z00-Z99)

Persons Encountering Health Services For Examinations (Z00-Z13)

- Z00 Encounter for general examination without complaint, suspected or reported diagnosis
- Z01 Encounter for other special examination without complaint or suspected or reported diagnosis
- Z02 Encounter for administrative examination
- Z03 Encounter for medical observation for suspected diseases and conditions ruled out
- Z04 Encounter for observation for other reasons
- Z06 Infection with drug-resistant microorganisms
- Z08 Encounter for follow-up examination after completed treatment for malignant neoplasms
- Z09 Encounter for follow-up examination after completed treatment for conditions other than malignant neoplasms
- Z11 Encounter for special screening examination for infectious and parasitic diseases
- Z12 Encounter for special screening examination for malignant neoplasms
- Z13 Encounter for special screening examination for other diseases and disorders

Persons With Potential Health Hazards Related To Communicable Diseases (Z20-Z28)

- Z20 Contact with and exposure to communicable diseases

Z21	Asymptomatic human immunodeficiency virus [HIV] infection status
Z22	Carrier of infectious disease
Z23	Encounter for immunization
A28	Immunization not carried out

Persons Encountering Health Services In Circumstances Related To Reproduction (Z30-Z39)

Z30	Encounter for contraceptive management
Z31	Encounter for procreative management
Z32	Encounter for pregnancy test and instruction
Z33	Pregnant state
Z34	Encounter for supervision of normal pregnancy
Z36	Encounter for antenatal screening
Z37	Outcome of delivery
Z38	Liveborn infants according to place of birth and type of delivery
Z39	Encounter for maternal postpartum care and examination

Encounters For Other Specific Health Care (Z40-Z53)

Z40	Encounter for prophylactic surgery
Z41	Encounter for procedures for purposes other than remedying health state
Z43	Encounter for attention to artificial openings
Z44	Encounter for fitting and adjustment of external prosthetic device
Z45	Encounter for adjustment and management of implanted device
Z46	Encounter for fitting and adjustment of other devices
Z47	Encounter for orthopedic aftercare
Z48	Encounter for other surgical aftercare
Z49	Encounter for care involving renal dialysis
Z51	Encounter for other aftercare
Z52	Donors of organs and tissues
Z53	Persons encountering health services for specific procedures and treatment, not carried out

Persons With Potential Health Hazards Related To Socioeconomic and Psychosocial Circumstances (Z55-Z65)

Z55	Problems related to education and literacy
Z56	Problems related to employment and unemployment
Z57	Occupational exposure to risk-factors
Z58	Problems related to physical environment
Z59	Problems related to housing and economic circumstances
Z60	Problems related to social environment
Z61	Problems related to negative life events in childhood
Z62	Other problems related to upbringing
Z63	Other problems related to primary support group, including family circumstances
Z64	Problems related to certain psychosocial circumstances
Z65	Problems related to other psychosocial circumstances

Do Not Resuscitate Status (Z66)

Z66   Do not resuscitate

Blood Type (Z67)

Z67   Blood type

Persons Encountering Health Services In Other Circumstances (Z69-Z76)

Z69   Encounter for mental health services for victim and perpetrator of abuse
Z70   Counselling related to sexual attitude, behavior and orientation
Z71   Persons encountering health services for other counselling and medical advice, not elsewhere classified
Z72   Problems related to lifestyle
Z73   Problems related to life-management difficulty
Z74   Problems related to care-provider dependency
Z75   Problems related to medical facilities and other health care
Z76   Persons encountering health services in other circumstances

Persons With Potential Health Hazards Related To Family and Personal History and Certain Conditions Influencing Health Status (Z79-Z99)

Z79   Long-term (current) drug therapy
Z80   Family history of primary malignant neoplasm
Z81   Family history of mental and behavioral disorders
Z82   Family history of certain disabilities and chronic diseases (leading to disablement)
Z83   Family history of other specific disorders
Z84   Family history of other conditions
Z85   Personal history of primary and secondary malignant neoplasm
Z86   Personal history of certain other diseases
Z87   Personal history of other diseases and conditions
Z88   Allergy status to drugs, medicaments and biological substances
Z89   Acquired absence of limb
Z90   Acquired absence of organs, not elsewhere classified
Z91   Personal risk-factors, not elsewhere classified
Z92   Personal history of medical treatment
Z93   Artificial opening status
Z94   Transplanted organ and tissue status
Z95   Presence of cardiac and vascular implants and grafts
Z96   Presence of other functional implants
Z97   Presence of other devices
Z98   Other postsurgical states
Z99   Dependence on enabling machines and devices, not elsewhere classified